MY MEN ARE MY HEROES

THE BRAD KASAL STORY

★ ★ ★

AS TOLD TO
NATHANIEL R. HELMS

★ | MEREDITH® BOOKS
DES MOINES, IOWA | ★

Meredith Books
1716 Locust Street
Des Moines, Iowa 50309–3023

Cover photo by Lucian Read.
Photography courtesy of Sgt. Major Brad Kasal, Lt. Col. Willard "Willy" Buhl,
and photojournalist Lucian Read.

Printed in the United States of America.

ISBN-13: 978-0-696-23236-7

DEDICATION
★ ★ ★

This book is dedicated to the memory of the members of 3d Battalion, 1st Marines who gave the ultimate sacrifice in the fight for Fallujah.

Headquarters and Service Company

SSgt Russell L. Slay

SSgt Trevor L. Spink

Sgt Krisna Nachampassak

Cpl Bradley T. Arms

Cpl Nicanor A. Alverez

Cpl Terry Holmes

LCpl Louis W. Qualls

LCpl James E. Swain

PFC Christopher J. Reed

Weapons – George Company

Sgt Byron W. Norwood

Cpl Brian Oliveira

Cpl Steven Rintamaki

LCpl Joshua W. Dickinson

LCpl Abraham Simpson

Kilo Company

Sgt Christopher T. Heflin

Sgt Morgan W. Strader

LCpl Jeramy A. Ailes

LCpl Juan E. Segura

India Company

Cpl Dale A. Burger Jr.

LCpl Justin D. McLeese

LCpl Andres H. Perez

LCpl Joseph T. Welke

LCpl Phillip G. West

PFC Fernando B. Hannon

PFC Geoffrey Perez

Lima Company

Sgt Juan Calderon Jr.

Sgt William C. James

Cpl Theodore A. Bowling

LCpl Benjamin S. Bryan

LCpl Luis A. Figueroa

LCpl Michael W. Hanks

LCpl Nicholas D. Larson

LCpl Nathan R. Wood

SPECIAL THANKS
★ ★ ★

From Sergeant Major Brad Kasal:

The Marines and Sailors of Weapons Co. and of 3d Battalion, 1st Marines, "The Thundering Third"

Lou Palermo

John and Cathia Sylvester

Ian and Tia Welch

Jim and Linda Arslanian

Ed Sparks

Hope Petlock

Roy Lundstedt

SSgt Nic Fox and wife Sarah

SSgt Sam Mortimer and wife Christy

SSgt Chris Lopez

GySgt Chad Wade

1st Sgt Wayne Hertz

Sgt Major Tim Ruff

1st Sgt Scott Samuels

Sgt Major Rob Cadle

Lt Col Willard Buhl

Lt Zach Iscol and family

Major Rob Belknap

Gary Munstermann

Shawn Essy

Patricia Driscoll

Geoff and Clyrinda Milke

Nurses and corpsmen of Ward 5c, Bethesda Naval Hospital

Cmdr Frank McGuigan and staff

Lt Cmdr P.J. Girard

Lt Maurer

Staff of Aav School, Camp Pendleton, California

Soldiers Angel Organization

Semper Fi Foundation

MSgt Kelley Ramsey

Sgt Robert Mitchell

Alex Nicoll

Sgt Chris Pruitt

SSgt Kris Korreck

Mary Medina

Sandy Dorothy and family

Heather Richardson

Sgt Major Ed Sax

Sgt Major Kent

Lt General Staettler

From writer Nat Helms:

Writing this book has been a remarkably rewarding endeavor. I would like to thank people who contributed so much to making sure this story could be told.

First I would like to thank Sgt Major Kasal for his patience, forbearance, and honesty. By nature he is a very humble man. It was necessary to remind him almost daily the book was about him; otherwise he might never have mentioned his own role in anything.

Kasal is a Marine's Marine and a warrior of unparalleled valor, honor, and honesty. His efforts were ably reinforced by Lt Col Willard "Willie" Buhl, Brigadier General John Toolan, and all the officers and men of the United States Marine Corps who directed me, patiently corrected me, and put up with all my questions for almost two years.

Also I wish to acknowledge the role of Lt Col Robert Brown, U.S. Army Ret, the publisher of *Soldier of Fortune* magazine. Without his advice and encouragement this project would not have gotten off the ground.

I'm grateful to our editors, Larry Erickson and Dan Weeks, who deserve much credit for the final product. During the production of this book Larry's son, Ryan, was fighting in Iraq and Afghanistan as a grunt in the 10th Mountain Division, no doubt making Larry's editorial task doubly difficult.

Finally I must mention my wife, Marsha, who listened to me rumble on far into the wee hours; my daughter, Cecily Daller, Esquire, who provided me legal advice and constant encouragement; and my son, Nate Helms, currently serving in the Coast Guard. It is men like Kasal and our sons and daughters in uniform who make it possible for the rest of us to pursue our dreams.

TABLE OF CONTENTS
★ ★ ★

FAILURE WAS NOT AN OPTION

The long white bone lying on the road looked like an enormous chicken leg that had been sucked clean and tossed aside— except for the gray athletic shoe on the rotting foot. The shoe and the leg had once belonged to a radical Muslim jihadist— a "holy warrior." The remnants of the rotting corpse had become breakfast for a pack of the starving, half-mad dogs that roamed the embattled city of Fallujah, Iraq, in November 2004. It was a city that thousands—perhaps tens of thousands—of warriors on both sides of the battle wouldn't exit in one piece, much less alive.

The last time Marines had fought from house to house and room to room for days on end was during the epic battle for the Vietnamese city of Hue in 1968. As it was then, the combat at Fallujah was ghastly and the casualties high. During the monthlong fight, at least 136 Marines were killed and more than 1,200 were wounded.

In both cities, pools of blood slicked the floors and stained the walls of embattled houses after the Marines surged through them.

Every alley was a death trap and every room a potential morgue. Dead men shared floor space with the living while cracking bullets zipped overhead and pinged around like castor beans in a cheap Juarez rattle. Walls of the rooms where the combatants took shelter suddenly collapsed, and roofs came crashing down without warning. A finely sifted frosting of concrete, dust, and sweat covered the living and dead alike, coloring everyone in the same dull gray. Every room in every house promised a fierce contest with only one outcome for the embattled Marines. To a man, they knew that failure was not an option.

Another gripping image from Fallujah—captured by a freelance photographer—depicts a terribly wounded Marine being assisted from a house by two comrades. He is bloody but still defiantly holds his 9mm pistol at the ready. The man's jaw is set in determination to come out standing up.

The riveting photo couldn't show it, but the Marine had been shot seven times and riddled with at least 43 grenade fragments during a struggle to rescue several wounded comrades from inside the house. His right leg was nearly severed by a burst of bullets from an AK-47 assault rifle, one that also wounded another Marine.

By all rights, he should be dead—he lost enough blood to kill most men while surviving a give-no-quarter shoot-out, point-blank range. The loser of that gunfight lay sprawled on his back in the shadows behind the Marine, seeping blood and brains from massive holes where the back of his head used to be.

That memorable photo—snapped by Lucian Read for *World Picture News*—stares at you from the cover of this book. You may well have seen it before, as it has appeared on hundreds of websites, magazines, and newspapers and was even made into a Marine Corps poster. The photo's subject, First Sergeant (now Sergeant Major) Brad Kasal, did make it out alive. Thanks to his death-defying bravery, cunning, intelligence, and raw grit, Kasal is now known around the world as the iconic United States Marine.

"Kasal is always ready," says Staff Sergeant Sam Mortimer, currently a drill instructor at the Marine Corps Recruit Depot near San Diego, where young men are forged into steel. "There ain't another Marine like him in the entire Corps."

This is his story.

CHAPTER 1

THE MAN AT THE POINT OF THE SPEAR

Friends and family call him "Brad." Marines now call him "Sergeant Major," the highest noncommissioned rank in the United States Marine Corps. Brad Kasal was promoted to that status after the Battle of Fallujah, but he will always be "First Sergeant" to the men he led into the fight there. They speak the title respectfully, almost reverently, as if it were reserved only for him.

Even before entering Iraq, Kasal was almost mythical among Marines, known for leading his troops at the front to ensure that he would always be the first man into a fight. In his mind, that is what Grunts do, and Brad Kasal is a true Grunt.

Unlike most career Marines, Kasal has always been an infantryman. With the exception of recruiting duty, he has spent more than 18 years in the infantry. That's not typical. The infantry is a young man's game. In addition to guts and brains, infantry service takes tremendous stamina. Most men simply can't maintain the pace of leading 18- and 19-year-olds—kids in their absolute physical prime—for nearly two decades. It's the same reason there aren't many 41-year-old Olympians—and even that comparison trivializes the physical challenges of the infantry.

Perhaps more important, infantry service takes tremendous courage to stand in harm's way. Death is always just around the corner. Kasal never seemed to notice. He chose the infantry because infantrymen live on the cutting edge of America's military might. The sharp point of the spear is where Kasal lives to be.

"Infantrymen are the troops who close with the enemy and kill them," Kasal says simply. "That is our only purpose."

ROBO-GRUNT

Until an Iraqi gunman shattered Kasal's right leg, blasted his ass with bullet holes, and riddled his head and back with shrapnel, Kasal could outrun, outfight, outshoot, and outthink the much younger men he led. Unlike the medical experts who urged him to accept amputation of his leg and retire quietly, his Marines expect he will one day lead again. If anyone can do it, they say, it will be Kasal.

Kevin Kasal, who served with his older brother at Camp Pendleton, California, recalls how Brad once motivated his men by picking up a lagging Marine and running to the top of a steep mountain trail with the trainee slung over his shoulder. Many of his young Marines still call him "Robo-Grunt" because he was able to run them into the ground long before he got tired.

You won't hear such superlatives from the man himself, however. "Leadership is not about ego," Kasal insists. "It is about taking men into battle and keeping them alive. The best warriors make the best leaders because they can think and function effectively when surrounded by the chaotic hell of combat.

"Marine Corps combat leaders are expected to lead from the front, so they have to be the best. Green Marines need to see that somebody is there for them—somebody who will ensure they understand what they have to do."

Whether they're Marines or Army soldiers, infantrymen have been called "Grunts" since the Vietnam War, ostensibly for the sound they make when they shrug on 100 pounds of combat gear and stand up. In other times and other wars they were called doughboys and dogfaces, sad sacks, and GIs. The terms all mean the same thing.

Privately, infantrymen will tell you they're called Grunts because the name fits their unfortunate station. Grunts are the first into combat and the last out. They live in mud and dust, heat and cold, in wretchedness so complete that all they can do is grunt with despair. But the very misery they endure also makes them proud that they can take it—and cocky to the point of being eager for more. Grunts are weird that way.

Grunts march. And because they usually walk instead of ride, everything they need must be hauled on their backs. Sometimes Grunts have to carry 100 pounds of equipment, food, ammunition, and water for many long miles. They call it "humping."

Robo-Grunt is a supreme accolade among men who offer very few. Kasal earned it by consistently showing himself to be exceptionally tough and hard in a culture where strength and endurance are important measures of a man.

Just down the road from Kasal's hometown of Afton, Iowa, is the sleepy community of Winterset, birthplace of actor John Wayne. Wayne made Marine infantry legends more than 50 years ago in the role of Sergeant John Stryker in the World War II classic *Sands of Iwo Jima*. The movie is a fictionalized story about the conquest of the most expensive real estate ever paid for with the blood of Marines. Wayne's character was a hard-bitten three-striper who led a squad of 13 riflemen and machine gunners.

Being a Marine Corps squad leader is an exceptional honor and an apprenticeship for higher distinctions: Kasal's longtime job of first sergeant and his current rank of sergeant major.

The Corps is very picky about whom it chooses to lead its young warriors. When squad leaders make mistakes, young men die.

An infantry squad leader is usually the leader closest to the opposition. What he sees and what he knows are essential to the success of the mission, so he has to be smart and capable of keeping a cool head when bullets fly. John Wayne made it look easy, but in real life it's tough—very tough. In combat, an infantry squad is never far from the center of the fight. They live with the stink of death in their noses and taste it in the grit that comes free with their morning chow.

"We are usually very ordinary guys who have an extraordinary job," Kasal says. "All Marines wonder if they are capable of killing someone before it happens. Being curious about combat comes with the job."

Kasal had been curious about combat for a long time. Like most boys, he had watched Wayne's war movies and wondered what it would be like to be a tough-talking, two-fisted Marine. By the time Kasal reached high school, he had already decided to join some branch of military service. All that was left was choosing which one.

"My older brothers joined the Army, so I knew a little about the military," he says. "I had seen and listened to the Army, Navy, and Air Force recruiters when they came to my high school to talk about joining the service. They all emphasized education, seeing the world, and earning all the benefits of joining their particular service. None of them even mentioned war.

"The Marine recruiter came out in his dress blues and said that most of us weren't good enough to be in his Marine Corps. He didn't promise us anything except we would be the best trained warriors in the world when the Marine Corps finished with us. I decided right then I wanted to serve with the best."

Service is a Kasal family tradition. In addition to his three older brothers who joined the Army, their father once guarded

Soviet Premier Nikita Khrushchev as a member of the Iowa Army National Guard. Kasal's youngest brother, Kevin, was in both the Army and the Marine Corps and still serves in the Iowa Army National Guard. Brad's older brother, Jeff, was a paratrooper in the 82nd Airborne Division and fought in Desert Storm.

Marines and the other services "all fight together and we've all got a job to do," Brad Kasal says. "Each service does it differently. The Army trains for defense, and the Marine Corps trains for offense. Back during the Cold War, the American soldiers defending West Germany against the Soviet Union were taught to immediately go on the defensive and wait for help if the Russians attacked. Marines aren't taught that. We would attack."

That aggressive approach fits Kasal perfectly. "Nobody wins wars being a speed bump," he says. "Marines are trained to always attack."

The differences in military service were important to Kasal even before he joined the Corps. He spent a considerable amount of effort researching the various branches at the expense of his studies. As a high school student looking for a future beyond Afton, he saw that research as a reasonable trade-off.

LIFELONG OBSESSION

"I read every book on military subjects I could find at my local libraries," he says. "Whenever I could, I watched war movies on TV and at the theater in Creston, the closest town with a movie theater. I probably didn't know what the word 'obsession' meant at the time, but being a Marine someday was always on my mind."

Even now, at age 41, the obsession remains. "I spend my time training and studying and practicing things that make me a better Marine," he says. "In the days preceding the war in Iraq, I used to scuba dive, jump out of airplanes, ride my motorcycle, go fishing, and check out the ladies." He insists with a straight face that the last activity contributes to a Marine's performance.

"Ladies," he says, "are always good for morale."

And he still watches war movies. One of his favorites is *Heartbreak Ridge*, the fictional story of a Marine Force Recon platoon that wipes out the Cuban Army and their evil Socialist sidekicks on the tiny Caribbean island of Grenada. Clint Eastwood plays a Marine named Gunny Highway. "Gunny" is short for Marine Corps gunnery sergeant, a rank one step below first sergeant. In the movie Gunny Highway is a hard-nosed, foulmouthed "Old Corps" Marine who likes to get drunk and fight when he isn't savagely drilling his men.

Kasal isn't nearly as crude as Gunny Highway. He rarely drinks. He almost never swears in public. But he respects Highway's hard-core image—that last vestige of the "Old Corps" that was once the stuff of legends.

"Today's Marine Corps stresses professionalism and honor and duty," Kasal says. "When I was a young Marine, I got in more than my share of fights in liberty ports. I was lucky; for some reason I was never written up. I suspect it is because fighting is what Marines are supposed to do, and I only got into fights when I had to. The hardest part of learning that particular skill is knowing when it is appropriate to fight. A real-life Gunny Highway probably wouldn't make it in today's Marine Corps."

Gunnery sergeants remain legends, however, for ruling their young charges like kings of old. To most young Marines their Gunny is the nearest thing to God they will meet on this earth. Gunnery sergeants teach young Marines how to be warriors. Their job is to make tigers out of kids and do it with finesse. It is an awesome responsibility.

"Some of the stuff Eastwood does in the movie is good leadership technique and some of it is pure Hollywood," Kasal says. "One thing for sure is phony: Gunny Highway didn't get dirty, and he didn't get killed despite taking foolhardy risks that no Marine would undertake with the expectation of surviving."

Even without their faces full of dirt, Kasal thought both Wayne and Eastwood did great jobs promoting the Marine Corps—except when they glamorized combat. War can be exciting—but combat, from Kasal's perspective, is a foul business where people die horrible, gruesome deaths devoid of compassion and sympathy.

During the American Civil War, General William Tecumseh Sherman said, "War is hell," while defending his Union Army for sacking and burning Atlanta. It was hell then and still is, but Kasal says no image of war can compare to the gruesome intimacy of combat.

"War is hell and combat is a motherfucker," he says matter-of-factly. "There is no politically correct way to describe it. It doesn't deserve a kinder word. It is unrelenting, tremendously unforgiving, treacherous, and deadly. Good Marines quickly learn to understand and adapt to the dangers and intricacies of combat or face the consequences. Marginal Marines are liabilities that get good people hurt; it is as simple as that. Teaching young Marines to understand and recognize the subtle complexity of war is what keeps them alive, and keeping them alive is what leadership is all about."

Marine leaders exist to make sure their Marines do the killing and not the dying. Dying is reserved, whenever possible, for the other side. So Marines preparing for battle are trained to eliminate as many of the enemy as is humanly possible. If it is a legal killing, a Marine is expected to take the shot. "There is no place for mercy in combat," Kasal says.

Marines are taught that "sympathy" is a word found in the dictionary between "shit" and "syphilis." "It doesn't matter whether Marines kill with rocket launchers, artillery fire, a mortar, a rifle, a pistol, a grenade, a knife, a shovel, or simply grabbing the other guy and choking the living shit out of him until he dies," Kasal says. "In real war there is no other way to win, and Marines are trained to win."

CHAPTER 2

FALLUJAH: ACT 1

Operation New Dawn, the battle on which Kasal's fate turned, was known locally as al-Fajr (Arabic for dawn). Ironically it began near dusk at 7:00 p.m. on November 7, 2004—D-day in the ancient Iraqi city of Fallujah, a simmering metropolis in al-Anbar province roughly 43 miles west of Baghdad on the Euphrates River.

AN ANCIENT BATTLEGROUND

Anthropologists and archaeologists have discovered ample evidence that Fallujah is thousands of years old and was inhabited well before Babylon. Many scholars claim the origin of the town's name is a variant of its ancient Syrian name, Pallugtha, which is derived from the word "division."

If that is so, the name was prophetic as the city has been fought over time and again. Often the conflicts were religious: Fallujah hosted many important Jewish religious academies for several centuries before the bitter rivalry that grew between Islam and Judaism drove the Jews away.

At the close of the Ottoman Empire 80 years before the current conflict, Fallujah was an unimportant place, little more than a watering hole on one of the main roads across the desert west of Baghdad. When the British gained control of Iraq after the fall of the Ottoman Turks in 1920, competing tribes fought the British and each other for pride and plunder. The British government sent an expedition to Fallujah to quell a riot soon after taking over. The attempt led to a military disaster.

Leading the charge was famous British explorer Lieutenant Colonel Gerard Leachman, a senior colonial officer. Leachman was killed just south of the city in a fight with local leader Shaykh Dhari after underestimating the tenacity of his opponents. Next the British sent an army to crush the rebellion. It was barely enough. Before the battle was over more than 10,000 Iraqis and 1,000 British soldiers lay rotting in the desert heat.

In subsequent decades both Fallujah and the province capital at Ramadi were determined centers for the Arab nationalists shaping the political destiny of modern Iraq. Due to its proximity to Syria during the 1930s and 1940s, Fallujah was the center of Iraqi nationalism seeking to rid the region of its British and French colonial masters. During the turbulent 1950s the sheiks and imams of al-Anbar province opposed the secular Baathist Party because of its ties to the godless Iraqi Communist Party. But with the rise of Saddam Hussein—and the consolidation of his rule beginning in 1968 when the Baathists seized political power—the so-called "second" Baath regime was generally welcomed.

Fallujah has long been known as "the city of mosques" for the more than 200 houses of worship found there and in surrounding villages. It is one of the most important places in the region to Sunni Muslims. Before the war it had been a stronghold of Saddam Hussein's followers and therefore lavished with unusual prosperity.

By 2002 the city's population had grown to 350,000 in a conservative, devoutly Islamic region where medieval Sunni traditions coexisted with traffic jams, blaring boom boxes, and modern graffiti preaching Islam in wild bright paint. It was also a severe Islamic city where the Koran was understood literally and blasphemers dealt with harshly.

Fallujah's architectural makeup, coupled with its bloody history, made it well-suited to defending against a siege—even a modern, hi-tech siege conducted by the best-trained, best-equipped fighting force in the world. In addition to the many mosques with turrets that offered excellent sniping positions, insurgents had the advantage of block after block of one-, two-, and three-story buildings made from reinforced concrete—the same stuff used to construct bunkers and fortresses. Thick-walled courtyards surrounded the buildings, and everywhere ran a maze of alleyways, passages, and safe houses where radical Islamist warriors could flee and regroup to attack again. For an invading force, Fallujah was a deceitful, deadly place. Even without an entrenched opposition, an invasion here would be risky and tough.

A GATHERING STORM

The political reasons for the battle that erupted there in November 2004 are many, varied, and complex. Their various weights and merits are still being argued today.

The easiest reason to understand comes from the young Marines who were there: The bad guys were in Fallujah and the Marines had been called upon to kick them out. Even new recruits understood that rationale. Kicking ass is what Marines do.

The short story is this: Four American civilians from a private security company were ambushed and killed in Fallujah on March 31, 2004. After their fiery deaths their blackened bodies were strung up on a bridge into the city code-named "Brooklyn

Bridge" by the 1st Marine Division (1stMARDIV) Intelligence staff. The insurgents' barbaric actions enraged Americans and resulted in the Coalition's decision to invade the city in an attempt to quell its growing insurgency movement.

The first operation to retake Fallujah began with a bang and ended with a whimper in April. It started when several battalions of Marines from the 1st Marine Expeditionary Force (MEF1) and U.S. Army troopers from a variety of armored, infantry, and cavalry units surrounded Fallujah and then pressed inward.

Just as the force began to make inroads, the Coalition offered the insurgents a unilateral cease-fire. It was a big disappointment to the Marine brass, who knew they could take the city before the enemy had a chance to dig in. At the time, their enemies were still a disorganized mob of Sunni insurgents, even fewer Saddam loyalists, and a handful of foreign fighters who had infiltrated from Jordan and Syria.

But a relatively easy takeover was not to be. After the cease-fire came six months of negotiations to "free" Fallujah. The negotiations might have been comical had they not led to such a bloody end. A variety of Iraqi generals, imams, and wannabe politicians took turns negotiating with Coalition generals, Iraqi politicians, and moderate wannabe religious leaders. They were trying to convince Fallujah's predominantly Sunni population it wanted to be part of a "new Iraq." No agreement was reached and the months of negotiations allowed the insurgency to gain strength. They gathered weapons and manpower, fortified positions, laid explosives (the notorious improvised explosive devices, or IEDs) and other traps for the Coalition forces that would eventually invade.

Meanwhile 1st Marine Division's 22,000 troops were spread across 1,200 square miles of the most hostile region in Iraq. Major General J. N. Mattis, the commanding general of 1st Marine Division, told the press his division had two missions during the negotiations. First was to find and destroy any foreign fighters making their way to Fallujah or anywhere else in the province. Thus offensive operations were first and foremost. The division's combat-hardened Marines had marched from Kuwait to Baghdad the year before, and they knew how to fight. Mattis expected resistance but he knew his Marines were prepared to confront any opposition they would encounter.

The second mission was more complicated: win the hearts and minds of al-Anbar province's residents, many of whom were virulently anti-Coalition Sunnis. The aggressive Marines were instructed to seek common ground with their enemies. It was one of Kasal's jobs to make sure his men did.

"Our motto came from General Mattis," Kasal recalls. "He sent around a letter on our first deployment that said our motto was to be 'No Better Friend, No Worse Enemy.' My young Marines had to be trained—to be instructed—that we couldn't go around indiscriminately killing people. They understood that and did what they were supposed to do. But there were people there who were trying to kill us at the same time." Kasal underscores this dicey duality: "Leadership is important in that situation."

The Marines had reason to be leery of the locals. The Marines' headquarters was only 10 miles from Fallujah, and in the months preceding their impending attack, insurgents had often sortied out of the city to clash with Marine patrols in the endless sand and scrub.

"For five months we endured IEDs, snipers, and daily attacks on our convoys," says Kasal's boss, Commander Lieutenant Colonel Willard "Willy" Buhl. "We had 35 killed and hundreds wounded yet our Marines practiced remarkable restraint. I never saw a civilian woman or child killed before Fallujah during the battalion's second deployment. It was Kasal and the other NCOs' leadership that came into play. It was essential. They were instrumental in keeping our men low-key."

AN ENTRENCHED OPPOSITION

Meanwhile a growing number of experienced foreign fighters were making their way to Fallujah from Baghdad, Ramadi, and Mosul to the north. Exactly how many was unclear. Although the Coalition sent unmanned aerial vehicles (UAVs), Special Forces spooks, and informants to count the growing insurgent army, the reported numbers ranged from 1,500 to 15,000, depending on who was telling the tale. The most accepted figure was about 3,000 regular fighters and another 5,000 active supporters of the insurgency, although these numbers are still hotly debated.

Calculating more refined estimates of the opposition was doubly difficult because it was so diverse. Among them were soldiers, street criminals, politically motivated secular insurgents who wanted to rule, part-time neighborhood warriors looking for glory, vicious foreign fighters with murky agendas, and disenfranchised Baathists who did not necessarily agree with anyone else. There were simply too many factions with too many agendas to count them accurately. Estimates would have to do.

Some of the insurgents preferred rhetoric to combat, and others seemed almost eager to die. But not all were fractious amateurs. If that had been true, the battle would have been over in hours instead of weeks.

Marine intelligence officers identified jihadists from at least 16 countries. Among them were Saudis, Jordanians, Syrians, Yemenis, Pakistanis, Afghans, and Iranians. Many were veteran warriors who had fought in Afghanistan, Yemen, and Somalia.

Most notorious among those was the infamous Jordanian terrorist Abu Musab al Zarqawi. He had set up his al Qaeda network in Fallujah, and in the interval preceding the battle he orchestrated a few beheadings for al Jazeera television to let the world know he was back in action. At the same time Zarqawi and his followers made serious preparations for a fight-to-the-death invasion. They organized bomb-making factories, torture chambers, and booby-trapped death houses. They also intimidated the city's residents into joining, or at least not opposing, their cause. Zarqawi's presence brought even more attention to the situation. Everyone with a title in Iraq wanted to capture him. For the moment he posed a greater evil than Osama bin Laden himself.

Some of the Iraqi fighters were formidable as well. Among them were well-trained, well-equipped, battle-hardened soldiers who had been fighting the Marines for more than five months and other Marine Corps units before them.

In their own way the insurgents were as determined as the Coalition to prevail. To have even a small chance they had cobbled themselves together into die-hard squads and companies. Most would not survive the invasion.

"Some of them were well trained and some of them had never touched a weapon before," Buhl says. "But they were brave and willing to die. One time a squad of them blew down a house on top of themselves to kill Marines. At Fallujah I told my men to kill every one of them because if we didn't, they would be trying to kill us on our next deployment or the one after that."

To the insurgents defending Fallujah it all made sense. They believed that they were warriors of Allah, and Allah had a plan to defeat the Marines. Fortunately for the Marines and soldiers who would soon confront them, the insurgents were wrong.

"Every Marine knew that someday we were going to have to crush them," Buhl says.

A final battle was inevitable.

THE OLD BREED

Opposing the Islamic warriors was the entire 1st Marine Division, "The Old Breed," 22,000 marvelously trained Marines with the temperament of junkyard dogs.

All across the northern boundary they strained at the leash to get the on-again, off-again operation under way. The Old Breed made its reputation of handling its enemies with unparalleled toughness at Guadalcanal. Marines have been dying to preserve that reputation ever since. One Marine said he would rather chew off his arm at the shoulder than tangle with the 1st Marine Division.

The heart of the Old Breed is its infantry battalions. They are the "mailed fist." Their job is to root out the enemy and destroy them posthaste. Afterward the infantry occupies the conquered territory to provide absolute proof of who ultimately prevailed. In the battle of Fallujah, the Blue Diamonds, as the division is also called, fielded four superbly prepared, nearly self-contained battalions each with more than 1,200 highly trained Marine infantrymen. The attacking infantrymen intended to use rockets, grenades, small arms, and their fists to gain the upper hand in the city.

The 5,000 infantry were backed up by a host of supporting arms specialists including military police, recon, armor, artillery, intelligence specialists, radar operators, aviation mechanics, communication experts, aerial surveillance crews, supply units, engineers, construction troops, and linguists. These elements are designated "combat and logistical support" units and make up the essential "logistical tail" of the division.

THE THUNDERING THIRD

In the thick of the action was Buhl's "Thundering Third," a proud unit that keeps a bull for a mascot and a battle flag bearing a thick tassel of campaign streamers. In Marine Corps vernacular the Third is "Three-One," usually written "3/1" on maps and in logs and other places where formality is unimportant. The battalion's colorful battle streamers carry the names of almost every major American conflict around the world since the battalion was formed in 1942 at the beginning of World War II. Like most of the battalions in the 1st Marine Division, 3/1 fought in Korea, Vietnam, and Desert Storm.

In Korea 3/1 assaulted the fortified port of Inchon, helped capture Seoul after the landing, and cleared Hell Fire Valley on the march north to the Yalu River. The Thundering Third stayed through the war until Operation Boulder City when the last Chinese human wave attacks were launched immediately prior to the Korean armistice in 1953.

In Vietnam 3/1 fought brutal battles around An Hoa, Hoi An River, Goi Noi Island, and the terrible "Arizona" free-fire zone of immense proportions, where phantom armies and ghost troops endlessly haunted the U.S. forces.

During Operation Iraqi Freedom in the spring of 2003, 3/1 broke through fierce resistance at An Nasiriyah during the all-important fights for the bridges leading into the heart of Iraq. That fierce contest was one of the first big battles in the fledgling war, and news media from around the world focused on 3/1 Marines reducing the opposition to smoking holes while holding open the road leading through Iraqi lines.

In November 2004 3/1 was an awesome force of 1,245 Marines primed and cocked for battle. In its ranks were Grunts, combat engineers to destroy roadblocks and fortifications, and chemical experts to neutralize potential chemical weapons and biological agents thought to still be in the city. Amphibious assault vehicles (AAVs) from a Marine reserve battalion and two Iraqi National Guard (ING) companies with paper strength of 450 men each were also under Lieutenant Colonel Buhl's tactical control.

When the invasion started Kasal was still First Sergeant Kasal, the senior noncommissioned officer in 3/1's Weapons Co. That was a 170-strong team of superbly trained infantrymen who specialized in deploying the Corps' heaviest infantry weapons— mortars, rocket launchers, and automatic grenade launchers.

Buhl called the Weapons Co. the "power behind the punch."

And "punch" is a euphemism: The Thundering Third's only reason for being is to locate, close with, and destroy the enemy by fire and close combat. Before the sun would set on November 7 the Iraqis who dared stay behind in Fallujah would experience the mighty Thundering Third.

D-DAY

In the days immediately preceding the battle, in Baghdad and Fallujah proper, the antagonists rattled their sabers and postured for the media one final time, spouting rhetoric for the attentive press. On the Coalition side, sniper teams and specially trained reconnaissance units probed the insurgent defenses and performed so-called "demonstrations"—small limited-duration attacks—to confuse the enemy as to where the main attack would originate. In turn the insurgents set up IED ambushes, sniped at the Marines, and moved small units around the city for essentially the same reasons.

Then on November 7 a brigade from the Army's famed 1st Cavalry Division set up a cordon of interlocking fighting positions around the southern and western boundaries of the city to catch anyone fleeing the city there. To the north and east of Fallujah were Marines and soldiers doing the same thing. At the same time the Coalition announced that anyone staying behind in Fallujah after November 8 would be considered the enemy. The plan was to make sure the insurgents had nothing but a Hobson's choice: Surrender and face 30 years in prison or fight and die.

The Coalition had already identified most of the hard targets inside the city using UAVs and other sources. The 3/1 and everyone else in the attacking force knew generally where many of the suspected fighting positions were, as well as where the insurgents stored their weapons and supplies and where they assembled. It was time to take these targets out.

Soon Air Force and Marine Corps aviators zoomed overhead, shaping the battlefield with laser-guided bombs and Hellfire missiles. "Shaping" is a relatively new word in military vernacular. Its innocuous name disguises its terrible implications. Shaping means destroying every identifiable hard target inside the combat arena. To do it the Coalition used Joint Direct Attack Munitions (JDAMs), a type of deadly accurate GPS-guided bomb dropped from Marine, Air Force, and Navy fighter-bombers; Hellfire and TOW missiles from orbiting attack helicopters; aerial-launched unguided missiles of several varieties; and conventional 500- to 2,000-pound dumb bombs. They also used 30mm cannon fire from Air Force A-10 "Warthog" ground-attack aircraft and aerial artillery from AC-130H "Spectre" gunships—the heavily armed night-fighting version of the lumbering four-engine turboprop C-130 Hercules transport in service since the late 1950s. The Warthog's tank-busting cannon used depleted uranium-cored bullets to consume targets, and the Spectre used a battery of 105mm cannon as well as 40mm and 25mm automatic cannon.

Each aerial display brought home the sound of secondary explosions when the insurgents' ammo dumps, explosive-filled vehicles, and daisy chains of IED-laden buildings went up in huge, smoky fireballs. Adding insult to injury the Coalition aircraft destroyed all the vehicles that had been parked in the same location for more than three days on the assumption they were car bombs. Hundreds of insurgents died and plenty more lost their will to fight before the ground campaign had even begun. All in all it was a hectic day for Iraqi automobile owners. Even Kasal's Marines were impressed.

Meanwhile 3/1 wasn't just watching; its assignment involved taking out a huge train station. The ING would then follow behind the main force and seek out the hidden weapons and desperate insurgents left behind after the main attack. Leading them were two cobbled-together 20-man platoons from 3/1 charged with training their newfound Iraqi brothers.

BEHIND AN ARMORED SHIELD

The Thundering Third got busy at 3:00 a.m. on November 8, which was called "D+1," when it moved into its attack positions on the north edge of the city. The 3/1's first mission was to exploit a breach in the fortified line separating the combatants that Marine and Army engineers intended to blow the next morning.

In front of them all were Army M1A1 Abrams heavy tanks and Bradley Fighting Vehicles (BAFVs) from the 2d of the 7th Cavalry, better known as the "Ghost Battalion." The proud 2/7 Cav within the 1st Cavalry Division dates to the Indian Wars in the 1870s. The Ghosts were assigned to provide an armored shield for the Marines to maneuver behind when they entered the fortified city. The 62-ton M1A1 Abrams main battle tanks and 25-ton M2A3 Armored Fighting Vehicles filled with Army cavalrymen were both far more powerful than anything the Marines had within the battalion. The Abrams 120mm main gun was an irresistible force and the Bradley 25mm chain gun devoured soft targets as though they were cotton candy. Initially the armored vehicles staged behind 3/1's position where they set up their Tactical Operations Center (TOC). Until the fight commenced they were encamped about a mile north of Fallujah proper. They would move ahead of the Marines November 9 when the main attack commenced.

3/1's long-anticipated attack began on the ninth, a few hours after Iraqi interim Prime Minister Ayad Allawi gave the green light and the Marines and soldiers were finally unleashed. At the first sound of the guns the insurgents seemed eager to fight. They used the unexpected six-month political respite to turn Fallujah's 140,000 or so stout concrete buildings into death-filled fortresses. Armed with time and emboldened by the false peace, the insurgents were laying the fiercest battleground United States Marines would struggle over since their epic fight for Hue.

For once the weather was not a factor, although at night the Marines were putting on everything they could wear to keep warm. Temperatures were hovering between the upper 30s and low 40s after the sun went down. In the daytime temperatures rose into the 80s. For the encumbered Marines it was hot enough but not as stultifying as it would have been at the height of summer. Luckily the sky was clear and visibility was generally good. At night the stars brightened the sky and allowed the men using night vision goggles to clearly see when the enemy moved. As the battle progressed smoke, clouds, and billowing dust would become a problem, but that was still in the future.

The Marines and soldiers in Fallujah fought 24 hours a day clearing the insurgents from the city house by house and hole by hole. When they took heavy fire from a house or strongpoint, the Marines would call for tank support. The tankers in the 7th Cav were glad to oblige, opening up on the house with their 120mm main gun or their .50-caliber machine guns, literally knocking it to the ground. After a few minutes of suppressive fire the Marines would go into the problem building and clear it. There was rarely anyone left alive at that point. Unfortunately there weren't enough tanks to go around and the Marines were often forced to dig the enemy out with their personal weapons and guts. The fight would last until December 6 when the last insurgent had either died or, rarely, surrendered.

From that battle forth First Sergeant Kasal's life would never again be the same.

CHAPTER 3

GROWING UP IN AFTON

Brad Kasal was born to Gerald and Myrna Kasal in Marengo, Iowa, on a cold February day in 1966. There were three boys already in the clan when Brad arrived, and after a long drought, a fifth son would be born. Not too long after Brad's birth, the family moved from that small farming community west of Cedar Rapids to Afton in southwest Iowa.

Afton is a timeworn village of about 900 in northern Union County, a farming region where good brown soil competes with clay, rocks, scrub, and winding gulches. You can walk across town in 10 minutes. The Kasal farm rests on a hill overlooking a landscape of more rugged hills subdivided by fences full of hedge apples, junipers, old oaks, and an occasional walnut tree. Go a few miles in any direction and the terrain modulates to the gently rolling prairie and rich ground Iowa is best known for.

In the spring and summer the land around Afton renews itself. Redbuds and dogwoods and early spring flowers bloom. When the crops burst forth, the land turns dark green. When it gets warm, residents plant their sparse yards with bright annuals that compete with the occasional clump of perennials waving in the wind. Many Aftonians keep dogs and cats, cars and boats, and all manner of contraptions in their driveways and yards, adding both clutter and life to the place. The town's northwestern boundary is marked by an imposing row of raw concrete grain elevators; toward the center of town a diamond-shape water tower punctuates the otherwise uninterrupted horizon.

From the stand of ragged oaks on Highway 34 near the optimistically named Grand River, Afton doesn't look like a place where legends are born. Except for the occasional train that pounds along the old Burlington-Northern tracks, the town looks relaxed, an easy spot to spend a quiet life. On hot sunny days the turkey buzzards circle overhead waiting for something to die, and red-tailed hawks and an occasional eagle glide lazily by looking for something to kill. Not much else moves.

FROM BOOM TO BUST

Many Iowa families came to the state from somewhere else. So it was with the Kasal family. Brad's father, Gerald Kasal, is the descendant of a barely remembered Czechoslovakian immigrant that family legend says arrived in Chicago with a new wife to find a new life. After learning English and gaining his bearings, he moved to Iowa before the turn of the 20th century and bought a farm, and then another and another, until he was a respected and prosperous Iowan who raised grain, pigs, cattle, and strong, hardworking sons with equal success.

If you were lucky enough to know Gerald Kasal before he died in late April 2006, you could have asked him what kind of farmer he was. He would probably laugh and answer, "Apparently not good enough."

By the time Brad came along in 1966, the economic worm had turned. Like many small farmers, Gerald Kasal found himself farming almost 400 acres in a race with an unkind fate. Prices were perpetually down while costs were always rising. Over time the elder Kasal tried raising hogs, beef, milk cows, and grain to stay ahead in the agricultural game, but the luck and prosperity that had blessed his ancestors eroded away almost as fast as the land he farmed.

Soon after Brad joined the Corps, Gerald gave up farming. Sometime later, Brad's mother, Myrna, and Gerald split. Gerald referred to those unhappy events only as ancient history that he didn't want to discuss. Family business is private business in their households, and they expect others to respect that.

Nosy reporters won't learn much more by asking the locals. Aftonians prefer to brag about how Brad Kasal put their humble town on the map. Gossip in Afton is confined to friends who share over morning coffee at kitchen tables and the local convenience store. Only snippets are offered to strangers. They will say Gerald Kasal worked as hard as anyone to keep his farm, but small farmers didn't yet know how to compete with corporations. It didn't matter what kind of farmer he was. The heyday for small farmers had passed in Iowa, and they went under liked jumped checkers.

By the time Brad was in junior high school, he was old enough to understand that his father and friends lived to work and worked to live off waning fortunes. Even to a kid, it was evident that Brad's father was pouring his life into the earth so he could coax another crop out of the ground before the bank foreclosed and drove the family off the land. This hand-to-mouth existence convinced Brad he didn't want to be a farmer. He wanted to see the world as a Marine.

A GREAT PLACE

But what Brad wanted and what he got were two different things until he was old enough to vote with his feet. By the time Brad came along, the birth of another son was no longer extraordinary, and he was expected to pull his own weight as soon as he was able to work. Randy, the oldest boy, was the alpha dog in the family and used his dominance to lord over his brothers until they were too big for him to bite without a fight, Gerald Kasal said. Whether it was the hard work or the occasional fraternal scrap that toughened Brad, he soon grew extraordinarily strong and straight in a part of the world where strong backs are as common as red barns.

Afton, Iowa, was a great place to grow up. The town's children were carefully watched while they made their way from kindergarten to high school graduation. The town was too small for big secrets, and kids were always found out when they pulled one stunt or another.

"Everybody knew if we did something we weren't supposed to. Somebody would tell Brad or my dad," Brad's youngest brother, Kevin, remembers. "Somebody would stop by and mention whatever it was. We couldn't get away with too much."

Hardly a week went by from fall to summer that the kids in Afton weren't entertaining their parents and neighbors with plays, band concerts, or sports. And when kids weren't entertaining their families and friends, they were usually working for them—baling hay, caring for livestock, planting crops, and working at the grain elevator for money that went for cars, school clothes, and a bit of pocket cash.

WORKING BOY

Brad labored on his dad's farm because he had no choice. "Brad was a hard worker," Gerald said. "He was always working. As soon as he could do a man's work, he was out doing it. Brad was never one to sit around when there was a job to be done."

In high school Brad worked as a busboy and cook at a little Mexican restaurant in Afton called Chello's. At 16, as soon as he was old enough to buy a car, Brad got a job at another restaurant in nearby Creston called Lil' Duffers, a fast-food hangout all his friends visited for a handout. He started out on the counter and worked his way up to night manager, earning enough money to keep his car running and to buy nice clothes.

At Lil' Duffers Brad was generous to a fault, and his hungry friends never left without a free burger and fries, says Troy Tucker, one of Brad's well-fed buddies. "I was always showing up just before close to get a sandwich. Brad would give me something and then tell me to get out of there before he got fired. There would be a whole line of us getting free food. I used to wonder how he didn't get in trouble."

Most folks in Afton agree the virtues of plain, country living that attracted their grandparents and great-grandparents to Iowa were still intact in the 1970s and '80s.

"It was a great place to grow up," Brad says fondly. "We all hung out together. In the summer we hung out on the square in our cars, talking or driving around Afton. I had several really close friends I was usually with."

Brad and his friends somehow managed to elude the more dangerous temptations of modern life. Their world was cars, girls, sports, and hanging out in Afton's tiny town square. Sometimes they skipped school and goofed off. Like kids of any era, they liked music and parties. During the long summers they drove around on the gravel backroads. If you listen to their stories long enough, you might find yourself humming the theme song from *Happy Days*.

The town's one cop didn't bother them. "He kept us out of trouble but let us be kids," Brad says. "If we did a burnout or a doughnut on Main Street when he was around, he'd flash his lights and shake his finger at us, but he was smiling when he did it, and we'd say, 'OK, we'll tone it down.' We got along real well with him. We respected him, and he respected us."

Drugs were not an issue because nobody used them, or admitted to using them, and drinking was limited to some kids pounding down too many beers on a Friday or Saturday night.

"I hung out with the jocks, the average kids, and I was friends with the hoodlums," he says. "Because I was well liked and popular, I didn't have peer pressure to do drugs or drink. I could hang out at the parties and be with everyone and not have to get involved."

BRAD 'N' THE BOYS

That didn't mean, however, that Brad Kasal was a choirboy or that he hung out with choirboys.

One of his best buddies during high school was Randy Cornelison, now a 41-year-old self-described "gearhead" who lives near Adel, a small town north of Afton. Cornelison owned his own body shop for years before giving it up to run heavy equipment. Today he is married and has two sons. In high school he got into more than his share of trouble.

Kasal describes Cornelison as his occasional nemesis as well as one of his closest high school friends. He claims Cornelison and Troy Tucker were at the root of most of his minor scrapes with trouble. The big ones, Kasal jokes, he managed on his own.

All who knew the infamous trio remember the eyes of the teachers fastening on them when a disturbance unexpectedly broke out in the halls of East Union High. Whether it was skipping school, riding bicycles through the halls, or playing "grab ass" in the classroom, the three of them were usually involved in it together.

Kasal remembers Cornelison as a big, gawky kid with a crazy sense of humor and a strong devotion to his two best friends. Cornelison in turn recalls Tucker as a "wild man" and Kasal as the quiet type.

"Troy was a fast-driving, tough-talking country boy who didn't mind egging on his buddies to stir up some shit on Saturday night when things got a bit dull," Cornelison says. The three liked to play practical jokes on each other, get loud, and drive the nine miles to nearby Creston where they cruised the loop, driving aimlessly around on the main drag looking for girls or trouble or both.

Their behavior was nothing exceptional. Like millions of young men from Small Town, USA, fighting and fornicating were the two most popular pleasures of the day in the early '80s, although most of Afton's young men weren't usually successful in either pursuit. Kasal was an exception, Cornelison says. He backs up his assertions with stories from his private annals that present the trio as a cross between the Three Musketeers and the Three Stooges.

"Troy and Brad and I would be somewhere," Cornelison says. "Brad was such a nice guy he would never cause any trouble, but he was a tough guy—I mean tougher than shit. We would try and get him in a fight. We would walk up to some guy and tell him, 'That guy over there wants to fight you because he thinks you're a punk' or 'That guy over there has been checking out your woman.' Something like that. But that was back in the good old days when after a fight you would get up and shake hands. Nowadays you'd get shot."

MEMORIES

More than 20 years later Kasal hasn't forgotten his nights with Randy and Troy. The memories still make him chuckle, a kind of rasping sound he makes when he is telling a joke or relating a fond memory. He claims his life would have been much quieter if it weren't for the antics of his buddies.

"I would be standing there drinking a soda at the refreshment stand somewhere," he says, "and the next thing I know some big guy would walk up and tap me on the shoulder and say, 'Hey, I heard you want to fight me.' I'd think, 'that damn Cornelison.' Just about every time we went out, he would try and get me in a fight.

"He would walk up to the biggest guy he could find and tell him I wanted to fight him. Right away, we would be heading to the bathroom or out in the alley or somewhere to fight, and I didn't even know the guy."

Cornelison knew he was playing with fire. "Brad could kick me and Troy's ass at the same time," he says. Kasal played football and was a standout wrestler, gaining a cauliflower ear in the process. He lifted weights constantly and ran for pure pleasure.

"We used to give him hell," Cornelison says. "Troy and me were always hitting him or telling him we were going to kick his ass, or getting him in headlocks, and he never did anything to us. I think secretly he liked being a badass, even in junior high school. Brad was very timid and shy when you met him; once you open that door and unleash that beast, look out!"

Cornelison adds, "He could be one ornery son of a bitch. One time in school Troy and Brad put me in the trash can during break—put my butt in the can and Brad stomped me in until only my head and legs were sticking out. Then put me up on the sink. They did it more than once. Sometimes they would shut the lights off on me too. I would have to tip the trash can off the sink and fall on the floor to get out of it."

But Brad Kasal didn't just hang out with the guys. No one would expect that. Shawn Essy is a lifelong friend and a devoted follower of his Marine career. Back in high school she was Kasal's confidante and frequent companion. They shared parking spots on the square on summer nights under the big Iowa sky and talked about the future waiting for them. Although they have been separated by thousands of miles since Kasal joined the Corps, they have remained close friends.

TALK ALL NIGHT

"When we weren't working—especially in the summer—we would hang around the square," Essy remembers. "Brad would be in his Charger—later he had a Cutlass—and I would have my four-door Ford LTD, and we would sit on our hoods and talk and talk all night. Sometimes we would go to Creston and cruise around, but most of the time we hung out in town just talking."

Essy says Kasal showed a different side to the girls. "He was different than most of the other boys in Afton. By the time he reached high school Kasal was already confident and self-assured. He was already serious about what he wanted to do and how he intended to get there. He just didn't let people too close to him until he got to know them. In school he was fairly shy, but out of school he could talk your leg off."

Kasal says Essy was one of the few people he was comfortable confiding in. "She was my friend," he says. "I would tell her things; we were very close. It was a brother-sister thing."

Essy now lives with her husband and two sons near Randy Cornelison in Adel. On a shelf in the family room of her well-appointed home is a picture of Brad in formal dress looking boldly into the camera. Behind him are an American flag and the golden battle flag of the Thundering Third. To her two boys, Brad is a real-life, honest-to-God Marine hero, she says. They idolize him and Brad reciprocates with letters and emails letting them know what he is up to.

His stern countenance in the photograph is a far cry from the Brad she grew up with, Essy says. "If I could say one thing that I know we did, it was laugh. Brad could be a complete crack up when he wanted to be, when he got to know someone."

Essy's younger sister Tracey shares her sister's fondness for their favorite Marine. Tracey remembers how much pride Brad took in the appearance of his car. "Brad's cars were always in mint condition. His car was his pride and joy and always spotless.

He would go about 15 miles an hour when driving on backroads so the gravel wouldn't nick the paint."

Tucker and Cornelison razzed their buddy mercilessly about his cautious driving. "I could get out and run faster than he was driving," Tucker says with a laugh. "I did it one time, and he drove off and left me!"

Cornelison also gets a chuckle out of Essy's characterization of Brad's innocence. In Cornelison's memory Kasal was a bit of a rake in Creston. He speculates that at least some of the trouble Kasal found himself in while cruising the Creston loop came from his propensity for seducing local girls.

"When it came to women Kasal was something else," Cornelison says. "He knew how to turn on the charm for the Creston girls. We liked to watch him work. He wouldn't try anything with the girls from Afton because we were all too tight. We were very close friends, and everybody would have known what was going on. So we never really knew what he was up to, but we were like everybody else. We talked about cars, girls, and jobs, but mostly girls—except for Brad. Even then he was a gentleman. Brad wouldn't ever say anything. He would just smile."

KASAL AT SCHOOL

Male or female, Kasal's friends remember him as a natural leader at school. He never bullied anyone and he always watched out for his friends and classmates. Even though he could hang out with a rowdy crowd, he generally had a settling influence on the other students without being menacing.

Kasal wasn't particularly interested in high school except for sports and reading. He was a good wrestler and played varsity football, but he liked challenging himself better. "It takes more self-discipline to do hard things when nobody is making you," he explains.

Most of the subjects he studied in high school bored him almost to distraction, but he was very interested in history. He liked to read about military operations and wondered what it would be like to fight in battle. He discovered his heroes in the books he read about war and combat, particularly stories about Marines.

When his thoughts began to mature, he shared them with his friends. They say that by the time they were in high school they already knew he was going to be a warrior or a cop or something like that. They saw a sense of adventure already evident in their friend long before he knew it for sure; they just didn't know how to define it. Then he told them.

"Brad knew what he wanted and where he wanted to go," says Essy, "and he wanted to go in the Marines. He told me when we were maybe sophomores or juniors in high school, but he had mentioned that kind of stuff before then. I didn't understand it, but I could respect it. Most of us did. Brad was always a leader in school, and the Marines didn't seem too far-fetched for him."

There was one problem though, and Kasal finally got up the courage to admit it to Essy. He didn't know how to swim. In fact he was terrified of the water.

His other friends learned of his problem after his local recruiter informed Kasal that one of the tasks he absolutely had to complete in boot camp was to jump into a pool from the high dive while fully clothed. Worse, he had to then sink underwater, swim to the surface, and make his way to a ladder to simulate abandoning ship. There was no way around it. To graduate from boot camp, everyone had to pass the swim test—a time-honored tradition that has washed out more than one aspiring Marine.

"He came back from the recruiter and told us he had to swim, but he was afraid of the water," Essy says. "He had a hard time telling us because Brad wasn't the kind of guy who ever admitted being afraid of anything. So we decided we would teach him how to swim before he left. We told him we would take him to Shelley's—she was a girl we knew who had a pond on her property outside of town—and teach him how to swim, get him used to the water. He wasn't too crazy about that."

Tracey Essy picks up the story from there: "He didn't want to jump in because he didn't know how deep it was. We didn't really care because as kids, you know, we just saw water and jumped in. But Brad hated the water.

"It turns out it was pretty shallow. When I jumped in to show him it was safe, I hit the bottom so hard I had mud in my ear. After that I heard Brad say, 'Uh-uh, no!' He was fearful of it. He never did it that summer, but he did it in boot camp," Tracey says.

"He came home and told us he had done it," Shawn Essy adds. "He was pretty excited."

GOTCHA!

Before making it to boot camp, Kasal had to graduate from high school. That took him longer than it might have and not because of his academic record. While undistinguished, his grades were perfectly acceptable, but his reputation as a ringleader of the rowdy, along with one particular indiscretion put a six-month dent in his plans.

Kasal's nemesis in this case was a cranky high school principal, Mr. Goetche, a man the kids called "Gotcha Goetche" because he was always on the lookout for Brad and his buddies Cornelison and Tucker. Even Kasal's former teachers acknowledge the principal was a stern, uncompromising man who had little tolerance for the self-assured boy whose reputation preceded him. Kasal claims Gotcha was waiting for him to screw up so he could be made an example to the other rowdies. As a result Kasal and his friends were frequent visitors to Gotcha's office. Sometimes it was for licks from his wooden paddle; sometimes it was for detention. One thing was for certain, Brad remembers; it was never for a good thing.

"Gotcha Goetche didn't like me," he says.

Kasal found out exactly how much Goetche didn't like him when he was slapped with a six-month suspension for saying the forbidden word "fuck" in a classroom during the final semester of his senior year. Although his invective was aimed at Cornelison, his indiscretion became a terrible embarrassment and a huge inconvenience when it came time to enlist in the Marine Corps.

"I was all ready to leave for boot camp when I graduated in June, and then I got suspended and had to stay in school another semester after all my friends had graduated," he admits bitterly.

He went before the school board for a reprieve, but the sentence stuck. Kasal learned a big lesson about being a wiseass and swore to himself he was going to keep his mouth shut and get through his extra semester. Although he tried to act like it didn't bother him, it was a crushing blow for a young man who had his eye set on being a Marine as soon as he could.

Kasal accepted his sentence and graduated quietly from high school in December 1984. There isn't even a senior class picture of him in the school yearbook. He left for the Corps as soon as they were ready to take him. Gotcha never got a second chance at Brad Kasal.

BRAD'S LAST VISIT HOME

After Kasal joined the Marines he came back to Afton one more time on leave following boot camp. His friends found him to be different: more serious, less prone to carry on. If anything, though, he was both tougher and more gracious than ever.

"One time Brad and me were in a bar after he joined up and was back home on leave," Cornelison says. "We were playing pool when some scrawny little skinny guy got all mouthy. He kept calling Brad a jarhead and all sorts of names. Brad really hated being called a jarhead. All you had to do is look at him and know that calling him a jarhead is pretty stupid.

"So Brad was saying, 'Sir, please sit down. Sir, please sit down,' but the guy just kept it up until he really pissed Brad off. Brad ends up dragging this guy across the pool table by his neck and pinning him to the table.

"About then four girls—a couple of them worked there and two others who were just trying to break it up—climbed all over Brad and started pulling on him and yelling at him to make him let this little skinny dude go. By now the dude was lying on the table making choking sounds. But Brad is such a gentleman that he just turned around—still holding the skinny dude by his neck—and said, 'Ladies, please quit it; please get off me; don't do that.'

"He never raised his voice or got mad or anything. He said it so polite and all the time he is still choking the shit out of the skinny dude."

Although Kasal left Afton, Afton never let go of Brad Kasal. Everybody in town loves their local hero and they unanimously agree that Kasal makes a good one. When Read's famous picture appeared in the *Creston News Advertiser* and the *Des Moines Register,* all the old Kasal stories were brought out of the closet and dusted off. His picture appeared in windows and folks took an active interest in his welfare. Kasal and his family were flooded with well wishes and inquiries of concern. Most of the folks in town have since watched his story unfold in the coverage of newspapers, magazines, and television. Before his untimely death from cancer, Gerald Kasal made sure his famous son's circle of old friends was kept abreast of what was going on with Brad. Many of them drove out to the farmhouse to visit the ailing Kasal and to find out what had become of their famous classmate. Many more called or wrote short notes of encouragement that Gerald Kasal treasured until his death.

CHAPTER 4
★ ★ ★

JOINING UP

Like millions of young men who enlisted before him, Kasal eventually saw the day when he achieved his cherished goal of becoming a Marine. For Kasal that journey, which has not ended, began on a frigid Iowa morning in late January 1984.

"When I got on the plane in Des Moines it was 35 degrees below zero," Kasal says. "When I got off in San Diego it was 60 something. We are talking about a 90-degree difference in temperature. It was hot and humid when they bundled us up and put us on a bus through San Diego. The first thing I saw that made an impression on me—something I will always remember—is when we drove down the Pacific Highway. It was a place called Dirty Dan's—you know what that is? A girlie bar. When you are 18 and you come from Iowa, it's a big deal to see something like that. Anyway that was the last thing I would see of civilian life for three months."

BOOT CAMP

First stop for the recruit was the Marine Corps Recruit Depot (MCRD). A drill instructor (DI) jumped into the bus and started kicking everybody off. "He was yelling, screaming, the whole routine," Kasal recalls, "and he tells us to get on the yellow footprints.

"I was thinking, 'Holy cow. What have I got into?' All night long and for two more days we were getting our haircuts, getting our gear, getting our basic uniforms issued to us: cammies, socks, boots, stuff like that. Then came the medical examination, the dental examination—all this time the drill instructors and senior Marines are yelling and screaming. After Receiving we went to our regular platoon. There we picked up our senior drill instructor and our permanent junior drill instructors. For the next three months we trained with them."

Marine Corps boot camp is no garden party. Former Marine drill instructor and Vietnam vet-turned-actor R. Lee Ermey did a fair job replicating the conditions and treatment Marine recruits enjoy in Stanley Kubrick's *Full Metal Jacket*. This bizarre 1987 movie follows a fictional group of Marine Boots who endure the tortures of the damned while getting ready to go to Vietnam. Kasal likes the first half of the movie for its accurate depiction of boot camp.

Before Kubrick's surrealistic look, Jack Webb wrote, produced, directed, and starred in *The DI*, a sanitized 1957 version of Marine Corps boot camp that offered more promise than realism. Kasal's experience was somewhere between the two movie extremes. Most Marines say that the drill instructors were fearsome beasts who didn't care for "knuckleheads," "knot-heads," and far harsher names they bellowed into the recruits' faces. Most Marines remember the experience as somewhere between hell and damnation until they started feeling the pride of being Marines. Kasal remembers learning his craft and beginning to admire the drill instructors' skills and knowledge as boot camp dragged by. It went slowly and quickly at the same time, a dizzying schedule of off-and-on and hurry-up-and-wait that ran in an endless loop. Part of being a Marine is learning to cope with stress, and the DIs' pressure to the young recruits made sure they had plenty of it.

"Who joins the Marine Corps to be a computer operator?" retired Lance Corporal Alex Nicoll, who was in the Fallujah battle with Kasal, asks rhetorically. "I expected some pain. I wanted to be in the infantry. I wanted combat, and I expected to get my ass kicked. People know what they are getting into when they join the Corps, which is why they do it.

"I was a squad leader most of the time in boot camp, and I got my ass kicked double—once for what I did and then for the things my squad did. I was always getting my ass kicked. Some of the DIs were as straight as officers, but most of them knew how to kick somebody's ass when they couldn't be seen. They knew the system and how to pick who could take it. It was part of being a Marine. I got plenty of kicks to the shins and a few kidney punches when nobody was looking."

Kasal acknowledges the DIs occasionally reinforced their commands with strenuous punishment even though the practice isn't sanctioned. In today's Corps physical punishment is banned and violators are prosecuted, Kasal says.

Marines said the same thing about the physical realities of boot camp back in the '60s when more than one Marine graduated sporting a black eye or fat lip in his graduation photo. Pain is part of the process and it will never completely go away.

Usually, Kasal says, any physical abuse in boot camp arrives disguised as exercise, an unrelenting regimen of body-stretching, muscle-making drills followed by running and push-ups and more running. Between classroom instruction, outdoor classes, close order drill, and exercise periods, recruits occupy their time with bayonet training—learning to use their rifles as pugil sticks to batter each other. They also work on the fine art of hand-to-hand combat.

Repetition is how Marines learn, Kasal says. "Marines learn by doing things over and over until it is automatic, until their training just kicks in. In combat that is what happens: Training kicks in and Marines do what they are trained to do. That is why discipline and following orders is so important."

The entire process was a carefully choreographed routine to turn them into neophyte Marines, although many green recruits never recognize a method to the madness around them. The unrelenting regimen toughens them mentally and physically. They are taught to be aggressive, to attack, to go for the jugular. They become killing machines under contract to their government. That is what Marines do and boot camp pushed Kasal and Nicoll to the top level of proficiency.

Kasal says he had a good experience at MCRD and he was meritoriously promoted to Private First Class (PFC). "I won't say boot camp wasn't hard, because it was very hard. But I was already in good physical shape," he says. "I had played football and wrestled and worked out on my own year-round. Even in the winter I would be out running on the country gravel roads in snow, jogging to stay in shape, so I was already fit when I went there. On April 12, 1985, I graduated and got 10 days' 'boot leave'—the leave Marines get after boot camp."

As Kasal expected, his two best friends kidded him unmercifully while he was home. The high school trio tried picking up where they left off, but something had changed. Kasal was a Marine now, and Marines are no longer mere civilians.

Cornelison immediately sensed Kasal had outgrown cruising the loop in Creston. Although Kasal enjoyed seeing his friends, he was anxious to get to his destination: the School of Infantry (SOI) where Boots learn to be riflemen—"mud Marines."

"To me being a Marine is being a Grunt," Kasal says. "But my recruiter told me I had to join open contract, and when I got to boot camp our senior drill instructor told us that anyone on open contract was going to be a cook. I was on mess duty for one week, but it was a week too much."

Mess duty is anathema to a warrior. Duties are varied but equally bad. You might be "Admiral of the Vessels" in command of the dirty pots and pans floating in the sink or a dining room orderly ensuring the milk machines are filled and the tables and chairs are precisely lined up. Or for 12 hours a day, seven days a week you might mop the floors, clean out grease traps, and carry away the garbage under the gaze of a scowling mess sergeant.

"So I spent the next month sweating it out, waiting for the end of boot camp when they tell us what our Military Occupational Specialty (MOS) is going to be. And then they told me I was going to be a Grunt. I was a really motivated Marine then. I had really sweated having to be a cook," says Kasal.

SCHOOL OF INFANTRY

West Coast Marines selected to be infantrymen go to the School of Infantry (SOI) at Camp Pendleton, California, before being deployed to permanent duty stations. The motto is "Every Marine a Rifleman," and the trainers at SOI take their mission very seriously. Unlike other branches of service every Marine is a rifleman first—a distinction Kasal points out with pride.

The School of Infantry's beguiling setting belies its very serious nature. Camp Pendleton is about 40 miles north of San Diego along the rugged Pacific Coast. In winter its lush green hills turn dull brown, but with the coming of spring Pendleton turns into a riot of competing colors when the wildflowers blossom and the grass turns a lush green. At first glance it doesn't appear to be the home of warriors.

In peacetime it is home to the 1st Marine Division as well as to a variety of schools, logistic facilities, aviation assets, and support operations for the Marines' worldwide mission. More than 125,000 acres and approximately 200 square miles big, it is arguably the most important Marine Corps facility in the United States. The stretch of shoreline along the base—17½ miles—is the largest undeveloped portion of coastal area in Southern California. Within its confines are training areas, administrative buildings, an air base, ship docking facilities, dependent quarters, and a variety of off-duty recreational opportunities new Marines occasionally get to look at on their morning runs.

The skyline is marred by "Mount Motherfucker," an especially steep mountain where Marines climb for glory on forced marches, conditioning runs, and long humps. On any given day visitors at Pendleton are treated to squads, platoons, and companies of physically fit Marines marching by loaded down like pack mules or jogging in formation to the rhythm of gravelly voiced sergeants calling cadence.

The first stop for PFC Kasal was the Infantry Training Battalion (ITBn). The ITBn's mission is to train and qualify Marines in the MOS of 0311 Rifleman, 0331 Machinegunner, 0341 Mortarman, 0351 Assaultman, and 0352 Anti-Tank Guided Missileman. Those five specialties are the heart and soul of a United States Marine infantry division. For 52 days young Marines are taught how to use the weapons they will ultimately shoot in the field.

Kasal was selected to be a 0351 Assaultman firing antitank rockets. An Assaultman in 1984 was responsible for the tactical employment of the shoulder-launched multipurpose assault weapon (SMAW) and the M-47 Dragon medium assault antitank weapon, which is now obsolete. Assaultmen provide antibunker and antiarmor fire for infantry units in attack and defense. Assaultmen are assigned to weapons platoons and weapons companies.

Marine infantrymen provide antitank capabilities using several man-portable and vehicle-mounted antitank systems including the SMAW and the mighty M-220 tube-launched, optically tracked, wire-guided missile (TOW) that can pierce any known armor or knock down a building, depending on what the Marines need it for.

The SMAW is the smallest antitank rocket in the Assaultman's inventory. It is a single-man-fired 16.5-pound weapon with a maximum range of about 500 meters when used against a tank. The almost 50-pound TOW is the largest. Both are deadly and Kasal would get plenty of time—both in training and in combat—with each of them.

Dragon was replaced by Javelin, another man-portable weapon and a favorite of Marines fighting in Iraq and Afghanistan. The Javelin is a Dragon with a brain. It is a "fire-and-forget," shoulder-fired antitank missile with a range of 2,500 meters. As soon as it is fired the gunner ducks—a big advantage when fighting an enemy tank or trying to destroy a machine-gun position. In the Javelin gunner's case he uses a sophisticated sight to take a picture of the target, which he transfers to the guidance system in the missile's warhead. After the gunner lets fly the Javelin homes in on the target using the locked-in image for guidance and recognition. The Javelin system is even tougher to hump but much more deadly. At Fallujah the Marines fired dozens of them with telling effect. Jihadists detested the Javelin and ran when they saw it being deployed.

Kasal's long runs back in Iowa with logs on his back paid off at the SOI. The Dragon's 32.1-pound weight and nearly 4-foot length made it just as cumbersome as a log and just as hard to hump—especially when a gunner is carrying all his weapons and ammo, personal gear, water, and rations. The gunner is accompanied by a second team member who carries one of the weapon's various day and night sighting devices.

Kasal learned quickly how difficult it was to be an Assaultman. "It was very hard, very physically demanding and there was a lot of knowledge to learn," he says. "I was already very physically fit and I didn't have any trouble keeping up physically, but it was hard. They ran us everywhere. We ran with all our gear on, all our weapons. They taught a lot to us in a very short period of time."

Seven weeks later Kasal was SOI's honor graduate and a full-fledged Marine. All he needed was a little salt and he would be seasoned to perfection.

Getting to his first duty station wasn't too hard. Kasal was assigned to the 2d Battalion, 1st Marine Regiment (2/1) at Camp Horno, a lodgment area within Camp Pendleton and the home of the 1st Marine Division.

A PROUD HISTORY

Second Battalion was activated August 1, 1922, at Santo Domingo, Dominican Republic, and deactivated two years later. The regiment first gained notoriety when it was part of a joint Navy-Marine Corps task force that seized the Mexican port of Veracruz.

During the Great Depression the regiment's colors stayed mothballed until the threat of war in the Pacific brought it back to life on February 1, 1941, as part of the 1st Marine Division. The 1st Marines' first campaign was on Guadalcanal from August until December 1942. Its last battle was at Okinawa, the longest and fiercest Marine contest in the Pacific war.

Arguably its most illustrious commander—and perhaps the most famous Marine of all—was Lewis B. "Chesty" Puller. He spent 37 years in the Corps during which he received five Navy Crosses, the nation's second highest award for valor, behind only the Medal of Honor, before retiring at the rank of lieutenant general.

In 1949 the 1st Marines was again briefly deactivated until shortly after the outbreak of the Korean War the next spring. On September 15, 1950, the 1st Marine Division assaulted the beaches of Inchon.

During the Vietnam War the 1st Marine Division first fought around Chu Lai, in Viet Cong-infested southern I Corps. In January 1968 the Communists launched their all-out Tet Offensive during which the old imperial capital of Hue was overrun and occupied by the Communists. Between January 31 and March 2, 1968, the 1st Marines, along with other Marine elements, as well as South Vietnamese and U.S. Army troops, fought to regain control of the city. When the battle ended more than 1,900 enemies had died. It wouldn't be the last time Marines would take a city; the 1st Marines just didn't know it yet. The 1st Marines were the last Marine infantry unit to depart Vietnam.

When Kasal reached 2/1, 1st Marine Division in June 1985 he was a PFC assigned to Weapons Co. as a Dragon gunner. He couldn't have asked for more.

"Ever since I had learned about the Marine Corps, I had learned about Camp Pendleton. It had a certain mystique about it, and I had always wanted to be there. That is when I checked into Weapons Co. as a young PFC and started getting the reputation—so they say—for always humping extra gear," Kasal recalls.

During training the Marines took 20-mile hikes with all gear. "When we went on humps, I would carry the weapon and the sight just so I could outdo someone else. It would be a bet. People would say it couldn't be done. We would hump up Mount Motherfucker and I would race up to the top to try and beat everybody. And then when I got up there I would howl like a coyote to kind of motivate everybody else."

Kasal's extra efforts were noticed, although he wasn't working hard for a promotion. He just liked being a Marine. He liked the "esprit de corps," the challenges, and the competition to be the best. Kasal was meritoriously promoted to Lance Corporal in August 1985, about two months after he checked into the company. He had been a Marine for eight months.

SHIPPING OUT

Weapons Co. trained until June 1986 when Kasal's battalion deployed to the Western Pacific (WESTPAC) as part of the ground combat element of a Special Operations Capable (SOC) Marine Amphibious Unit (MAU). The MAU name was subsequently changed to Marine Expeditionary Unit (MEU) to emphasize the expanded capabilities of such a unit beyond amphibious landings. With a strength of approximately 2,200 personnel an MEU is normally commanded by a colonel and built around a reinforced infantry battalion, a composite aircraft squadron with both rotor- and fixed-wing AV-8B Harrier II "jump jets," and an MEU service support group. The Marines live on ships and crisscross the Pacific, training with allied nations and showing the flag in less receptive places.

The designation SOC is never granted until a unit successfully completes a special training regimen. This prepares the SOC to perform 18 special missions including amphibious raids, limited objective attacks, noncombatant evacuations, and a host of other operations, including Military Operations on Urban Terrain (MOUT), special demolitions operations, and "in-extremis" hostage rescues. In short, Kasal's team was a highly trained, remarkably able, self-contained attack formation with multiple capabilities, ready to kick ass anywhere, anytime.

For Kasal the deployment was a great training experience and a place to show his skills. His unit visited ports in Australia, Singapore, Thailand, Hong Kong, and the Philippines. He went on joint infantry training exercises with soldiers from other nations, practiced beach assaults and aerial envelopments using helicopters, and simply hiked over miles of rugged terrain carrying huge equipment loads to simulate a real combat deployment.

"I liked deploying," Kasal says. "I like Third World countries. People are really nice to us and welcome us. They are usually very curious and follow us around so close we can't train. I like being there better than training in more modern countries where everything is the same."

PARTY TIME

There was a lot of work, but all work and no play makes "Private Schmuckatelli" a dull Marine indeed. Marines never get too crotchety or too old to remember when they were young Marines. "Sometimes we trained and sometimes we would just pull into liberty ports and party," Kasal recalls. "Life is simpler in Third World countries. All the time we would be out somewhere and people would just come up and bring us food. They would want to talk. At the end of the day we would just stop and hang around talking to the local people."

Partying in exotic ports is always interesting, Kasal says. Everything is different. From street signs to far more mysterious pleasures and pursuits, the sights, tastes, smells, and sounds are completely foreign. New American guys on liberty for the first time in Bangkok, Hong Kong, Subic Bay, or any other Asian port on the Pacific archipelago won't quickly forget what went on. They might not tell their mothers and sisters, but it is a unique experience.

In September 1986 Kasal won a Noncommissioned Officer (NCO) of the Quarter award and was meritoriously promoted to Corporal. It was his third meritorious promotion, putting him ahead of the curve for career Marines. More important he was now officially a Marine combat leader. All he needed was some leadership experience to make it all work.

He quickly found out that being a corporal definitely has its rewards. They are still subtle—it isn't time to kick back in the sergeant major's quarters sucking down a cup of coffee while bad-mouthing the boots and making fun of the junior officers— but there are benefits nonetheless. For Kasal the shit details like standing guard, working mess duty, and lifting and toting supplies and equipment diminished, and the first sergeant took an interest in his behavior. Corporals are probationary members of a closed and cloistered system bound by customs and traditions as old as the Corps itself. Entrance is limited to the chosen few so the enlisted leadership has to know if the junior Marine is going to make the cut.

Getting promoted has other benefits as well. One is having more time in liberty ports for personal pursuits. Young Marines are on a tight leash most of the time and get edgy like overtrained thoroughbreds. For weeks at a time they are confined to eight-man and 10-man spaces that would instigate a lawsuit if they were inmates in a county jail. They are stressed, denied sleep, and roused at all hours of the day and night during training exercises. Sex and food, sex and drinking, sex and training, sex and cars, and just plain sex are the usual topics of conversation. When it comes time for a little relaxation after all this, Marines have a long, proud tradition of how to go about it.

Depending on what port they pull into and what kind of ship they are on, Marines either go ashore over the brow—a platform from the ship to the pier—or in liberty boats, landing craft designated for transporting Marines ashore from a ship in the harbor. While the ships are in port the Marines receive mail, put aboard supplies, pull guard duty, and prepare for the next port of call. Civilians pulling into the same ports spend thousands of dollars for the opportunity. Marines pay in sweat and toil and deadly serious training.

"While we were on my first WESTPAC is when I got introduced to partying," Kasal says. "I never used to drink until I went to the Philippines the first time. That corrupted me for partying for about five or six years. We would go to Subic, Barrio, Olongapo, places like that. We would go out, drink, party, stay out all night, and stagger back to the boat about 5 in the morning. Then we would be tired and half-dead all day waiting for liberty the next day, and then we would be all wide-eyed and bushy tailed and do it again.

"When I was 18 or 19 years old, I could do that. We would go out in groups, three- or four- or five-man groups, and drink and party all night. Now I would have to have a four-day recovery."

Another well-known pursuit in liberty ports was fighting. Marines like to fight. Because they are trained to fight, disagreements over who is the best and who is the worst and I-just-don't-like-your-face opinions erupt into fights. Servicemen from rival branches of the military make good targets. But Marines would fight each other if no one else were around. Even officers aren't immune. When one highly placed officer was rousted in front of a urinal in a Filippino bar by an enlisted Marine, the recalcitrant young Marine ended up cleaning the urinal with his face.

"It would have been the end of my career right there," the officer later admitted privately, "but nobody identified me."

For the young Marines brawls were the stuff of legends until they got back on board and sobered up. Then it was time to face the wrath of their commanders, which could also be legendary. However more than one Marine surmised that his commanders would have been even angrier if the Marines were forced to admit they had been subdued by "doggies" (Army soldiers), "squids" (Navy personnel), or civilians instead of holding their own in impromptu tough man contests.

More than once Kasal found out the hard way that the local authorities have little patience with wild-eyed Marines on liberty. "I was arrested for fighting in a bar in '86 in the Philippines by the Navy Shore Patrol and held overnight and released the next morning," he says. "I was charged but it got dismissed. In fact I have been arrested for fighting in four different countries: Okinawa, Mexico, the United States, and the Philippines. But like I said, you get in a partying phase. I got into it for a few years and then I outgrew it. After I was 26 or 27, I never did it again."

In December of 1986 Kasal returned to Pendleton. Almost immediately he was assigned to be a team leader for a Dragon section. In January of 1987 he was appointed to be a section leader, a staff sergeant's billet and one responsible for leading three squads—a heavy duty for a 20-year-old Marine.

"All of '87 I was a section leader and we would do training at Camp Pendleton," he says. "That is also where my reputation for never getting tired and the whole routine was made. In January 1988 I was meritoriously promoted to Sergeant. In June of '88 we deployed overseas again. My section was attached to Fox Co., 2/1 on the USS *Fresno*. We would do the same thing, pull into a country, do training, go on liberty, and then back to sea."

Kasal's youthful vision of being a Marine was now realized. He was a sergeant of Marines, an infantryman, and a locked-and-cocked warrior ready for war.

CHAPTER 5

THE LONG HAUL

For most of the next five years Kasal did what Marine infantrymen do in peacetime—he trained. He went from ship to shore and back in routine cycles of training and forward deployment. One ship that made a lasting impression on Kasal was the USS *Fresno,* a landing ship-tank (LST) he sailed on in 1988. Decommissioned now, *Fresno* was an ungainly looking craft with a portable landing ramp that looked like an alligator's snout poking into the air. *Fresno* was 522 feet long, had a beam of 70 feet, and displaced 8,500 tons. She was rated with a top speed of 20 knots and carried a crew of 14 officers, 210 enlisted sailors, and approximately 350 embarked Marines and their equipment. Aboard *Fresno* Kasal found a home away from home.

"I loved LSTs," Kasal says. "They were my favorite ship. The bigger the ship you go on the more brass you have, the more people you have, the more crowds, bigger chow lines, longer mail call, and the more people to screw with you. On an LST it was your company and that was it. It is the difference between living in a small town and living in L.A."

Fresno was part of a five-ship amphibious-ready group that usually included a "big deck" helicopter carrier or an amphibious assault ship plus a group of smaller vessels.

The Marines had everything they needed and nothing that wasn't required for a seagoing deployment. No gourmet meals. No tastefully decorated staterooms. No plush bathrooms. Only a steel box designed to carry bodies with the highest efficiency and lowest possible cost. There was no privacy, no space to stretch out, and very little to do except be a Marine.

Certainly great chow wasn't what drew Kasal to the life of a combat Marine. "You eat Navy chow," he says. "The first week you are out at sea the food is pretty good. After that it is rice and hot dogs every day, rice and chicken, or rice and rice. The longer you are out, the lower the supplies get. After a while there is not as much to eat."

Being on a bigger ship was not the solution either. Grunts still lived in tiny berthing spaces crammed with their gear and themselves regardless of the size of ship. The chow wasn't any better or more plentiful either.

Life on board Navy ships at sea had a dull sameness to it. Kasal's company trained in any open space they could find to keep themselves occupied. "We would find a corner of the ship where we could do push-ups and pull-ups and maybe run around the deck when they were not doing flight ops," Kasal recalls. "You clean your weapons, and you find little nooks and crannies on the ship to give classes about tactics, weapons, riot control— sometimes we did hand-to-hand combat training, anything we could think of."

Toward the end of any deployment the tension among the men would begin to build. It was a time that tested leadership among the NCOs and officers.

"The cramped quarters, everybody tired of being gone, looking forward to going home, all these things added friction—especially looking forward to going home," Kasal says. "We weren't always on this ship—we'd go ashore for a week at a time to train and take liberty in Australia, Thailand, the Philippines. But still, by the end of six months we were ready to get off the cruise."

Fresno took Kasal and his Dragon team to many of the world's most exotic ports of call. Australia was nice, Kasal remembers, particularly the girls. He liked Hong Kong the first time he visited there and Thailand every time—and the Philippines, especially the Philippines, where the young ladies warmed many hearts, including his.

"Thailand and the Philippines were fun," he says. "I liked them because they were cheap, and I liked Third World countries. You go to Hong Kong or Sydney or any developed country and a city is a city—full of people, high prices, cops, cars. One developed country is like the next developed country. Skyscrapers, shopping malls—they're all the same.

"You go into a Third World country and you never know what you are going to pop into. In Thailand they had snake shows, king cobra shows—or you could walk down the street with a monkey, ride an elephant, or go on a jungle safari. Third World countries were better."

RANGER SCHOOL

In February 1989 Kasal attended Ranger School at Fort Benning, Georgia. The Rangers are the Army's shock troops—rugged, hard-charging soldiers who take things away from a reluctant enemy with surprise and firepower. It is a grueling three-month, four-part course that many soldiers argue is the toughest training course in the Army. Kasal was selected from his battalion for the assignment for his hard work.

"Ranger School impressed me mostly because all the people I saw had problems," Kasal says. "SEALs had a high dropout rate. Navy SEALs don't do well at Ranger School. They think they are the best and when they get there, they have a problem keeping their egos in check. They are not team players and Ranger School is all about teamwork, leadership, attention to detail. That is what Marines are good at, what Rangers are good at, but SEALs aren't. They are more individual types.

"Army Rangers wear a shoulder tab showing they are Rangers. In the Marine Corps we don't wear anything. It is just more training, another tool to put in your toolbox. Some Marines put a Ranger tab underneath their pocket. I never did. Number one it is not regulation, and number two I am not a Ranger; I am a Marine. If I was going to wear a tab I would wear one that said I am a Marine.

"The Marines at the school formed together to support each other. For example, you are supposed to go down the 'slide for life' and yell 'airborne.' We would all yell 'Marine Corps.' When you do push-ups you are supposed to say, 'One Ranger, Two Ranger.' We would say, 'One Marine Corps, Two Marine Corps.' The instructors would get on us but it actually motivated us. The Ranger instructors expected that; they knew we would never forget we were Marines."

MOUNTAIN TRAINING

Not content with merely knowing how to sneak into places, swim, and assault and destroy the enemy from either land or sea, Kasal chose to attend the Marines' eight-week-long Winter Mountain Leadership course in Bridgeport, California, to be a Winter Mountain Leader instructor.

"Winter Mountain instructors learn scout skiing, learn how to be a skiing instructor for a unit. You learn winter survival, winter bivouacs, and tactics, so if your unit ever deploys to a winter mountain environment, you can be the expert," he says. "When I got there I had a hard time learning to ski. They told me I was going to be kicked out, sent back without graduating unless I learned how to ski. I tried real hard and became one of the best skiers there."

The following August and September, Kasal took the Summer Mountain Leader course. He thought it was a little bit easier because it wasn't so cold. He learned rappelling, rock climbing, assault mountain climbing, medevacs, and gorge crossing.

"Assault climbing is where you start at the bottom of the cliff and are the lead climber," he says. "You climb first setting up the ropes. When you get to the very top, you anchor the rope off so the other Marines will have a rope to use. I loved doing that."

The school's finale was glacier crossing and ice climbing on 14,000-foot Mount Shasta. Kasal had to march back down the mountain to graduate.

From mountain climbing school, he returned to Pendleton to Delta Co., 1st Battalion, 4th Marines, the famed "China" Marines of old. Kasal was the platoon sergeant of 2d Plt., D Co., 1/4, a sergeant E-5 holding a staff sergeant's position. Things remained essentially the same until 1/4's WESTPAC deployment in August 1990. Although Marines, soldiers, airmen, and sailors were dying in minor skirmishes and quick, testy firefights all over the world, the United States was officially at peace.

DESERT STORM

On June 20, 1990, the 13th MEU and Battalion Landing Team (BLT) 1/4 deployed for a routine WESTPAC training in the Philippines when Saddam Hussein decided to send his minions for Kuwait's oil. The battalion got the word almost as soon as President George H. W. Bush declared Hussein's invasion would never stand.

"We were training in the jungle when we got a call to return to the ship," Kasal says. "When we pulled out to sea, the Commanding Officer [CO] told us what was going on. He told us that Kuwait was invaded by Iraq, and we were setting sail to go to the Middle East."

Kasal was thrilled, excited, and eager like everyone else in his battalion. He was still itching for a little payback for the notorious attack on the Marine barracks in Lebanon and all the other humiliations that jihadists had heaped on the United States for 20 years. It was an anxious time for his young Marines.

"Once we got on board ship we had a lot of gear preparation, a lot of packing, a lot of 'what if' scenarios, a lot of everything. My young Marines would take me to the side and ask me questions," he says. "They wanted to know what combat was like, what it was like to kill an enemy. I would tell them to depend on their training and their leadership."

The battalion was destined to stay in the Kuwaiti desert from late August until April 1991. The time in between was an endless cycle of alerts, training, more alerts, and more training until the war finally broke out. Kasal was a sergeant by then, a platoon sergeant, and ready.

"We didn't actually do too much in Desert Storm," he says. "There was not much combat. It was 100 hours and it was over."

What with burning oil wells and Iraqis surrendering to anyone they could find, "it was more like a training exercise than a war," says Kasal. "My young Marines were a little disappointed that we weren't more involved, but in the Marine Corps you go where you are ordered and do what you are told."

After 11 months of sweat, flies, filth, hot water, and loneliness, the battalion returned to California. By the time they arrived the Desert Storm victory parades were over.

INFANTRY INSTRUCTOR

Following Desert Storm Kasal returned to Camp Pendleton and became an instructor at the School of Infantry. He was detailed to be Platoon Commander in 1st Platoon, Charlie Co., Infantry Training Battalion.

The training ran in six-week cycles. Every 43 days Kasal gathered up another group of fresh-faced Marines eager to learn from the old salts.

"My job was basically to train them," he says. "I would get them up in the morning, take them to chow, get them from Point A to Point B, and then bed them down at night. The job is similar to drill instructing, except you're not always yelling at them. You train them and motivate them, put stress on them and discipline them, but they are Marines now."

Kasal's younger brother, Kevin, was a PFC undergoing training at the SOI when his older brother was pushing troops there. Kevin remembers his brother as a hard-charging troop leader who drilled his Marines mercilessly. Kevin thinks this is where his brother was dubbed Robo-Grunt.

"It spread from there," Brad Kasal says. "The privates would call me all sorts of stuff—Rock Jaw, Captain America, things like that. I would step off for a hump maybe an hour and a half early and take a roundabout way—the hilly way—to get there. I would go up over the ridges and the mountains, come out way over on the other side, and come back just to push the privates harder.

"Every cycle we would take three company hikes led by the CO. We would do a 6-miler, a 15-miler, and a 20-miler. When we would do a 20-mile hike we would always hike past the obstacle course on the way back."

It was a good place for Kasal to give his tired Marines a little extra motivation.

"That last mile or two is when the privates start dropping out," he says. "They can't take it anymore. So as they were walking by, I would run the full obstacle course and then climb the rope to motivate the privates and show them that 'Hey, this ain't that hard. You can make it.' It wasn't normal, and most of the troop leaders didn't do it, but it motivated my Marines."

In January 1993 while still training troops at the SOI, Kasal was promoted to Staff Sergeant. Now he had three stripes and a rocker, and he was ready to step on the first rung of the ladder to senior status among NCOs. He was ordered to 3/5 Marines as an infantry platoon sergeant, his home from August 1993 to November 1995.

RECRUITING DUTY

Career Marines are expected to be well-rounded individuals, as skilled in dealing with the civilian public as they are at commanding troops; so at some point in their careers, they usually get assignments that put them in the unblinking public eye. The Marine Corps believes recruiting duty is an ideal training ground for such experience. It is duty that Kasal had tried—successfully so far—to avoid. His natural reticence recoiled at the idea of dealing constantly with the public, and he knew that performance on recruiting duty could make or break a career. But during the summer of 1995, he received orders to report for recruiting duty. It would be his lot for the next three years.

Being selected for recruiting duty also snatched away Kasal's opportunity to serve beside British Royal Marines, an honor and privilege reserved for a very select few.

"They needed someone who had been to the Mountain Leadership course, so I was in the process of getting my orders for spending three years overseas with the Royal Marines," Kasal says.

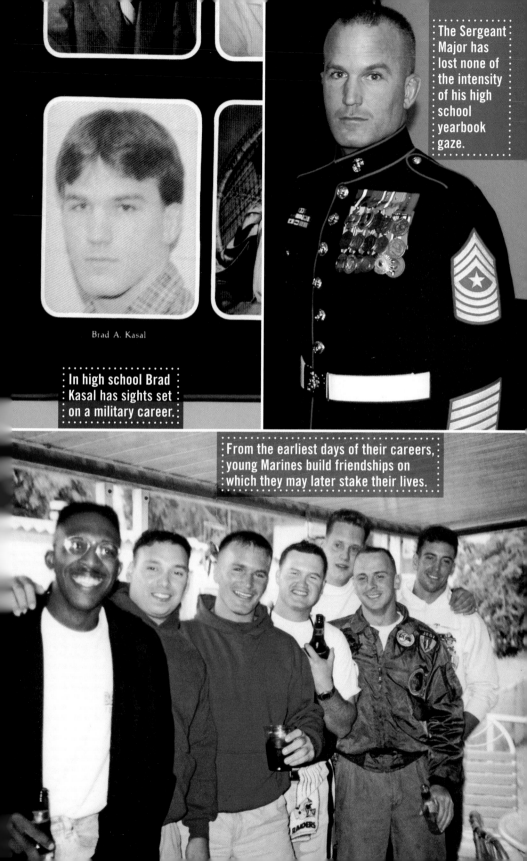

Brad A. Kasal

The Sergeant Major has lost none of the intensity of his high school yearbook gaze.

In high school Brad Kasal has sights set on a military career.

From the earliest days of their careers, young Marines build friendships on which they may later stake their lives.

Phuket Zoo

Exotic animals and faraway lands, such as Thailand in October 2000, brought new horizons within reach.

Foreign ports offer relief to sea-weary Marines.

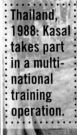

Thailand, 1988: Kasal takes part in a multi-national training operation.

In 2002, Kasal found himself training in Hawaii, here with SSgt Van Daele.

Shipboard life puts Marines in a much different type of environment.

Kasal enjoyed the time spent traveling the world aboard Navy ships such as the USS *Fresno*, designed to deliver 350 combat troops and their equipment.

During the March 2003 invasion of Iraq, Kasal and the Marines of Kilo Co. pause along the road to An Nasirijah.

1st Sergeants Kasal and Ruff with a well-armed vehicle in June 2003.

Kasal, center, joins a pair of Marines for a moment's rest between patrols.

An 81mm mortar team sets up on the outskirts of Fallujah.

Mortimer and Kasal pose with Iraqi children.

August 2004: Kasal takes time for a photo after a long patrol.

Roadside explosives can be devastating, as shown by the wreckage of SSgt Christopher Viklund's Humvee. One Marine was killed; Vicklund and three others were wounded.

This large and isolated train station, north of Fallujah, would become a staging area for the assault to take control of the city.

Marines move warily through deadly streets, clearing buildings one by one, leveling as many as necessary.

Smoke billows from a strike on a mosque where insurgents had hoped to find refuge from the advancing Marines.

Marines advancing through Fallujah were under the command of Lieutenant Colonel Willard Buhl, shown at right and, leading the assault, below right.

CITY OF AL FALLUJAH, AL ANBAR PROVINCE
"OPERATION AL FAJR" 7 NOV 2004 – 25 JAN 2005

Using satellite imagery as the basis for their tactical maps, commanders marked off a grid pattern to identify sectors of Fallujah for a comprehensive door-to-door campaign.

D-1 AT 0300 3/1 OCCUPIES ATTACK POS

D-2 AT 0900 TASK FORCE 3/1 BEGINS IDENTIFYING INSURGENTS IN ZONE UTILIZING UAV'S AND COMMENCES REDUCTION OF TARGETS

AR RAMADI 40 KM
HUSAYBAH SYRIA 280 KM

AXP
1/RCT-1

LD EAST
PL APRIL
PL ABE
PL BILL
PL CHARLES
PL DAVE
PL ETHAN
PL FRANK
PL GEORGE
PL HENRY
PL ISAAC

ECP-2
ECP-3

D-1 AT 0600 RCT-1 & 3/1 ENGINEERS COMPLETE BREACH. 2/7 CAV BEGINS MOVEMENT THROUGH BREACH LANES ENDURING ENCOUNTERS LIGHT RESISTANCE CLEARING THE TRAIN STATION. REG OBJ B TASK FORCE 3/1 ESTABLISHES FWD CP BAS ASP

D-3 TASK FORCE 3/1 FIS OF 2/7 CAV, WITH INDIA AND KILO CO'S. FORWARD, AND LIMA CO. BACK, OFFSET TO THE WEST.
CO.I ENCOUNTERS HEAVY RESISTANCE FROM FIRE TEAM TO SQUAD SIZE INSURGENT UNITS AND ACCURATE IDF

D-4 CONDUCT BHO AND COMMENCE ATTACK TO CLEAR JOLAN DISTRICT 3/1 (ME).
CO. K ENCOUNTERS LIGHT RESISSANCE SECURING REG OBJ D.

REG OBJ BRAVO "TRAIN STATION"
REG OBJ CHARLIE "CEMETERY"
REG OBJ ALPHA "APARTMENT COMPLEX"
REG OBJ DELTA "KABER MOSQUE"

DIV OBJ 1 JOLAN AREA

ECP-1

At ease: Moments of rest often come uncomfortably to troops in combat—on an abandoned swing set or, below, on a protected rooftop.

"Marine humor" is the way Kasal describes men relaxing with a radio-controlled toy that they found and promptly equipped with a very real grenade.

Something for a guy to read, especially a letter from home, offers real relief from combat.

The burden of battle can weigh more heavily than any Grunt's gear.

Lt Col Buhl steps lively with troops dancing on the eve of their assault on Fallujah.

In searing sunlight or in a fog of smoke and dust, Marines move in teams, protecting one another as they claim the gritty landscape of Fallujah, one city block at a time.

As troops push forward, all barriers must yield, whether they are walls to be tumbled by machine or doors to be opened by manual force.

But his battalion commander, himself a recent recipient of orders to recruiting duty, had other plans for his staff sergeant. Being a good officer the commander realized the need for good men under his command.

"Lieutenant Colonel Donohue got orders for recruiting," Kasal says. "Miraculously, after he got out there, my name appeared for recruiting even though I was already pending orders to go to the exchange program. I tried everything I could to get out of it. There wasn't anything I could do about it; it was a done deal and I was going."

It was the only time in Kasal's career he was unhappy being a Marine, he says. "I was pissed off and even demotivated. I had no intentions of being a recruiter. But eventually I accepted my orders because that is what Marines do. I am not the kind of Marine that pulls that punk card that says if you make me a recruiter, I am going to get out. It's not Burger King where you can 'have it your way.' "

Kasal set aside his disappointment and reported to the six-week Recruiting School at MCRD in San Diego in the fall of 1995. He graduated fourth among 290 students and headed north for recruiting duty at Recruiting Station (RS) Twin Cities, Minnesota.

Staff Sergeant Kasal soon discovered Marine Corps recruiters walk in the public eye every day. They are expected to act with great decorum and unceasing respect. Marine recruiters don't drink from containers while walking in public or smoke on the street while in uniform. They keep their field scarves (neckties) tightened, their blouses (shirts) buttoned, and their covers (hats) on or off as appropriate. They become marvelously adept at listening earnestly to stupid questions and endless stories about someone's uncle who was in the Corps. It is all part of the Marine mystique that makes women smile and men suck in their guts. Unfortunately it doesn't always attract recruits or convince their parents the Corps is the right choice.

"Recruiting duty is a tough and demanding job," Kasal says. "I always believed the best way to do it was for the Marines to sell themselves. Being out in the public eye in a Marine Corps uniform is like being a walking billboard. However a lot of the young individuals didn't have a clue what to do, so it was my job to give them direction."

After just two months in the Twin Cities Kasal was suddenly transferred to St. Cloud, Minnesota, to be Noncommissioned Officer in Charge (NCOIC) of a recruiting substation that hadn't "made mission"—produced its quota of recruits—in 11 months.

"The first week I was NCOIC we made mission, but I never had a day off," Kasal says. "I worked seven days a week until ungodly hours. I detested it—but like I said, I am a Marine."

Leaders have problems that aren't included in the job description. One of Kasal's biggest headaches was the wife of a below-average recruiter who wanted her husband home for supper. "She would call up every day about 3 o'clock wondering if he was coming home, wondering if she should come into the office to get him," he says. "She did nothing but bitch, bitch, bitch. It was almost as bad as combat!"

Marine Corps protocol demanded that Kasal be discreet. Privately he told the henpecked recruiter he needed to get his wife in check before it affected his career.

"WE'VE BEEN ROBBED!"

Kasal was on the telephone when one of his recruiters breathlessly entered the recruiting station and told him somebody had just been robbed. The recruiter, a staff sergeant named Perry, was too excited to explain the problem coherently. Kasal followed Perry to his car and jumped in.

"All I could make out was 'get in the car, we've been robbed,'" Kasal says.

Perry peeled out in pursuit, rapidly filling Kasal in at the same time. "He said that while he was in the barbershop sitting in the chair a guy came in, pulled out a .45 handgun, and asked for all the money in the cash register—about $110 or $115. The robber put the money in his pocket and took off on foot. Staff Sergeant Perry jumped out of the chair, jumped into his car, and came back and got me."

No sooner had Perry finished his tale than Kasal spied the robber at the end of an alley.

"Before the car stopped I had jumped out the door and was running after the guy. He pulled the gun so I disarmed him, threw the gun on the ground, and tackled him. Then I grabbed the guy and held him there in a choke hold. By then the police had been called and they showed up, cuffed the guy, and picked up the weapon."

The good citizens of St. Cloud were grateful and so was the Marine Corps. "The City Council, the Chief of Police, and everybody else gave us a bunch of awards and plaques," Kasal says. "The Marine Corps gave us the Navy Commendation Medal for conspicuous gallantry. The newspaper showed up out there right after it happened and took a picture of me giving a statement to the police."

Kasal says he and Perry just did what anyone would do. "That was our barber he was robbing," Kasal says. "I liked the barber. He was a nice guy."

After three long, hard years, a promotion to Gunnery Sergeant, and a Navy Achievement Medal for being the Recruiting Station NCOIC of the Year, Kasal finally got his wish and left the role of recruiter behind him, thinking it was gone for good. It had been a tough duty but one he was ultimately proud of.

THE THUNDERING THIRD

After another tour with 1/4 as a gunnery sergeant and another round of deployments in the western Pacific, Kasal was promoted to First Sergeant and transferred to 3d Battalion, 1st Marines—the Thundering Third. Kasal was appointed First Sergeant of Kilo Co., one of four companies in the battalion. He was the junior first sergeant in the battalion and had a lot to learn in a short time. No sooner had he settled in when the battalion headed into harm's way.

The one thing Kasal had going for him at Kilo was his time being a Grunt. Many first sergeants reporting to infantry companies are not Grunts. In the Marine Corps a first sergeant is a military occupational specialty (MOS) as well as a rank. First sergeants are expected to be capable of overseeing any Marine unit with a fine hand.

Kilo was sent to Camp Lemonier in Djibouti, Africa. It was a desolate, primitive place of mud huts, plywood shacks, gravel roads, shale, and scrub. In addition: "Djibouti is right on the equator and hot as hell," Kasal says. "Temperatures can peg daytime highs of 130 to 145 degrees." The people looked poor, hungry, and tired. They dressed in a variety of fashions from flowing robes that suggested traditional garb to mismatched shirts and pants and tennis shoes. A few drove battered trucks and utility vehicles but most walked or rode camels or burros.

Djibouti is the home of the 13th Demi-Brigade of the French Foreign Legion (13e DBLE), the legendary mercenary force charged with keeping the peace in the remote reaches of French-patrolled Africa. When Kilo arrived the Legionnaires were their hosts. Kilo was there to practice the black arts of raiding with various Special Operation units stationed there—U.S. Army Special Forces teams, the Army Rangers, and the Delta Force—all supersecret elite "operators."

This three-month mission was secret, the training was hard, and the Marines were dead serious. Operations included infantry training that focused on maneuver, urban fighting, combined arms exercises exploiting joint infantry, armor, artillery exercises, as well as combat assaults of several kinds. "We practiced raids on air bases, [body] snatches, stuff like that. The land was arid, dead, and empty, perfect for preparing for a Mideast war," Kasal says. "We were training for Operation Enduring Freedom, basically to hunt and kill terrorists."

FAILAKA ISLAND

"While we were down here two of our companies, Lima and India, were up in Kuwait training, doing exercises, and supporting Operation Enduring Freedom in the Middle East. And that is when the incident at Failaka Island and First Sergeant Ruff occurred," Kasal says. "The second war in Iraq started there."

In October 2001 the U.S. and Iraq were still pretending to talk in the United Nations. At the same time U.S. Army and Marine Corps combat units were training in Kuwait for the prospect of war in Iraq. Failaka Island was a designated military training area in Kuwait.

In better times it had been a quiet island of fishing villages. Between the two Iraqi wars its population had been evicted so Kuwaiti, Coalition, and American troops could train in an environment that allowed for both amphibious and land warfare exercises.

The exercise began simply enough. India and Lima companies went ashore on Failaka Island on October 7, 2001, for several days of training exercises.

The senior NCO on the island was First Sergeant Timothy Ruff, at the time the first sergeant of Lima Co. He had 24 years service. Lima was his first infantry company. A short and powerful man with a quiet voice, he has a careful disposition. One enlisted Marine says Ruff is "so strong he had muscles in his shit." Kasal describes Ruff as a by-the-book Marine, a mentor, and one of the finest Marines he ever served with.

Also at Failaka was Ruff's good friend and fellow First Sergeant Wayne A. Hertz, who at the time was the company Gunnery Sergeant for Lima Co. Hertz is a brawny, full-of-life Marine with more than 20 years of infantry savvy who loves his craft. (He was stationed with Kasal at Camp Pendleton after Kasal was wounded and helped him recover.)

"Those two are about as good as they get," Kasal says of his fellow Marines.

"Our guard was still up from 9/11 when we went to Failaka Island," Hertz says. "We had been training in the desert for two weeks. Our companies had been rotating for two weeks at Failaka Island and two weeks in the desert. We took buses out of the desert and then we took ferryboats to Failaka.

"There had just been an incident in Kuwait with alleged terrorists, so we made sure we took some security ammo with us. All the officers and some of the staff NCOs had loaded 9 mils [9mm Beretta pistols], and we had Marines on sentry duty with live rounds—a magazine of 30 rounds of 5.56mm for each sentry's M16A2.

"As I remember there was only supposed to be some caretakers and a few shop owners on the island. We saw some young men driving around in a small white truck scoping us out when we were setting up, but we weren't expecting trouble. I thought they were probably just curious about Marines."

Hertz remembers seeing the same two Kuwaiti males a second time. "On the night of the seventh I wasn't feeling so good, so I went to the portable toilet to do my business. It was almost dark, but I noticed two guys near the road around our area. They began watching us from real close. It was somebody right across the street."

The next morning the training schedule resumed as planned. The nocturnal visitors were forgotten, Hertz says.

"Two platoons ate their meals ready to eat [MREs], packed up water, and went into town to train. One of the platoons we kept back. That platoon had turned in their live ammo and was unarmed. They couldn't defend themselves."

Suddenly shots rang out. Hertz was mystified. There was not supposed to be any firing around the encampment, he says.

"Not more than maybe five minutes later, about 75 meters from our position where there was a road, I hear some shots. They were popping. Somebody was shooting a lot. I know the shots are coming from the right."

Ruff says he wondered: "Why are the other platoons training in this area? It is a residential area. I was going to find out about it."

Hertz immediately got mad. He wanted to know what knucklehead was shooting so close to Marines.

"I was kind of pissed off," he says. "The shots got louder. It was two different gunmen. I recognized that they weren't blanks. From the corner of my eye I noticed a small white pickup truck.

"I said, 'These guys are shooting!' At the same time I was going for my pistol."

Ruff drew his sidearm and began firing at the terrorists as bullets were burning through the tent they were standing in.

"It drew fire onto us," Hertz says. "I still think they were shocked that we were armed. All I had was my 9 mil; at the time it seemed like bringing a knife to a gunfight. I started shooting as well and so did at least one of the sentries. I started seeing our rounds striking the vehicle. We started to bound and cover. I could see the Marine sentry from 3d Platoon with his M16A2 firing. He ultimately disabled that vehicle. At the time, it was driving slowly by with both alleged terrorists firing at Marines. It rolled to a stop. Our rounds were hitting, cutting through like butter. The two guys inside were still shooting with their AKs.

"Before the truck started moving by the tent we were all thinking the same thing: There is no fucking way we are going to die in that tent. I remember that well before they finished shooting we had 75 or 80 cases of soda being shot up. I saw it out of the corner of my eye. I was thinking, 'those bastards!' Shooting up our soda was really pissing me off. We had ice locked on and everybody was looking forward to a cold soda. There was powdered Gatorade all over the place."

Ruff and the other armed Marines mounted an attack. They formed a line and assaulted the truck, Hertz says.

"We continued to put rounds in the vehicle. First Sergeant Ruff called out he was going to take the passenger. I was going to take the driver. One terrorist started crawling out of the vehicle on the passenger side—he was full of holes. While First Sergeant Ruff fired a couple of more rounds into him I opened the door to the driver's side, but Ruff was too close so I could not engage. We dragged the driver out of the vehicle, and then I heard the most chilling words you ever want to hear out of a Marine: 'Corpsman up!' You know it wasn't for some Marine needing Motrin."

His worst fear was quickly realized: Two Marines had been shot. One of the officers summoned Hertz to help.

"I ran over to Corporal Antonio Sledd; he was wounded the worst. He was white and pale, hit all over the place. Marines can be as tough as woodpecker lips, and I thought he was going to live," Hertz recalls bitterly.

Within 10 minutes an Army medevac helicopter flew in for Sledd and Lance Corporal George Simpson, who was shot in the arm. He wasn't as serious, but he was hurting, Hertz says.

Ruff still calls the confrontation the "worst day of my life." He adds, "I am still not really sure why they did it. I just know Marines started taking fire and went to cover. They were blasting and blasting; Marines were taking cover and then returning fire. They do it because of their training, the core values they are instilled with by their recruiter and their drill instructors."

Despite the quick arrival of the Army rescue helicopter time was running out for Corporal Sledd. Hertz was with him until the chopper took off.

"'You're a Marine, motherfucker,'" Hertz told him. "He squeezed my hand as hard as any healthy Marine could do. They flew him to the hospital in Kuwait City," Hertz says. "Later we heard Corporal Sledd had died."

The next day U.S. Central Command issued a brief description of the encounter that was carried by the major wire services. Defense officials said the Marines were attacked while participating in an urban warfare exercise on Failaka Island.

The U.S. Navy confirmed that Corporal Antonio J. Sledd, 20, of Hillsborough, Florida, died from wounds received in action, and Lance Corporal George R. Simpson, 21, of Dayton, Ohio, was wounded in a firefight while participating in an urban warfare exercise.

The first shots of the second Iraqi war had been fired and nobody at home could hear them. The 3/1 Marines knew that they were going to be revisiting Iraq. Other Marines were already fighting in Afghanistan and it was only a matter of time before the inflammatory rhetoric from the antagonists ignited the fuse that would send the Marines into battle. Since 9/11 the preceding year the Marines had been praying for war—anxious but hungry for a fight.

CHAPTER 6
★ ★ ★

THE BRIDGE FIGHTS

Kasal was First Sergeant of Kilo Co., 3d Battalion, 1st Marine Regiment when Operation Iraqi Freedom kicked off on March 20, 2003. Kilo Co. was a 246-man rifle company—then as now a potent killing machine. The Marines who filled 3/1's ranks had no idea their battalion would soon make headlines around the world. An Nasiriyah, Al Kut, al-Anbar province, Fallujah, and Haditha—now known for infamous battles—were then simply names of obscure places very few Marines had heard of.

3/1 moved out in a convoy that included the entire 1st Marine Expeditionary Force (I MEF), a huge assemblage of approximately 68,000 Marines and British soldiers that included Task Force Tarawa (TF Tarawa) from the 2d Marine Division, the 1st Marine Division, the British 1st U.K. Division, the 3d Marine Air Wing, and the First Service Force Support Group and attendant Reserve units.

The Thundering Third was part of Regimental Combat Team 1 (RCT1), a 5,000-man combined arms force built around the 1st Marine Regiment.

THE BATTLE PLAN

According to the original plan, the U.S. Army's 4th Infantry Division and the Brits would move south into Iraq through Turkey while the 3d Infantry Division took An Nasiriyah.

That changed when the Turkish government said no to the Coalition's using Turkey as a jump-off point a few weeks before the invasion began.

The new plan called for the Marines to move north into Iraq and destroy Saddam Hussein's army. Their first waypoint was a pair of important bridges in the city of An Nasiriyah that spanned the Euphrates River and the Saddam Canal. The bridges were divided by a 3-mile stretch of road. The Marines were to hold the bridges and the road while the entire Marine contingent moved north toward Baghdad. Before the Marines reached the bridges, the Army's 3d Infantry Division, part of the so-called "left fist" of the U.S. Army's attacking force, was supposed to check the bridges to make sure the route was passable.

Meanwhile V Corps—essentially the entire U.S. Army invasion force with the exception of an airborne brigade that would strike northern Iraq—would move into the country from the west to threaten Baghdad using traditional invasion routes along the Tigris River. It was a sophisticated plan that very few Marines in 3/1 except senior officers knew anything about.

Before March 20, Kilo, 3/1 was laying up along with the rest of the 1st Marine Division behind the last berm-and-barbed-wire fence that marked the border between Kuwait and Iraq. The company had been mated with a platoon of reservists operating the thin-skinned amphibious assault vehicles (AAVs) that would drive them to the war. The reservists' job was to take Kilo's Marines into combat much as their fathers and grandfathers had in previous wars. Only this time they would be driving across sand instead of swimming across the sea in front of them.

WAITING FOR ORDERS

There wasn't much new for 3/1's Marines to look at while they waited for the war to start. For as far as the eye could see was tan sand rolling along in gentle, undulating ridges. Somewhere ahead of them was the entire Iraqi army. Behind them and on both flanks was the multinational Coalition force.

The air hummed with anticipation. Every Marine was doing something. Some halfheartedly practiced donning their hated gas masks; others cleaned their weapons. Still others packed and repacked their 80-pound rucksacks full of ammo, food, water, candy, cameras, underwear, socks, and other personal gear. Some roughhoused their way into a state of hypertensive relaxation. All were tired of training and eager to go to war.

Their eagerness to get moving was heightened by the constant threat of missile attack. Saddam's army was equipped with Russian-designed intermediate-range ballistic missiles code-named "SCUD" by the North Atlantic Treaty Organization. SCUDs were relatively primitive but quite versatile: They could carry high-explosive gas, biological, and chemical warheads.

Four times that morning the Marines dove into their gas masks when "Lightning! Lightning! Lightning!" crackled over the battalion radio nets warning of incoming SCUDs. Despite the potential danger, the Marines hated the gas masks and hated the mission oriented protective posture (MOPP) suits designed to protect them against gas, biological, and chemical agents.

By evening everyone knew the war was on, Kasal says. Each Marine looked inside himself and decided he had a war to fight. All the loud, angry bullshit, the snapping orders that stung like hard rain, all the endless, repetitious training was behind them. It was time to man up. Before Kilo's men mounted their AAVs, they were told to make a formation between their respective paths so Kasal and Captain Michael Martin, their company commander, could make a final inspection before they departed.

Kasal was just as ramped and ready to go as his young Marines, but he couldn't show it. They looked to him and the other NCOs and officers in the company for guidance. If the leaders seemed rattled in any way, the men would be upset, and now was not the time for histrionics. Kasal stayed calm and exuded a self-confidence and pride in his men that eased their minds and left them determined not to fail the company.

Kasal had been in their boots before. He knew they were jittery, uptight, and eager to show their stuff. He was also well aware that nervous energy was not the best driving force to motivate young warriors. It leads to mistakes, and mistakes lead to tragedy. Kasal intended to share his lessons learned with the young men now looking to him for guidance. He had learned that being an infantryman is a unique craft, a skill that combines cunning and combat coolness with white-hot, carefully controlled aggression. Every gesture he made, every word he said was designed to teach that craft, to impart that knowledge, to model that unique mental state.

The command group shook each man's hand. It was never said but always understood that Martin and Kasal were saying their last goodbyes. Every Marine in the company knew what they were doing and appreciated the gesture, Kasal's men recalled later.

Kasal knew something else for certain: The time for training was over. Kilo was as good as it was going to be when it crossed the line of departure to begin the fight to liberate Iraq from Saddam. The moment of truth was at hand.

FORWARD!

The first day of war in Iraq was relatively uneventful. Kilo Co. headed north in their uncomfortable, overstuffed AAVs along with a rolling city of 68,000 other Marines that flowed across the desert at the excruciatingly slow pace of about 15 miles per hour. They were stuffed in the trucks like sardines, and unless the men had security watch and stood up to look outside, they remained packed inside trying to sleep or scratch their asses without smacking someone. They still wore their MOPP suits, body armor, and helmets. Weapons were clutched in every pair of hands. Several more false gas-attack alarms had reminded them that they were in a combat zone, so their despised gas masks were always near.

All day and night the endless convoy started and stopped, started and stopped, occasionally deploying in various defensive formations only to start and stop again. Occasionally Kilo Marines would see a distant smoke plume or pass a smoldering car or truck. They even rolled over a few squashed bodies and passed beside dead Iraqis baked into the road from conflicts with the infantry battalions ahead, but the heavy combat the young Marines anticipated had not yet developed.

Kasal sensed the war was getting closer because increasing numbers of Iraqi soldiers in dirty civilian clothes and cheap civilian shoes were surrendering to the units leading RCT1 up Route 8. Reports coming back to 3/1 identified the Iraqis as the first deserters from the 8,000-man Iraqi division in An Nasiriyah— a division that, it was rumored, would surrender rather than fight when the overwhelmingly disproportionate Coalition force got closer to the bridges at An Nasiriyah.

Even without combat, Kilo's men were already tired, dirty, hungry, and stressed. Kasal and Martin were not much better off. They had already run for more than 24 hours on caffeine and catnaps. Kasal knew that the infinite boredom of the road march could be as deadly a foe as combat itself if it made the men complacent and dull. He was determined not to let that happen.

"Marines in combat need to be constantly reminded of what they are doing," he says. "They get tired and bored and sleepy and don't pay attention. The section leaders and squad leaders have to make sure they don't get that way. The platoon sergeants make sure the squad leaders are doing their job, and my role was to make sure they were all doing their jobs."

Any Marine will tell you that riding in an AAV rolling across the desert is not pleasant when shared with 19 or 20 other guys, their equipment, extra food and water, ammo, and a three-man crew. Lance Corporal Alex Nicoll, a rifleman in 3d Squad, 3d Platoon, Kilo, remembers some of the tracks were stuffed with as many as 28 or 29 men.

"Hey, when your track breaks down, you have to ride somewhere," Nicoll explains. "So we would just get in another track. It's better to be in a firefight than crammed into a track all day. You breathe exhaust fumes and get a terrible headache, and the noise and movement gets terrible."

The only good thing about riding instead of walking was not humping their 80-pound rucks in the withering heat, Nicoll says. The AAV's roof opens up, so several Marines at a time could get some fresh air while serving as lookouts—except when the wind blew exhaust fumes in their faces.

"After a day everyone had black faces," Nicoll remembers. "The exhausts were perfectly aimed to hit us in the face. After the deployment they sent around a questionnaire asking about what could be improved. I hope the exhausts got fixed."

The view outside was just about as bad as what they couldn't see inside. The Marines who rode across Iraq compare the scenery to a giant, stinking landfill occupied by dirty, scared people and unfamiliar animals. They frequently use the words "garbage," "filth," "poverty," "devastation," and "emptiness" to describe the view. Incongruously, running through this emptiness was a four-lane superhighway that would have been perfectly normal in Arizona or Utah.

Taking a turn as a lookout was marginally better than being

cramped down below with only what passed for fresh air moving across their tension-tightened faces. The sun was hot, the MOPP suits were hot, their helmets cooked their brains, and sand fought to penetrate every uncovered orifice. Already men were dealing with pus-filled eyes contaminated with grit and lungs irritated by inhaled sand that caused hacking thick green phlegm. Even with their heads outside the track, the fetid air was filled with dust, bad breath, and the stench of rotting flesh, burning oil, and indefinable smells as rank as the garbage that filled the countryside around them.

AMBUSH!

On March 25, 3/1 got the word that 1st Battalion, 2d Marines had gone into An Nasiriyah and taken heavy casualties. It had been hit on Route Moe, the city street in An Nasiriyah that RCT1 had to traverse before it could cross the Saddam Canal to the north. 2/1 was not going to be able to complete its mission to secure the southern bridge for the 1 MEFs passage because of heavy contact they were already facing.

3/1's convoy slowed to a stop. The desert horizon to the north rocked with explosions marked by black and brown plumes of greasy smoke—proof that the war had begun in earnest and that a battle lay ahead.

In fact the bridge battles actually began when the 507th Maintenance Company, a rear echelon Army unit formerly based at Fort Bliss, Texas, was ambushed south of the first bridge across the Euphrates. The 507th was on a road march with the 3d Infantry Division when somebody driving the big trucks made a navigational error and took a wrong turn into An Nasiriyah, where an Iraqi trap was waiting for them. The shock of the ambush sent its soldiers scurrying for cover.

When Alpha Co. 1/2 arrived on the scene, they discovered the Army troops burrowed in the ditches on the side of the road near their burning vehicles. The Euphrates River was still ahead. The Iraqis had set up a defensive position on the approaches to the bridge to deny a crossing. It was a risky tactic because it is easier to defend the approaches from across the river, but it worked well enough to decimate the soldiers who had no idea they were lumbering into an ambush instead of traveling a safe route. The Americans engaged in a fierce firefight with the Iraqis for more than an hour and suffered many wounded and dead. Other soldiers were missing and presumed captured.

The 1/2 Marines were just as mystified as the soldiers of the 507th by the ambush because they thought the Army had secured An Nasiriyah. Intel reports circulating among the 2d Marine Regiment had suggested that approximately 8,000 soldiers from the Iraqi 11th Division intended to surrender there.

But as Task Force Tarawa closed in on the city, they didn't find any surrendering Iraqi soldiers. Instead they found burning American Army trucks, dead and wounded American soldiers, and mayhem.

The Marines from Alpha 1/2 did their best to help the injured, two of whom were critically wounded. The Iraqis only increased their rate of fire as the Marines moved about on their mission of mercy. During the rescue an Army officer reported that half the soldiers in the ill-fated convoy were missing. (The situation became a world-shaking event when Army brass revealed later that several women were among the dead and captured soldiers in the unfortunate 507th. Most famous was Private First Class Jessica Lynch, who was awarded a Bronze Star and a Purple Heart after her daring rescue from an Iraqi hospital.)

Marines from Alpha Co. brought forward their corpsmen to treat the critically wounded soldiers and called for helicopters to get them out. Other Marines fanned out in search of the missing soldiers. Five were found hiding in a nearby swamp; several of their dead were also discovered. Later, America would learn from an Iraqi newsreel that a number of captured soldiers had been executed. The Marines kept fighting, taking the Iraqi ambushers' fire and starting a struggle that went on for days.

As soon as the soldiers were under the Marines' protective wing, Alpha was told to move on to An Nasiriyah and take the southern bridge.

THE STREETS OF AN NASIRIYAH

Soon AAVs filled with Alpha Co. Marines pushed across the Euphrates River bridge. Bravo Co. was right behind them. As soon as the tracks got across the bridge, the lead AAV was challenged by a rocket-propelled grenade (RPG) shot from a white van with a blue stripe. The track's driver swerved. The RPG missed. But the tension was palpable, and soon there were other obstacles: The tracks encountered mud and broken sewer mains that turned the ground they were crossing into sludge pits. After penetrating into the eastern edge of the city the tracks began getting stuck.

Meanwhile, Iraqis were firing RPGs out of windows, doorways, and cars. Alpha called for reinforcements and got M1A1 Abrams main battle tanks for support. The tank's 120mm stabilized main guns, coaxial machine gun, and the always fearsome M2 Browning .50-caliber heavy machine gun—better known as "Ma Deuce"— are great equalizers. The tanks belonged to a company of Marine Reserve tankers assigned to Task Force Tarawa. Their firepower was a greatly needed addition to Alpha's limited means. The tanks allowed the badly hit Marines to hold their ground while reinforcements moved up. But within a few minutes the same bad luck hit the reinforcing tanks—they got mired in the same mud and muck.

1/2's original mission—to secure the southern bridge across the Euphrates and push on to the Saddam Canal bridge—was a bust. Now their best hope was to hang on to the southern bridge and push another company to the canal bridge and hold that as well. Charlie Co., in trace behind the now mired Bravo Co., got the call. When Charlie's AAV started taking hits and several Marines died, even that became questionable.

Adding insult to injury, two Air Force A-10 "Warthog" attack aircraft strafed Charlie's column with their 30mm Gatling guns, destroying two AAVs. An accident investigation by the Department of Defense and Central Command released March 29, 2004, exonerated the Air Force, deciding the unfortunate combat mishap was a consequence of the fog of war. Before the fight was over, 18 Marines were killed and 17 were wounded.

3/1 AT THE LINE OF DEPARTURE

In the late afternoon of March 24, 3/1 received word that the 2d Marines Division had taken heavy casualties. 3/1 was ordered in to open up Route Moe.

Lima Co. was ordered into the city first. First Sergeant Ruff, who shot it out with the insurgents at Failaka Island, was still ramrodding the company. He had come to Lima from a cushy assignment teaching at the Naval Reserve Officer Training Program and was not an infantryman. This was a big challenge, Ruff admits.

"Learning what to do as an infantry first sergeant was tough," he says, "but I had the help of the other first sergeants in the battalion, especially First Sergeant Cadle and First Sergeant Kasal."

Lima's Marines were still riding in their AAVs when they arrived at their departure area near the bridge. Ruff supervised their dismount and watched while his NCOs got them into the appropriate order and led them off to battle.

Ruff says they were receiving "a little bit" of fire. The battalion logs show that the Marines were taking automatic weapons fire, mortars, RPGs, and sniper fire. After Lima's Grunts got organized into a solid line, the tracks moved up behind them to provide suppressive fire from their heavy weapons. It was a gutsy move by the track crews: Despite their size and bulk, AAVs are not tanks and are not intended to defeat heavy fire from mortars and RPGs. The proof was already burning just to the north of the southern bridge where two AAVs were still cooking off.

Lima was assigned a 700-meter stretch of Moe to secure. India Marines leapfrogged across Lima's line to form another line farther north. Kasal fidgeted all night waiting for Kilo to get orders to join in, but India's position was as far as 3/1 moved until dawn. All night, dug-in enemy pounded them with mortars, RPGs, and harassing fire. It was a tough place to be, even for seasoned veterans, and most of the young Marines in 3/1 were facing combat for the first time.

The tracks faced west and east to protect Lima's flank and rear along an exposed line that meandered beside Route Moe for about a mile. Fortunately the AAVs met only sporadic fire as they rolled into town behind Lima and India's protective screen. An occasional RPG raced past, and a few more skipped along the road or flew overhead without doing any damage. More fire came from small arms. Ruff was on foot moving up and down the company line encouraging his Marines, keeping them under cover, and directing whatever fighting was going on.

Kilo spent the night south of the bridge listening to the clamor of war, itching to get into the fight. Kasal and the other staff NCOs and officers kept busy making sure the company was ready to enter the cauldron the next morning. They passed out ammunition, went over the rules of engagement, checked the men's equipment, and checked and rechecked their maps and orders. Kasal slept when he could—a few minutes here, a few more there—something he says didn't bother him all that much. Almost two decades as a Marine had taught him how to catch catnaps that kept him alert.

When they moved into the city just after dawn, Kilo's job was clearing the street to the west of Route Moe. That road was now almost 4 kilometers of wall-to-wall enemy with automatic weapons, RPGs, heavy machine guns, and a few automatic cannon that could cause real pain. So-called Saddam Fedayeen (freedom fighters)—young Sunni supporters of the regime trained to fight as guerillas infested the town. The buildings and walled squares where the insurgents were hidden was an ungraceful collection of one- and two-story boxes made with thick walls and roofs to keep out the unremitting heat.

The buildings made great fighting positions. Iraqis could move from window to window without being detected or hit, and even from house to house through a maze of connecting alleys. An Nasiriyah was a perfect warren for the Saddam Fedayeen.

Kasal was in the thick of it from the first light of day. "We had to clear out all the buildings within a block in the whole length of the street, including the southern bridge across the Euphrates all the way to the bridge at the north end of the city," he says. "What we did was clear houses, city blocks, everything. I ran from position to position directing fire, helping Marines, inspiring Marines. It was the first time any of my Marines had been in combat."

As the fighting grew fiercer, Kasal got busier. Thankfully it was in the mid-80s and not as hot as it would be later, but running in the sun wearing the impermeable MOPP suit and weighted down with at least 80 pounds of body armor, ammo, weapons, and other gear made it sweltering just the same. Adding to everyone's discomfort was the constant incoming small arms, RPGs, and mortar fire that splashed on the baked ground, spreading white-hot shrapnel and snapping bullets through the smoke-filled air.

Occasionally the Marines would spot their tormentors. Most of them were wearing civilian clothes or all-black ninja-style suits that marked their antagonists as the ruthless Fedayeen —Saddam's youthful hired thugs emboldened by drugs and

Baathist rhetoric. The Marines' Rules of Engagement (ROE) prohibited them from simply killing anyone they saw moving about. A Marine had to see a weapon or some activity smacking of hostile intent before he could open fire. Obeying the ROE was a vexing, complicated situation for the young Marines, and it required constant leadership to enforce—especially after Marines started taking casualties from Iraqis who fired on them, then put their weapons down and walked away. The enemy knew what it was doing.

Corporal Nicoll was a rifleman on a fire team in Kilo when it went into the city. A fire team has four men and is usually the smallest maneuver element in a rifle company. He remembers his first combat as surreal. "They were playing AC-DC's "Hells Bells," Nicoll recalls of the trip in. "Somebody played it over the loudspeaker. It was hurry up and wait, hot as shit. We wore MOPP suits and spent our time breathing exhaust fumes. Three days is a long time all packed in there. People would get claustrophobic and start hitting the walls, freaking. We were glad to get out and fight.

"We sat outside of An Nasiriyah that night," Nicoll continues. "They told us what had been going on. I talked to Staff Sergeant [Christopher] Pruitt, my platoon sergeant. We were just watching the tracers and artillery. We were far enough from An Nasiriyah not to get shot at. I wanted to do it, get it over with. I kind of knew I was going to do okay—I knew I was going to because I was with my boys.

"We drove into the city on tracks. We started taking fire so we pulled off, the doors dropped, and we all got down on the street and shot people as they popped out. It was amazing. There were people all around us. One gunner left a pile of dead bodies, six or seven bodies right in front of us. It was incredible."

When 3/1's Grunts identified shooters, they took them out with M-16s, SAWs, M203 grenade launchers, hand grenades, and shoulder-launched multipurpose assault weapons (SMAWs)—the Marines' favorite building busters. Backing them up was Weapons Co. armed with Ma Deuce, 81mm mortars, 40mm automatic grenade launchers, and TOW and Javelin antitank missiles that would definitely do damage when they found the enemy. Weapons Co. in turn was backed up by the powerful gunners on the AAVs and Abrams tanks.

Unlike the enemy, the Marines of Kilo were lying in the street, totally exposed to the Iraqis. It was a tough place to be a Marine and an even tougher place to be a Marine first sergeant. Devoid of cover, Kasal, Ruff, and the other leaders moved from position to position completely exposed to enemy fire. Worse, their constant movement identified them as leaders, earmarking them for special attention. Kasal and Ruff both say they never gave much thought to being exposed because it was the only way they could direct their men.

"If I would see something wrong, I would run over and correct it—misaimed fires, uncoordinated fires, whatever," Kasal says. "I would go with a squad to clear a building, help evacuate wounded—basically try to be everywhere, directing, guiding, encouraging, inspiring. The only cover we had was what we could find: a wall, a fence, the side of a building. Sometimes I was just out in the middle of the street."

That's the way it went as they progressed through the city clearing buildings, securing the route, and ensuring an uncontested passage for the units that followed them. Eventually they made it out the other side of the city. Incredibly, 3/1 escaped without any fatalities.

TOO EASY

After An Nasiriyah the division encountered only light resistance and sporadic hit-and-run ambushes in central Iraq. The anticipated hard combat the Marines expected never materialized, but they soon outran their supply. They were down to eating one or two MREs a day and using their water sparingly. The battalion had to slow down until they received some support.

Kasal was glad for the pause. His Marines would finally get some time to take off their boots and change their socks and at least get out of some of their clothes for a few hours. They were still wearing MOPP suits and all their armor. Even then, the war was never far away, he says.

"We did an operational pause just south of Al Kut," Kasal says. "We set up a defensive perimeter. While we were set up there, this car comes down the road toward us. Behind it was an Iraqi truck. We kept trying to get the car to stop, but it wouldn't stop. The next thing you know, the truck starts shooting at the car."

The Marines turned their machine guns on the truck and destroyed it, Kasal says. "We lit up the truck, and a bunch of Iraqi troops jumped out and we lit them up and killed them. Then we ran out to the car. There was an Iraqi family inside—an old man, his wife, and his two daughters. The wife was killed and the daughters were wounded when the Iraqi soldiers opened up on the car. We medically treated the two daughters, and then we took the girls with their father and medevac'd them back to the rear for treatment."

Kasal later discovered that the unfortunate family were Shiites fleeing the Iraqi army. The predominantly Sunni soldiers had been raping and torturing the Shiites as they retreated. The victimized family hoped to reach the Marines before the Iraqi soldiers captured them. To Kasal's deep disappointment it was not to be.

Intelligence later revealed the bulk of Saddam Hussein's military forces had either melted away or retired to Baghdad for the final fight. The foreign fighters had not yet arrived in strength and the only real resistance was from the Saddam Fedayeen,

Kasal says. Most Iraqis still smiled at Americans. Most Marines thought they had won the war and the Army would now move in and administer the peace.

Despite the euphoria Kasal had reservations about celebrating the conclusion of the war. Things had just been too easy. Everybody with weapons had disappeared. Somebody had to have them. Kasal figured 3/1 would be back sooner than later.

"I didn't think it was over," he says. "I was more worried about going back to Pendleton because the battalion was going to lose a lot of good people who were waiting for discharge or schools or getting transferred when OIF started. I was worried about what would happen to the battalion. It was the senior battalion in the regiment and the best battalion I had ever served in."

Except for the Marines and soldiers who still mourned their dead, the nation quickly forgot the cost of the seemingly easy victory. In terms of history it was almost a bloodless war. For a time it seemed peace and stability would soon follow.

It was not to be, of course, but the shooting wouldn't resume again for a while. 3/1 went home by plane in late May 2003. After a month stand-down while everybody took leave, the battalion reformed at Pendleton. As Kasal had feared, the Thundering Third swiftly changed its face as more and more men left for Civvy Street, schools, and assignments that had been on hold while they fought the war.

They didn't know it yet, but the war had barely begun.

CHAPTER 7

BEFORE FALLUJAH

Kasal's world in the months preceding the battle for Fallujah revolved around a single reinforced battalion of Marines, the Thundering Third. His focus was on his men. They were spread over 850 square kilometers of inhospitable ancient Mesopotamia full of Iraqis who alternately loved, hated, attacked, or ignored the Marines. 3/1 was irrevocably mated to the rest of the 1st Marine Regiment for support, the 1st Marine Division for direction. Above the fighting Marines was a maze of commands and commanders debating over the best ways to control the burgeoning insurgency.

THE HOTTEST SPOT IN IRAQ

When 3/1 arrived in al-Anbar province in June 2004 the gruesome murders of four American civilian contractors on March 1 that fired the Marine occupation of al-Anbar province in the first place had fled the front pages. Where their burned corpses had been hung in the wind on the infamous "Brooklyn Bridge" in Fallujah only a painted-over eulogy remained. The rage that followed the disgusting events had been replaced by more rage over equally despicable acts in the region. Tensions were high and secular violence was on the rise. So fittingly the Marines were dropped into the hottest spot in Iraq, al-Anbar province, the home of the Sunni minority that had ruled Iraq for almost four decades.

Despite the carnage that hovered over Fallujah and the rest of the province, there was new thinking from up high that embraced benevolence, patience, and fair play when the Third arrived. Restraint was the order of the day. The Marines were there to "win the hearts and minds" of the Iraqis, certainly many of whom detested them. It was a jaded phrase and a tenuous proposition—and it was orders. The Marines were told to play nice with their Iraqi neighbors or pay the price.

At the time of OIF 2 deployment the Thundering Third was commanded by Lieutenant Colonel Willard "Willy" Buhl, a mild-mannered Californian of medium height who still carries the build of his wrestling days on his stout frame. Like all Marines Buhl stays sharp and neat but without some of the excess starch that stiffens so many others. His personality was perfect for the situation in al-Anbar province. By nature he is a friendly man who looks for the best in other people. Perhaps because he is also half Sicilian and half Irish, he has a dark side as well as a quick smile and a gift for gab. More than a few Iraqis who confused kindness with weakness would one day pay the price for their mistake.

Any Marine who served with him will say Buhl wasn't made in the ordinary mold of Marine officers. He is outwardly friendly, relaxed, and full of modern ideas about personal relationships and the art of command. He doesn't bark, snap, or snarl to expend his nervous energy. He burns it up visiting his troops, getting to know them, finding out what makes them howl. Buhl believes foremost in leading from the front, and that is where he was usually found. Kasal remembers him in his Humvee darting between companies under fire to discover for himself what was happening. At first Kasal wasn't sure whether his new commander's approach would work, but after studying him carefully, he decided Buhl's methods worked pretty damn well and the two men worked closely together to mold the battalion to fit its new mission.

"In the beginning we butted heads over a few things," Kasal recalls. "But as I grew to know him more and watched his leadership in combat, I found him to be a very adept and aggressive warrior who believed in taking the fight to the enemy and cared deeply for the Marines under his charge. I grew to respect him very much. He was always up-front."

By the end of the long, hot summer, Buhl could see that 3/1's Marines in al-Anbar province were slowly roasting in the desert heat under increasing numbers of sneak attacks and deadly ambushes. The battalion had lost 10 men, and there was no letup in sight. Some of the Marines were getting testy and more than a few simply wanted to kill somebody. At least one senior NCO was heard in Regimental Headquarters lamenting over his inability to kill someone or something. In Texas they call it buzzard's luck when you "can't kill nothin' and won't nothin' die!" Buhl kept a close watch on the temperament of his men to make sure they maintained their composure.

"You have to be careful with your anger because it can easily cloud your judgment," he says. "For me anger actually enabled me to remain calm. We're trained to think clearly under stress, but to really go through it, to live it, is another world."

UNPOPULAR PULLOUT

Buhl's Marines knew about the first attempt by 2/1, 1/5, and the Regiment's 1st Recon Battalion to take the ancient city of Fallujah the preceding April. That the mission was aborted pissed them off. Although their predecessors were already gone, it was no secret that the fight started April 4 during a handover ceremony with the Army's 82nd Airborne Division when an enemy mortar wounded several Marines. It ended with the testy Devil Dogs grudgingly pulling out while they were in the midst of some serious ass kicking. The Marines had the upper hand in Fallujah when they were suddenly—some say inexplicably—told to leave.

The order came from 1st Marine Regiment Combat Team's commander, Colonel John Toolan, who got it from Major General J. N. Mattis, and so on all the way to its source among the grand strategists in Baghdad. Toolan was ordered to hand over the parts of the city his Marines had just captured to so-called Iraqi National Guardsman and local police. The idea galled the Marines who swore the same guys had been shooting at them the day before.

The universally admired Toolan was still in command in al-Anbar province when 3/1 arrived. He would go home in September before seeing his mortal enemies get what he thought they deserved. In spring of 2006 Toolan was promoted to Brigadier General and reassigned from Director of the Marine Corps Command and Staff College for what he thought was a plum assignment as Assistant Division Commander of the 2d Marine Division. Later these orders would suddenly change, and he would find himself back in the bowels of the Pentagon. He didn't get a general's star being meek and mild. His Regimental Combat Team in June 2004 was more than 6,000 Marines strong and the absolute power in the region.

Toolan didn't say whether he agreed with the new methods that followed the so-called unilateral cease-fire that went into effect after his men pulled out or whether he preferred a more direct approach to settling up in Fallujah. Insurgents and Marines were still exchanging heavy fire every day over the berms and at the hard points where the Marines kept watch on the city. The

Iraqis took full advantage of the unilateral part of the cease-fire to blast away at the Marines whenever they thought they could get away with it. Those who saw Toolan work generally go with the notion he would have preferred to go back as soon as possible and finish it up before things got out of hand. Toolan is a big, powerful Irish rugby player who doesn't look like turning the other cheek is central to his personality. To slap Toolan would be like slapping John Wayne.

However, he made it clear to 3/1's Marines they had a new mission and new methods to employ. "Honestly, we didn't go in there with the intent of crushing the Iraqis," he says. "We went in there with the concept that we were going to win them over with a patient, persistent presence. Our first objective was getting them jobs. We knew where the jobs were, so our first objective was to get to get the factories in and around Fallujah going."

Toolan found himself in the limelight again in September when the press began speculating on a second run on Fallujah. It made perfect sense: Most of the action was in al-Anbar province, and Toolan was the sheriff. Now it looked like Toolan was approaching high noon again.

CLEAR ORDERS

The Thundering Third's orders were clear and concise:

- Deny indirect fires on essential installations by proactively seeking insurgent mortar and rocket firing positions and personnel;
- Ensure freedom of movement along the main supply routes and lines of communication;
- Locate, capture, and kill insurgents using raids and cordon-and-search procedures;
- Train and integrate Iraqi forces;
- Provide a secure environment and facilitate government of officials and agencies.

Then there were the so-called "implied tasks," including:

- Provide counterintimidation through aggressive patrolling, interdiction missions, and intelligence gathering;
- Initiate civil affairs projects;
- Develop actionable intelligence;
- Develop counters for improvised explosive device (IED) attacks;
- Provide force protection and firm base defense using both line company Marines and support personnel to man Marine base facilities.

FINANCING THE INSURGENCY

Buhl's job description didn't include questioning the new mission; his job was to carry it out. Regardless of the undertaking Buhl intended to see that 3/1 did it better than the soldiers and Marines who had preceded them. It was a lofty goal indeed in a sand-covered haven for every kind of malcontent in Iraq.

The battalion's arrival fresh from Camp Pendleton and six months of intense training for the mission was useful. They initially intended to cool off the insurgency with a combination of power, understanding, and lots of money. That plan never worked because the Sunnis couldn't be bought off easily. Indistinct groups of insurgents with different agendas were emerging throughout the countryside to take advantage of the American changing of the guard underway across Iraq. Bloodied Marine and Army combat formations all over the country were changing places with fresh combat commands. 3/1 was just one of many units replacing tired formations in al-Anbar province. The insurgents knew it was happening and took whatever advantage they could. The enemies' emerging skill and persistence were a growing problem.

"There is an amorphous network of cells throughout Iraq, but there wasn't any one singular leader, in my estimation," Toolan says. "This was still a concerted effort for them [insurgents]. They said, 'Hey, this is a good opportunity to make those guys pay' because there was such a huge change of guard. And so as soon as we got there we were intent on civil/military operations. They were intent on putting some stresses on our command and control just as we were taking over. So there were some renewed ambushes, IEDs, indirect fire attacks on Forward Operating Bases (FOBs). There was a big spike in these events during turnover."

A VICIOUS FIGHT

Between June and October Captain Jeffrey S. McCormack, the battalion's intelligence officer—the S-2 in Marine parlance—logged 207 indirect fire attacks, 95 IED ambushes, and six vehicle-borne IED and suicide attacks while discovering dozens of significant arms caches. Many of the senior Marines in the battalion said they'd never seen so much arms and ordnance even after the fall of Baghdad and Desert Storm. Indirect mortar and rocket attacks had jumped from 19 in June to 56 by October, and more than 100 1st Division Marines had been killed or wounded. The fight at al-Anbar province was turning vicious.

Not everybody was at risk. The locals had a fondness for the battalion civil affairs officer, nicknamed "Moneybags." His job was spreading around reconstruction money. He and his team would mount their Humvee and visit the sheiks and village administrators to pay for redevelopment projects that were part of the Coalition's carrot-and-stick psychology.

Moneybags' security team included a black Marine turret gunner. McCormack remembers him well because the only time the civil affairs officer was ever attacked was the day the turret gunner was replaced by a white Marine. "They never got hit," McCormack says. "They would go into some of the most godawful places and never be attacked, except once. He normally had an African-American as his turret gunner. Well, that Marine got sick for whatever reason that day so they had a different kid up there, and they got IEDed. We were sure it was because they didn't have that African-American kid up there. The insurgents knew that if the kid in the second vehicle was black it was the civil affairs officer. They called him 'Moneybags,' and they weren't going to IED Moneybags."

Despite handing out money, patrolling vigorously, increasing the use of aerial reconnaissance, and using intense political negotiations, the situation for 3/1 in al-Anbar province never improved. The rot radiated outward from Fallujah to infect the satellite towns surrounding it.

Marine intelligence knew that only 20 percent of the insurgents were foreigners and 80 percent of the trigger pullers were Iraqis. They also knew the foreigners were facilitating the war by bringing in money and weapons. The money, often crisp new American $20 and $100 bills, was being funneled to the insurgency from both Arab and Western contributors. The Marines also recovered donated medical supplies and food that, McCormack discovered, had been purchased off the black market with American dollars and brought into al-Anbar province by couriers.

Like most plans based on unrealistic expectations, the plan to pacify Fallujah and rid it of insurgents was conceived in presumption and executed with dysfunction. Arguably parts of the plan were working, but winning the hearts and minds of the insurgents wasn't one of them. McCormack, as a part of S-2, was one of the guys who had to figure out why.

"We talked to people who told us they could make $6 a day working for a Coalition contractor, or they could make $100 placing an IED," McCormack says. "Where's the choice? These people didn't have anything. Just a few people had all the money. You could tell because they were fat. They had enough to eat. They were paying for the insurgency."

McCormack's intel shop determined 3/1 was facing multiple four- to eight-man insurgent cells that had the ability to regenerate. They were well paid from caches secreted away during the Saddam regime and from contributions collected worldwide and filtered into Iraq from foreign sources. It was nothing extraordinary to find a furtive foreign fighter with $20,000 in American money destined for payrolls that enticed the unemployed Sunni malcontents.

"The insurgents knew the terrain much better than the Marines," McCormack says. "We said they had the jungle working for them. They could hide weapons and people out in the countryside."

Catching the bad guys was a challenge because they were so hard to identify. Residents were permitted to keep rifles for self-defense, so they were only implicated if they were caught carrying a detonator, planting an IED, or linked to large caches of arms.

They hid their caches away from their homes and yards, McCormack explains. Weapons and ammunition could turn up anywhere—near roads, alongside canals, even hidden in the furniture of homes in Fallujah.

Intimidation was a key factor in the insurgents' success. Local leaders would play both sides, according to McCormack. They took money from the foreign fighters supporting the insurgency as well as from Moneybags. "Sometimes they did it to survive," he explains. "If they said no to the insurgents, particularly the foreign fighters, they were killed. But some of it was because they agreed with the insurgents and because they earned a lot of money working for them."

LEADERSHIP UNDER FIRE

Toolan was aware of the political realities of al-Anbar province and it concerned him greatly because the insurgents' tactics incited his Marines. The pinprick attacks were wounding and killing his men and they couldn't respond. In his estimation they showed considerable restraint despite provocations that made the young Marines pray for payback. They held to it in part because Americans have a certain standard of decency and in part because NCOs like Kasal kept them in check, Toolan says.

"There is this guy, Jim Collins, in *Good to Great* [Jim Collins, *Good to Great: Why Some Companies Make the Leap*, Audio, Jim Collins 2005]. He speaks of the Level Five leadership, which is the highest. He says there are two components of the leader who not only can take an organization from good to great but who can transform the organization. In other words he can go from traditional combat to this crazy form of warfare we now have in Iraq. Collins' study was pretty extensive—several years, I think—and he found that the Level Five leaders had an overwhelming will to get something accomplished. Add to that humility and you have got a leader of an organization that can do just about anything. Kasal fits that description of a Level Five leader pretty well."

Kasal had his work cut out for him in Weapons Co. The young 3/1 Marines said they didn't know exactly what their mission was after a few months of the mushrooming insurgency. It certainly didn't seem to be about creating jobs and earning people's trust. Lance Corporal Alex Nicoll, in Kilo, didn't buy it at all. He figured that the whole place would fall apart eventually and they would be killing each other; he just didn't know when.

"When the IEDs and all that started, it was more about staying alert," Nicoll says. "We knew we had a pacification mission, but we also were told we better pay attention and keep our shit together."

Most of the young Marines claim they didn't start out hating the Iraqis when they arrived in al-Anbar province. The ones who remembered OIF 1 and their triumphant reception in Baghdad two years before had good memories of Iraqis greeting them as liberators. Some even compared their experiences to the jubilation in the cities of Europe during World War II. Kasal said it was such a powerful feeling he volunteered to go back again.

"I saw what we were doing for the Iraqis was helping," he says about his first deployment in Iraq. "They had been oppressed for 30 years, especially the Shiite areas in the south, and they were thanking us. They viewed us as liberators. The media made us out like we weren't liberators and in the Sunni areas they were right. We took away their corruption and their criminals and their money and everything else by throwing Saddam out of power. They thrived on Saddam because they were the thugs. But the rest of the country—the Kurds up north and the Shiites in the south—they are thriving. They were really helping us."

Not all the Marines shared Kasal's optimistic view. Many distrusted the Iraqis, insisting they were sneaky liars. They tried to be friendly anyway because that was the mission, but the young Marines weren't always convincing. The hate started when their buddies began to die and the Rules of Engagement (ROE) prevented them from retaliating. The resentment was hot in 3/1 before Fallujah burned.

Many of the Marines were bitching that the ROE were too rigid. Corporal R. J. Mitchell and Nicoll said they were getting ready for some payback. All the line companies were taking hits on the roads between Fallujah, Al Kharma, and Ash Shahabi to the west. The roads in between—called "Ratlines" among Marines—were named Michigan/Chicago, Michigan/Pittsburgh, Santa Fe, Richmond, and the River Road. On one 2,100-meter stretch of Michigan east of the infamous Abu Ghraib Prison, the Marines encountered 24 IEDs, one for every 100 meters of road. That kind of death-dealing situation has a strong effect on young men who can't adequately fight back.

Kasal and the other Weapons Co. NCOs spent a lot of time counseling young Marines who were getting too aggressive. Long-term mission objectives and lofty ideals are hard to see amid the dust of incoming mortars, burning vehicles, and fellow Marines writhing in agony. It was his job to see they kept those objectives and ideals in mind.

"I believe that when wearing the uniform and standing up front as a leader, it is vital to show confidence and instill in your men an attitude that they are the best," Kasal says. "Your men are a direct reflection of you. What they know is what you taught them. If they're out of shape, you allowed it. If you don't know them, you've failed. And their confidence and pride comes from you, the leader setting the example by your own actions and putting them through challenging and hard training so they have a sense of accomplishment and continue to learn."

Kasal has always taken that responsibility seriously: "Whenever I would take over a new unit, starting from a fire team leader to a company first sergeant, I would always push my men hard and set extremely challenging yet attainable goals for them. And every time it was the same. In the beginning there would be widespread grumbling and bitching about why they had to do this or that. But the grumbling only lasted for a short time before the unit would start seeing the improvements and the hard work pay off. They would then develop a tighter unit cohesiveness and pride in the unit—even to the point of making fun of other units for not doing as much."

Part of Kasal's strength came from other members of 3/1's leadership. They were all professionals with more than a century's combined experience. Kasal credits their leadership as much as his for the capabilities of the Thundering Third.

"Once a week in Iraq each company's staff would meet together with the battalion staff to do planning and operations briefs," he says. "It was a good time to get organized. Each company in the battalion spread out and separated over the entire area of operation [AO]. It was a good time to catch up with the other four companies' first sergeants.

"They were a very professional and proficient group I was proud to call my friends. I looked forward to the days we all were able to get together. We'd tell stories and joke with each other in typical Marine fashion. It was also a time I could let loose and share emotions of war I never would openly do in front of my Marines."

Tim Ruff was always there. Kasal called him "Shorty." Wayne Hertz would lend his martial spirit. The others included First Sergeant Scott Samuels, a rough and gruff Marine Kasal "trusted immensely," and First Sergeant Wayne Miller, Kasal's replacement in Kilo and a brave Marine who was wounded earlier in the year and stayed with his Marines instead of going home. Kasal called his action "a testament to his character."

"I was blessed to serve with these men," Kasal says.

"NO BETTER FRIEND"

By November all the 3/1 Marines were salty, hard-core, and seasoned by five months of pain, policing insurgents who used sneak attacks and hidden explosives to bedevil the Devil Dogs at every opportunity. 3/1's Marines were hurting for payback.

Lieutenant Jesse Grapes was Kilo Co.'s third platoon leader in the months leading up to the Fallujah fight. He and Kasal went all the way back to OIF 1 when Kasal was the first sergeant of Kilo. They shared a mutual admiration for each other's combat talents.

"We made an attempt, an honest attempt, to win the hearts and minds of the Iraqis," Grapes says. "We got some real good cultural training, and the first three or four months we went out of our way to win their trust. My best mission over there was when we guarded the civil engineers building a water project. These people hadn't had running water for 30 years. They were grateful."

In the five months preceding the second Fallujah battle, 3/1 was involved in small operations performing raids, cordon-and-knock missions to capture enemy suspects, and ambushes that kept the insurgents off balance. What the Marines were itching to begin, though, was large-scale operations to clear the area of the insurgents who were inflicting casualties.

"We had to keep the Marines focused on the current mission without straining their aggressive emotions. That is what leadership is all about. You set aside your personal feelings for the mission—the mission itself always comes first. I wouldn't just tell my young Marines; I would lead by example," Grapes says.

Being restrained was particularly hard on the young riflemen who stayed on the firing line day after day. Their life was an endless round of patrolling, ambushes, listening posts, and roadblocks. It was dirty, dangerous work that was getting deadlier every day. They wanted to kick some ass, take some names, and get some payback. Alex Nicoll was among them.

"It gets tedious. Fucking ambushes, patrol, hang out, and then go back on patrol. The officers and NCOs would remind us about not killing the Iraqis. They were shooting at us all the time—IEDs, snipers, mortars—but it was really boring most of the time," he says. "We would go out at night with our night vision and try and sneak up on some dude, an insurgent, and the damn dogs would start barking. Nasty dogs, not like pets; the Iraqis kept them around for barking. They hate dogs. And we would find some guy, and he would have his papers, and we would detain him anyway because he would fit the profile. It was considered a good mission, but the real guy we were looking for would be gone.

"It was mostly the dogs. They would start barking. I must have shot a good six of them—loud dogs. They would bark, and the bastards would take off running. Sometimes we could see them in our night vision running away. We couldn't shoot unless they had a weapon."

3/1's Marines could take the pain and uncertainty. They could even grudgingly take the boredom; after all, enduring pain and boredom is an important part of the traditions Marines hold in reverence. In a fight they never stray far from the customs and rituals of Marine Corps history. The most irreverent Marine knows that the discipline is what makes the Corps unique among famous fighting formations around the world.

Even so, things started getting confusing while they patrolled al-Anbar province. Before OIF 1 Major General J. N. Mattis had released a letter to his 1st Marine Division Marines urging them to be "no better friends" to the Iraqis who welcomed them and "no worse enemies" to the ones who didn't. His mandate was the ultimate double-edged sword. The restraint inherent in his order was considered a noble concept by many of the forward-thinking Marines in 3/1, but it was also one the insurgents viewed with contempt. Strength is a virtue in that part of the world. The Marines could not let themselves be considered weak. Weakness invited attack.

"No better friend was certainly our first and foremost objective, but we also knew that we could be their worst enemy if they decided to make life difficult," Colonel Toolan says. "In Bing West's book [*No True Glory: A Frontline Account of the Battle for Fallujah,* Bantam, 2005] he brings out the combative nature of Marines. Let's face it—that is what we are all about. But we spent an amazing amount of time and energy getting the Marines mentally ready to be their friends. Maybe friends is a bit of an exaggeration, but at least be present and earn their trust and confidence that we would be there. Instead of an insurgent, a Marine would be there and their family wouldn't be abused in the night or threatened or whatever. That was our going-in objective.

"The problem is," he adds, "the attacks just increased. It would have been a sign of weakness to them if we hadn't responded. We didn't have to respond with violations of land warfare, but we had to respond in kind."

By November infrequent incidents had melded into constant agitation. Weapons Co. Marines riding in Humvees with TOWs and other heavy weapons were constantly in contact. Kasal's Marines were spread thin, running around the entire AO while setting up road checkpoints and providing security, and they were being faced with more and more difficult circumstances.

"Our CAAT [combined anti-armor team] platoon would get some Arabs who would cross trigger lines—lines that if they crossed they would be shot," Grapes remembers. "There would be signs warning them, and they would ignore them, and they would get shot. It was still justified. The first time one goes to war there is a bit of hesitation. Later on there is no hesitation. Even those aggressive Marines with a rifle had a sense of compassion, but over time as you see more and more of your friends getting hurt, the hesitation diminishes. There is a distinction between losing hesitance and taking it too far and doing the wrong thing. Prior to going to Fallujah we didn't have an enemy."

Trying to be everywhere to ensure that his Marines complied with the ROE was a major part of Kasal's job. While constantly in the field and performing his regular duties as a first sergeant, he would go on missions with Marines. He was on the run 24 hours a day, living on 20-minute catnaps. He consistently went without rest so he could be with his Marines.

"Sometimes it was okay," says Kasal. "Sometimes we would get four or five hours of sleep. I learned to adapt. Marines learn to adapt to anything."

There was no time for too much else. His Marines were spread across an area roughly half the size of Rhode Island. Keeping them together was an important part of the job.

"A first sergeant should be there to lead and inspire," he says. "Before pinning on first sergeant stripes you have to be a leader. Just being with your Marines and letting them see that you are enduring the same hardships and dangers as them will lift their spirits in even the hardest of times.

"When I would go out with a platoon or a squad I would always have a pocketful of candy. I used to tell my Marines that I believed in General Mattis' statement about no better friend, no worse enemy than a U.S. Marine. I kept telling them that when you go out there, you be warriors and you be ready. If the enemy even thinks about blinking, you be the most ferocious thing he's ever seen and you kill the little bastard.

"At the same time I'd tell them to try to make a new friend every day," he adds. "If you just go out there every day and piss people off, you are going to have a long, hard war ahead of you. The only way you are going to win this war is by winning the populace, and that means when you go out on patrol, don't be abusing people and kicking things in and trashing places."

In October Weapons Co.'s 81mm mortar platoon suffered a killed in action (KIA) and multiple wounded in actions (WIAs) from an enemy mortar round inside their compound. While out on patrol with one of his sections, Kasal learned that the Marines from the 81s stopped combat operations to mourn their fellow Marines. Kasal came off the mission he was on and headed to the 81's compound. He pulled the NCOs together and gave them a brief lecture on combat leadership. Never let your Marines mourn immediately after a loss, he told them. Keep them focused on the task at hand. There would be time for mourning after the fight.

LOOKING AHEAD

Kasal realized the growing combat they lived every day was tough, scary, and lonely, but he also knew that it was nothing compared to the hell that was about to arrive. To make sure his own Marines kept their heads in the war, he turned to his gunnery sergeants and other staff NCOs to help him.

In al-Anbar province in October 2004 Chief Warrant Officer 2d Class Christian Wade was a gunnery sergeant, or "gunny," in Weapons Co. It was his fourth time in combat. Wade, originally from Bozeman, Montana, had sweated out Somalia and fought in Task Force Ripper during Desert Storm and during 3/1's first deployment in 2002. After getting wounded in al-Anbar province by an IED and staying on to get in on the fight in Fallujah, the former sniper was nominated to be a Marine Corps gunner, a rank of rare and exalted status. Wade went to Quantico, Virginia, to train for his new role.

"By the time it came around we were praying to go to Fallujah," Wade says. "I wanted my Marines to be aggressive. The Rules of Engagement were still pretty liberal. I encouraged my Marines to shoot and kill and destroy as much as possible.

"With First Sergeant Kasal leading the way, I didn't have a choice. He established a from-the-front style of leadership. I would hear things like 'What the hell is First Sergeant Kasal doing out there getting shot to hell? That isn't a first sergeant's job.' Kasal thought his job was being out with the men."

By the end of October Kasal and Wade already knew through the NCOs' grapevine that they were going to take out Fallujah.

Wade was more than ready, tired of daily firefights with no clear victory. The Marines in his platoon felt the same way. He rode them hard—he says sometimes too hard—making sure they stayed focused on the mission. The constant combat was grinding everybody down.

"I was going out with my CAAT teams to make sure that they had everything they needed and to show them we were all in it together," he says. "Even when the sections were running on their own they felt better because the gunny was out there.

"I had done some checking and found out that in the unit we replaced, the gunny I was replacing didn't leave Camp Abu Ghraib. I wasn't going to do that. I went out to keep an eye on my men, making sure the Marines were cleaning their weapons, doing their maintenance. I kept dialed in on four sections. Three had staff sergeants and one had a sergeant running them."

Wade confesses: "I had the habit of interfering when they weren't doing right, when I thought I saw something interfering with the integrity of the section or platoon. Kasal talked to me about it. When Kasal told me something I listened because he was right. I had to let my sections run themselves."

Kasal remained everywhere all the time. He went from platoon to platoon and section to section making sure Weapons Co. Marines stayed in the loop. He never tried to diminish his young Marines' fears about the upcoming fight with bullshit. He told them that good Marines are prepared Marines. Their training was the best weapon they had. He made sure they understood it.

Despite the Marines' combat anxiety they weren't running scared. Every insurgent assault was met with force and 3/1 stung the insurgents plenty of times. The snipers of H&S Company (Headquarters and Services) were especially effective taking out pesky insurgents keeping an eye on the Marines. Even so, before the battle for Fallujah broke, no one in 3/1 knew that one day the name would become immortalized in the annals of the United States Marine Corps. All they knew was that other Marines had been there before and were ordered to give up ground they had taken with their blood. That was enough to pray for payback.

The men in the Thundering Third were also too busy surviving to suspect that the Old Breed's battle for the ancient Islamic city would in the future simply be known as "Fallujah" and uttered with the same reverence as Veracruz, Chateau Thierry, Iwo, or The Canal. And it was still much too early to know that the Marines who died there would be enshrined in its lore and that Fallujah would claim its place in the proud litany of battles already admitted to the pantheon of the Corps' cherished fights. They would have laughed in the face of anybody who even suggested it.

CHAPTER 8

★ ★ ★

MOVING UP

On October 24, 2004, Lieutenant Colonel Willy Buhl and Lieutenant Colonel Patrick Malay, the CO of 3/5, accompanied Colonel Mike Shupp, the new commander of RCT1, on a mission designated Operation Team Comanche to reconnoiter a huge train station slightly north of Fallujah. Colonel Toolan had unexpectedly turned over command of 1st Marines in September to Colonel Larry Nicholson. Shupp replaced Nicholson, who was severely wounded on his first day of command.

At Shupp's direction Buhl and Malay joined C Company, 2d Tank BN, RCT1 while it executed a carefully orchestrated feint at the train station to determine if it could be used as a jump-off point to attack Fallujah. Team Comanche had been rehearsing the ruse for several days with the fast, wheeled light armored vehicles (LAVs) from 3d Recon. BN and was ready to move out. In the April battle the Marines had attacked Fallujah from the northwest with 2/1, from the south with 1/5, and later the east with 3/4. The insurgents seemed to expect any second attack from the same general directions. To repel attack they had massed their forces in the southwestern part of the city and along the Euphrates River on its western edge. They had even prepared positions to repel AAVs swimming across. Shupp wanted to surprise them.

Officially Captain Robert Bodisch, the C Co. tank commander, was leading the combined arms team of tanks, LAVs, and a tactical Psychological Operations (Psyops) team. The mission's primary purpose was to identify key objectives in north Fallujah and locations to establish breach lanes for follow-on operations. Breach lanes are paths cleared through obstacles to allow tracked and wheeled vehicles to attack a specific point.

Commanders and staff officers had varied views on the mission. Some believed it would telegraph the Marines' moves without any tangible gain. Others thought it was showboating to send an armored column unnecessarily into harm's way. They felt the intelligence information was available through other means.

TAKING FIRE

Buhl found himself the designated loader in an Abrams commanded by an experienced gunnery sergeant named Juhl. Juhl had just finished a tour as a tank instructor at the Army's Armor School at Ft. Knox, Kentucky. For the rest of the day Buhl was under Juhl's command. His job was to look out the gunner's hatch in the turret to make his reconnaissance and to load the main gun if called on to do so.

"We went up there with tanks and LAVs," Buhl recalls. "The insurgents were building up in the southern part of the city and along the river. The area where they were concentrated had been the scene of heavy fighting with 2/1 in April.

"It took us some time to maneuver toward the train station. The insurgents had some people where 3/5 later penetrated. They were shooting at us. Eventually the fire built up as more and more insurgents arrived. They were coming in from all over the city. It was sort of like, 'Hey, come over and take some shots at the tanks sitting by the train station.'"

The tanks stopped just east of the train station. While they waited, drawing small-arms fire, their Forward Air Controller (FAC) and artillery Forward Observer (FO) worked up an air strike and artillery attacks instead of just using the main guns on the tanks.

According to the official After Action Report Team, Comanche immediately came under "accurate and continuous mortar and rocket-propelled grenade fire coupled with sniper and small-arms fire." Buhl's perspective was that of the lance corporal who normally manned his position in the tank. His only view of the action was through the tank's optics.

"We sat there for 10 minutes taking fire from these bastards," Buhl says. "RPGs were hitting our tank; they make a peculiar sound when they strike the armor. The RPGs were coming from the northeast and northwest. The LAVs backed off out of range until just the tanks remained. By then the insurgents were bringing in adjusted 82mm mortars. At that point I thought that the insurgents could be bringing up something bigger. There were Milans [Italian-made guided antitank missiles] in Theater.

"I was concerned about a mobility kill. I thought we would have a tank struck with an RPG and have a track drop. Then we would have to get out and secure the tank, and it could be a big fight. We also considered they might try and swarm us if that happened."

Buhl knew as well as anyone that nothing was more deadly to a tanker than being immobilized with a broken track. The insurgents had been known to swarm over disabled tanks with the hopes of killing the crews working to recover them. So far that had not happened here and Buhl hoped it remained that way.

"In a previous operation we had already had a tank damaged and immobilized when it hit a mine while under heavy small-arms and RPG fire," he says. "The gunnery sergeant in my vehicle had been involved in that previous operation and he was very concerned. There were some tense moments."

Buhl's telescopic view from inside the tank brought the entire city into precise focus. What he could see was eerily medieval— a ponderous, lurking fortress of thick-walled buildings and tall, menacing minarets surrounded by ancient walls. From the minarets at the corners of the fortress city, its defenders could see the attackers long before they arrived at the gates.

"Someone could easily signal across the city via the mosque minarets just as they had done since medieval times," Buhl says. "In effect, with observers in these mosque minarets, there was no way to approach Fallujah without somebody seeing us, particularly enemy FOs."

As Buhl was peering through his scope Captain Bodisch directed his Fire Support Team (FiST) to suppress and, he hoped, destroy the insurgent positions while pulling back from the main line of resistance. Bodisch ordered his tanks to open up with their turret-mounted coaxial machine guns and suppress or kill as many of the insurgents attacking them as they could.

After the RCT1 engineer officer determined which enemy obstacles needed to be destroyed by his engineers, and Buhl and Malay had adequately studied their lines of approach, Bodisch ordered Team Comanche to beat feet.

Getting the order to leave didn't break Buhl's heart. As an infantryman he wasn't comfortable being inside a tank taking fire. Buhl later remarked, however, that a redeeming part of the experience was getting to load a round into the main gun and let it rip. He even saved the ejected cartridge for a souvenir.

It wasn't as if Buhl and his infantrymen didn't appreciate the Abrams' 120mm main gun, its magnificent array of optical wizardry, or its deadly coaxial machine guns. But infantrymen have understandably mixed feelings about tanks because tanks often draw fire. Marines call them "mortar magnets" for good reason. Every time tanks came in their area they received incoming mortar and rocket fire. It didn't bother the tanks too much, but it could be really tough on the mud Marines.

The insurgents hated tanks and they expended huge amounts of ammunition at great risk trying to wound or destroy one. Mortar magnets or not, tanks in Fallujah were worth their weight in gold to the Marines, and the men in Bodisch's C Co. earned the respect and admiration of every member of the Thundering Third.

Shupp later deemed the mission a success for identifying the key objectives and breach lanes that were ultimately used. Additionally the tankers killed seven insurgents and destroyed four fortified positions without getting bogged down in a slugging match. Shupp credited the mission with setting the conditions for penetration of Fallujah from the north two weeks later.

"The best thing about the mission was that we got a good look at the train station and the approaches to it," Buhl agrees.

KASAL TAKES CHARGE

By late October the battle plan was complete. The Third was given the all-important task of taking the Fallujah train station the night before the battle began in earnest. Success would depend on two untested Iraqi National Guard (ING) companies performing as advertised. Both were being trained by Marines from the Weapons Co., 3/1, former mortar platoon members out of work in al-Anbar province because of the ROE. India was the ING company led by Lieutenant Zachary Iscol and his ad hoc advisory team.

If the Iraqis were successful the Thundering Third would plunge headlong into the killing ground where unprepared insurgents would die. If they weren't successful things would get a lot messier. Weapons Co.'s newly minted advisors had a month to get ready.

Part of Kasal's job as first sergeant of Weapons Co. before the big fight for Fallujah was to keep it all communicating so that each element of the company meshed with the next. He had sections of TOWs and Mark-19 automatic grenade launchers perched on turrets in Humvees, and man-portable Javelins, and good ol' Ma Deuce, that big hunk of copper-spitting, twin-handled precision steel that had been sending the enemy to death for almost a century. In addition he had three platoons of 81mm mortars, a poor man's artillery that can be devastating. All of it was tied together with computers, radios, and satellite pictures. Above them were fixed-wing attack jets dubbed "fast movers" and attack helicopters on call. To make sure Weapons Co. was in the right place at the right time the chain of command went like this: The company commander issued the orders he received from the battalion commander. Kasal's NCOs led the squads, sections, and platoons to make sure the men were ready. Finally Kasal made sure they were all where they were supposed to be.

Kasal was also a confidant of Sergeant Major E. T. "Ed" Sax. Together with the other officers and senior NCOs, they were charged with leading mostly teenagers—18-, 19-, and 20-year-old Marine Corps riflemen—who were fighting as much for each other as for any other cause. The most experienced of them had fought with Kasal during OIF 1; the least experienced among them were barely out of high school. But to a man they were all Marines.

In the final days and hours before the looming battle, the young Marines privately took inventory of their leaders. They willingly followed Kasal and the other professionals in Weapons Co. because they knew they were tough, hard, unrelenting officers and noncommissioned officers. They did it out of respect and even a bit of awe. However there were always plenty of young Marines trying to buck the system.

Sometimes good field Marines don't fare so well in the rear

where peace tends to reign and mayhem of any sort is frowned upon. Like Animal Mother, the fierce Marine in the movie *Full Metal Jacket*, they need somebody throwing grenades at them occasionally to feel engaged. Kasal didn't mind coming around to explode in their faces when he deemed it necessary.

Corporal R. J. Mitchell knew something about Kasal's explosive capability, although he says it never arrived undeserved. "First Sergeant could really chew some ass," he remembers. "He could go crazy. Then he would tell you what you needed to do to correct it. First Sergeant could chew ass with the best of them."

Under their leadership the proven warriors of 3/1 had fought the good fight for more than five long months and were ready for more. A rare few of them didn't want to fight and more of them faced the realities of concentrated combat with a terrible dread. They all knew that the professionals among them had gladly chosen the unforgiving life of a field Marine so they could lead them into battle. No matter what their personal feelings, the younger men had no intentions of letting their leaders down.

Some who have experienced combat say there is no prouder action a man can take. Some who have witnessed combat leaders plying their craft say there is no more noble a profession. To a man, the officers and noncoms of 3/1 stood proud and straight and walked with a particular certainty that is almost chilling to the uninitiated. Even the young leaders, the first-term corporals and sergeants who had earned their stripes in training, were all about being professionals. Like all the Marines who have passed before them, the Third's leaders at Fallujah remembered that duty and honor were never far away.

Kasal considers his service with the Thundering Third at Fallujah the most rewarding of his career. "It was an outstanding battalion," he says. "We had the best men, NCOs, and officers in the Marine Corps. Lieutenant Colonel Buhl was a great officer and every man in Weapons Co. was outstanding. We had trained together for a long time. All the first sergeants were excellent, and Sergeant Major Sax was a fine sergeant major. We knew each other and knew our mission."

Buhl, a former NCO and Force Recon Marine who was no combat slouch himself, describes Kasal as "mentally and physically the toughest staff NCO I have ever served with.

"Kasal is larger than life with the young Marines. He praises them and kicks them in the butt when required," Buhl says. "He is everywhere all the time, and that becomes apparent to the young PFC—that First Sergeant Kasal, now Sergeant Major Kasal, is there for the young Marines all the time."

Buhl says Kasal always knows what he is talking about before he opens his mouth, an important asset when seconds count. And he says the rugged Marine had an uncanny ability to be wherever he was needed the most. Whatever the situation, the first sergeant of Weapons Co. would be part of the action.

Kasal says he was simply checking on his men just like any other first sergeant would do. The fact he always found himself in the thick of things was coincidental.

"Weapons Co. Marines supported all the companies," he says. "I would hear something on the radio, or Major [at the time Captain R. H.] Belknap or maybe even Colonel Buhl would require something and I would head that way. The sergeant major was out there and so were the other first sergeants. 3/1 was always that way. We all talked to each other."

Buhl says Kasal had been on the firing line in every fight Weapons Co. was engaged in since they landed in Iraq. On his first combat deployment he performed exactly the same way while leading Kilo Co. Every one of the officers and men who spoke about Kasal described him as a tough, tenacious fighter and a merciless hunter. His men stood in awe of him then and now. Even today, long after some of them have left the Corps, they still call him "First Sergeant" in a familiar way that sounds like

"Firs Sar'ent." Far from being a slight, it is the manner in which Marines show unmitigated respect to their noncoms. NCOs that didn't add up were quickly forgotten. In the lexicon of their lives "First Sergeant" is First Sergeant Kasal.

Mitchell, who would play a huge role in Kasal's future, says Kasal was one of the biggest influences in his Marine Corps career. "In Fallujah First Sergeant Kasal was in Weapons Co., not even in my company. He would just show up and fall in like a lance corporal," Mitchell recalls. "I would tell him what to do and he would go off and do it. He was awesome. If we had to take down a house he would do it. He had the TOWs and Javelins.

"One time some dude with an AK or something was firing out of this house in Fallujah—maybe the second or third day—and we couldn't see him because he was backed up into the room or something. I was going to take it out with a team until the first sergeant had a Marine fire a TOW missile into it. I was talking to him on the radio. It imploded the whole fucking house on this dude. Then several of us ran up to shoot him to be sure. Me, Kasal, Nicoll, and another Marine moved forward, but we couldn't find the guy because the whole house was a big rubble pile."

Kasal's leadership impressed Mitchell, especially his style of correcting an error or instructing a subordinate to improve his performance. "If I screwed something up or did something he thought was wrong, he didn't start yelling or correcting me in front of the other Marines," Mitchell explains. "Later he would say something and see if I agreed. You could tell him why you did something, and if he thought you were correct he would say so. I was a corporal then and there weren't too many first sergeants who would do that. He could chew some ass; he could go crazy, but never in front of anyone."

Mitchell adds with a tone of admiration: "I never minded when Kasal showed up. He could kick some serious ass. He was just a bad dude."

CHAPTER 9
★ ★ ★

SNIPERS, SNOOPERS, AND SELLERS

The campaign to retake Fallujah officially began November 1, 2004, and would capture the world's attention for nearly a month. That day Marine Corps Forward Operating Base (FOB) Delta took two rounds of incoming mortar fire from insurgents. Delta was located in the city of Al Kharma, 30 miles west of Baghdad, near Fallujah in the middle of the desert.

One result of the pinprick attack was that somebody far higher up the food chain than 3/1's Marines decided enough was enough. The Marines were finally going to put a stop to the insurgent activity bedeviling al-Anbar province. Fallujah was the viper's nest; insurgents had been operating there with impunity for six months.

First, though, there was much work to be done to prepare for an attack. 3/1 contributed on several fronts: Scout-snipers probed the insurgents in small deadly teams to determine their whereabouts, response times, communication methods, and strongholds. Snoopers of various kinds infiltrated the city, listened in on cell phone and two-way radio transmissions, and flew unmanned missions over the city, taking pictures. Finally Marine leadership endeavored to sell the idea of the occupation to the local leadership—sometimes the very people who were trying to kill the occupiers.

SNIPERS

In the weeks before the battle for Fallujah the scout-snipers were used to deceive the enemy about where the Marines intended to strike. Their job was part of a larger deception plan to confuse the insurgents about the location of the main attack.

Officially military records say these operations "served to attrite the enemy, stimulate electronic communications which revealed enemy command and control nodes, and to determine enemy reinforcement response times and basic operational capabilities."

More specifically their job was to scout for the company they were attached to and perform any other reconnaissance missions assigned: report intelligence information, seek out enemy snipers, and serve as overwatch for Marines on patrol to make sure the Iraqis didn't sneak up on them. An especially popular task was taking out Iraqi snipers if they got into contact.

Chad Cassidy was a corporal in H&S Co.'s scout-sniper platoon when the battalion geared up for Fallujah in November of 2004. His radio operator and spotter at al-Anbar province was Lance Corporal Russell Scott.

Cassidy and Scott were an inseparable team. Cassidy usually took the shots using a scoped, precision-built M40A1 bolt-action sniper rifle that can kill a man 1,000 meters away. Cassidy's job was to keep in radio contact with headquarters, spot targets, and provide added security. He also took an occasional shot. During Fallujah the team saw plenty of action before both men were seriously wounded the third day by shrapnel. They were medevaced home to recover. After healing Cassidy decided to try for an officer's commission. He attended Officer Basic Course at Quantico, Virginia, and earned a promotion to Second Lieutenant.

Scott's still-healing wounds remain quite painful, making being a Marine a lot tougher for him physically than it had been. He has been promoted to Corporal and is now helping to train Marines at Camp Lejeune's Special Operations Training Group. Scott plans to run out his military string, finish his interrupted college education, and get a graduate degree.

Cassidy and Scott are tight in a way only combat veterans can be. They fought together, got wounded together, and have survived their personal hells since by working it out together. In the spring of 2006 they met over breakfast at a hash house in Quantico, Virginia, talking to one another for the first time since they fought in Fallujah. Their sentences often drifted off before reaching the end—the listener simply nodding to indicate he already understood what the speaker had not yet said. They had perfected such silent communications in Iraq when talking any more than absolutely necessary might have gotten them killed. Watching and listening to their conversation it was easy to imagine them quiet and purposeful on a rooftop somewhere, waiting for the shot.

Both men were on the firing line almost daily during the month before the storm broke. 3/1's Cassidy, always quiet and controlled, says of his job in the time leading up to Fallujah: "It was a heavy and deadly responsibility, not some kind of twisted sport." But they also knew they had a moral responsibility to use their skills as justly as the rules of warfare allowed. It was a dangerous job that marked the men for a bad end if the Iraqis ever caught them.

As a result, Scott says, "We tried really, really hard to fit in with the Grunts." The signpost M40A1 rifle would be kept out of sight. "It was slung down the side," Scott says. "Unless somebody was really, really looking and had optics, they wouldn't see it."

But sometimes scout-snipers were forced into the open during cordon-and-sweep operations. That put their two- and four-man teams at risk because of their small numbers. Cassidy says the best way to handle that situation was to swagger their way through towns and villages.

"We'd walk like we owned the fucking street," he recalls. "The way we'd move our bodies, how we'd sweep, everything we did made it look like we were just daring somebody to come out in the street and do something." It was a bluff that got them out of several potential jams.

Their M40A1 rifles were deadly weapons in their own right, but scout-snipers' ability to call in the rest of the regiment's assets—mortars, artillery, and both rotary and fixed-wing aircraft—made them even more powerful.

In addition Cassidy says, "We knew the area that we worked in better than any Americans." Part of their scouting mission was to talk to the locals, many of whom spoke a little English. "We had conversations as best we could with Iraqi people," he says. "We knew who they were, and sometimes we would look for a specific guy because he would be known to be involved in something."

SNOOPERS

The intelligence that headquarters received from the scout-snipers about Fallujah was useful but it had its limitations. Scouts couldn't go into the city before the incursion—at least not without a serious fight—so the picture they provided of the insurgency was incomplete.

Fortunately there were several other sources of intelligence flowing back to 3/1 headquarters and a whole team of specialists whose job it was to gather and interpret it. Heading this Intelligence Section (S-2) was Captain McCormack, a former

Grunt who headed a group of more than 150 Marine technicians, mapmakers, photo interpreters, and radio intercept experts plying their black arts around al-Anbar province.

The input was diverse. In addition to the scout-snipers' intel, McCormack had human intelligence (HUMINT) coming out of Fallujah from spies. Some was good, some was flawed, and some was outright lies—the mix an intelligence officer expects from informants who are not particularly fond of those to whom they are giving information.

Army Special Forces and the supersecret Delta Force also had teams inside Fallujah that took huge risks to detect and identify high-value targets. That data had limitations: Bad guys move around a lot, and what was true today might be useless tomorrow.

The battalion also listened in on insurgents' cell phone conversations, although that traffic decreased dramatically after the power went off in the city and insurgents could no longer recharge phone batteries. The insurgents occasionally used radios and walkie-talkies, generally commercial sets that were easily identified and pinpointed. 3/1 listened to those conversations too.

Finally there were the visuals of real-time photographic and video downloads from unmanned aerial vehicles (UAVs). These ranged from 3-foot-long radio-controlled airplanes called Dragon Eyes, each carrying a tiny camera, to 450-pound, man-size Pioneers and huge high-tech, high-flying Global Hawks operated by the U.S. Air Force. All were orbiting Fallujah counting cars, people, mortars, insurgent cells, and men with weapons rolling in from Syria.

All sources revealed that there were a lot of bad guys arriving in Fallujah almost daily in the weeks before the attack—information that did not bode well for the 1st Marine Division Devil Dogs slowly circling the city like hungry wolves eyeing potential prey.

SELLERS

While the scouts were scouting and the snoopers were snooping the division leadership was driving from city to town and town to village selling the benefits of the Coalition occupation to the irascible Sunnis. Lieutenant Colonel Buhl headed up this effort and his mission was twofold: To soften the presence of the Marines with money, assistance, and medical care; and to seek out and destroy the Baathists and foreign fighters who had come to dominate the sheiks and imams. The latter were local leaders who might be willing to negotiate rather than fight if they weren't intimidated by the Baathists and foreign fighters who had taken control of al-Anbar province and Fallujah.

Buhl had to establish a relationship with these men, the same men who were trying to kill his Marines. One day he would be at the hospital at Camp Abu Ghraib visiting his wounded Marines and the next he would be breaking bread with the elders in the town where the Marines had been attacked. He couldn't allow his intense anger to overwhelm him. He constantly reminded himself he was doing it for his men.

Once a week McCormack joined Buhl in a city named Garma, where they met with the town council. McCormack quickly had to discern which of the many sheiks they met were important and which were merely window dressing.

"You could tell the wealthy guys because they were heavy," McCormack remembers. "They could afford to eat, so they were fat. In fact it was food that got us in with these guys. Buhl started having these things catered; we started feeding these guys with battalion money. Then they began showing up. They would bring in their bodyguards with them. Buhl would be in there smiling and shaking hands. That was okay because these sheiks weren't going to talk to you, but their bodyguards would.

"At the end of the day intel isn't rocket science; it is who you know. Buhl [knew that and] embraced town councils. At one meeting, a Shia meeting, he literally danced with a guy. He did good. We weren't getting attacked in these cities."

Out on the range in al-Anbar province Kasal was only vaguely aware of the machinations of the officers and locals going on about him. He was focused on making his rounds and keeping up with his teams. They had already suffered some serious casualties.

That's because having wheels instead of boots for transportation had both rewards and costs for the Marines of Weapons Co. Their AO extended from Fallujah almost to Baghdad. Weapons Co. had sections with every line company and two platoons of 81mm mortarmen advising Delta and India companies of the Iraqi National Guard. That meant the commanders had to travel the roads where IEDs, ambushes, and normal road hazards all presented dangers to the Marines in the Humvees.

Their vehicles weren't armored with the latest armor. Some of them didn't have any at all, some had bolt-on doors and other ad hoc setups, and a few had the upscale stuff just arriving in Iraq. With or without armor the Weapons Co. Humvees were still high-value support and targets of opportunity because of their impressive weapons. Everybody likes firepower and Weapons Co. offered it all.

RIGGED TO EXPLODE

3/1's first serious casualties were the result of an IED.

"Lance Corporal Paine and Gunnery Sergeant Christian Wade and their turret gunner were out on patrol and ran over a mine," Kasal remembers. The explosion blew the front off the Humvee and effectively destroyed what remained. All the men riding in it were hurt. "Paine took the brunt of it and he was our first serious casualty," Kasal says. "The explosion shattered his leg. He is up and around doing fine now. Gunny Wade had a concussion; the turret gunner got thrown out of the vehicle and also had a concussion."

In spite of the concussion that initially left him loopy Wade remembers the incident vividly. "We were going on a standard night patrol that ended at about 5:30 a.m.," he says. "We were all wearing night vision. We were on the road we called Mobile, a main highway that ran from Baghdad to Syria. We stopped in Abu Ghraib Prison to pick up some ice before going to our firm base—it was very hot. While we were there I talked to the section leader I was attached to. He said he knew a new shortcut so we headed back down the Mobile and tried his new shortcut.

"On the way we had to go through a fjord at a creek. It had high walls and you had to go through it. We got hit by double-stacked 5-inch-diameter PVC pipes about a foot long that were buried right where the vehicles had to cross over. They were filled with SEMTEC [an Eastern-Bloc plastique explosive] or something like it, all water-proofed with plastic bags. It was wired together with red British-style detonator cord.

"I think it counted our vehicles. It was a pressure fuse we had to drive over and it waited for the second or third vehicle before it exploded. I know what it was made from because only one deck detonated and I saw the other one."

Wade is, among other things, a weapons expert. This particular IED told him there were some very sophisticated terrorists in the neighborhood. "These were an experienced group," he says. "They knew our tactics—knew that the old guys usually rode in the second or third vehicle and knew where to place the device to do maximum damage. They had this one set to wait for the following vehicles."

ROADBLOCK ATTACKS

The attack on Wade's vehicle forever changed the trust he was trying to develop with al-Anbar's defiant citizens. It hardened the rest of the men in Weapons Co. too, Kasal says. The Marines were now more likely to shoot instead of watch a few seconds longer when something bad started happening.

"When we were doing road security we had weapons pointing down every road. If a car would all of a sudden turn right and head toward us, it would have got lit up before it made 10 feet," Kasal says.

Such quick-responding trigger fingers averted disaster for the Marines when an Iraqi died in a hail of gunfire for trying to ram a Weapons Co. Humvee. Pictures of the incident show a small car burned black with an equally destroyed human body next to it. Whatever possessed the man to try to ram an armed vehicle full of Marines disappeared in the fireball that engulfed him.

"They opened up on it with M16s, 9 mils, and ultimately a .50 cal," Kasal says. "It not only stopped the car and shot the guy, but it lit the car on fire. They were using incendiary bullets."

Buhl remembers many of the roadblock shootings with a touch of sadness. He thinks that some of them could have been prevented through better communication with the Iraqis because simple misunderstanding was often the culprit.

"Here in America we simply assume most people can see, hear, read, and comprehend while driving cars that have most of their normal safety functions intact," Buhl says. "We assume our brakes work and someone driving a car knows how to do it. It wasn't important to the Iraqis. They were trying to survive. The Iraqis don't always see too well, they have no glasses, and many are illiterate, and they are dazed and confused and bad things happened. They didn't always understand the signs because they couldn't read."

Presumed threats were fair targets out of necessity. Marines had to assume drivers failing to heed their warnings at roadblocks were acting intentionally and maliciously. To see it any other way was to invite American casualties, Kasal says. His Marines didn't want it that way, and he figures more than one Marine went home with some serious emotional baggage because of the violent nature of the encounters, but there wasn't too much time to make a decision.

"If it was a threat, for whatever reason, we had to stop the threat," Kasal says.

Stopping suspicious action was especially necessary because all too often the threats could be determined attempts on Marine lives. In September two insurgents blew themselves up in a twin suicide vehicle-borne improvised explosive device (SVBIED) attack during an incident at the 3/1 compound in Al Kharma. The vehicles were purchased there a few days before the attack. Post-attack investigation determined the two drivers were Syrian nationals on a mission to meet their maker.

Protecting the Marines was a HESCO barrier, named after the company that first manufactured them. A HESCO is a multicellular defense system, made of galvanized-steel mesh and lined with nonwoven polypropylene bags filled with sand. It's a sort of fortress-in-a-box. Behind the HESCO and sandbagged guard stations were Marines with automatic weapons.

The suicide bombers approached in two directions. Whether their intentions were to breach the entrances was a moot point because the Marines lit them up and they died long before they got that close. But the explosions were powerful enough to blow car parts, engine blocks, and parts of the Syrians all over the intended targets.

Other attacks were more successful. One SVBIED parked off the road detonated on the second-to-last vehicle in a convoy near Fallujah. There was a large amount of fuel in the vehicle, "which caused the Humvee to catch fire along with the Marines," the intelligence summary says. A picture accompanying the report shows the hulk of the insurgent vehicle 25 yards east of the road surrounded by puddles of unburned fuel.

All these incidents were undeniable proof that al-Anbar province was getting very dangerous. The Marines thought it was about time to do something about it.

BRING THE VIOLENCE!

Before the second battle of Fallujah broke, Buhl wanted his men to have a day to loosen up. Five months of intermittent combat had made the Marines edgy. Marines are like thoroughbred horses that can be trained too hard. Buhl was looking for a diversion. They needed to blow off some steam before they got in the big fight.

"These men were about to face the greatest professional tests of their lifetimes," Buhl says. "I needed some way to calm things down, to get the men thinking about something besides Fallujah. The younger Marines were especially aggressive. It could lead to some real problems."

It didn't help that the press was reporting 10,000 U.S. troops had encircled Fallujah to attack the insurgents. The media said it was all predicated on whether Iraq's interim prime minister, Ayad Allawi, gave the word. The tentative news reports weren't fooling the Marines. They had already packed their rucks and peeled down to their combat loads for the attack. Buhl didn't want them stewing over what might happen: He wanted their heads in the game when the attack lit off.

So Buhl decided that taking a page from the Hollywood epic *Ben-Hur* was just the ticket. He called for the "First Annual 'Ben-Hur' Memorial Chariot Race." More important, he had the horsepower to do it.

Over the preceding five months, the battalion had seized a number of horses from the Iraqis. Apparently even horses weren't immune from being suspects in the growing insurgency. The horses had been impounded temporarily when suspected infiltrators brought them around the FOB under the guise of collecting scrap. They were spavined creatures for the most part, more skin and bone than meat, but they had fattened up on Marine Corps chow. Marines with horse-handling experience cared for them in the weeks preceding the chariot race. They even had their own little stable inside the camp at Abu Ghraib. Meanwhile other Marines built chariots out of wagons.

Buhl thought the event would be as therapeutic for the men as it was for the indentured horses. The Marines had been in contact almost daily for five months and they were in a foul mood.

"Friends, Romans, Marines: Lend me your ears for the rules!" roared ringmaster Captain Jonathan Vaughn. "If all horses die before the finish line, whichever makes it the farthest wins!"

Then it was Alex Nicoll's turn. He stomped into view wearing a blue toga and a silver helmet, brandishing a broadsword and a great spike-studded club—the quintessential 10th-century wild-eyed Irishman. Nicoll got the Marines shouting with his lewd rendition of the famous victory speech by Scottish warrior William Wallace in *Braveheart*.

When Nicoll roared his defiance to the jihadists he raised his arms until his tattoos appeared: "Bring the," his right arm declared; "violence," his left arm replied. It was a magnificent performance that lifted the spirits of the Thundering Third.

Too bad Charlton Heston didn't show up. The insurgent Iraqi horses used the opportunity to try once again to defy the Thundering Third. One steed turned on its driver in the first race and tried to bite the Marine who forced him back with a wooden trident, drawing loud applause from the crowd. Another horse simply refused to participate. A third seemed confused about which way to run. When the contest was over a team from Weapons Co.'s 81mm mortar section, led by Staff Sergeant Sam Mortimer, had gained the victory and earned a rousing volley of cheers. It would be the last time they had anything to cheer about for a long time.

CHAPTER 10
★ ★ ★

THE OPENING GAMBIT

The eager Marines' opening gambit was played at 7 a.m. on November 7, 2004,—"D-day"—when maneuver elements began their work, rumbling across the desert to recapture the city. The sun was already setting when the Third Light Armored Reconnaissance (LAR) Wolfpack seized the peninsula west of Fallujah with its eight-wheeled LAVs to block the insurgents' potential escape route through that region. The idea was to initiate the battle incrementally to maneuver forces into final attack positions without overtly alarming the insurgents. Maybe they telegraphed the coming punch, maybe they didn't—that's a debate that is still argued among Marines. Regardless, Marines were uncoiling everywhere and the LAVs were fast and lethal.

All around Fallujah more Marine and Army units were closing up, tying into units on their left and right. The circle wasn't perfect but it was good enough to keep most of the insurgents from escaping. By the time the sun set the ring was constructed and the contenders were locked in their corners. Six months of bickering, backbiting, pointless negotiations, and on-again-off-again threats had produced a standoff. Now it was time to end it. Al-Fajr—The New Dawn—would rise tomorrow. Kasal, Weapons Co., the Thundering Third, and the entire 1st Marine Division were as ready as they could be. Now they awaited the opening bell.

During preparations Kasal was busy keeping track of where everyone was. "The company was spread out all over the place," he says. "I had 81s in firing position, then I had 81s with Lieutenant [Zachary] Iscol's group taking the train station and working with the ING, and then I had the FiST team with my CO and other personnel with the Alpha Command Group, and then I had four CAAT [Combined Anti-Armor Team sections] all split up. Three of them were attached one to each rifle company and the fourth one was in general support. I had units in eight or nine different locations."

Not only did he have to keep track of everyone's location, he says: "I had contingency plans for everything. If certain people got injured, who would replace them? If equipment failed or needed to be replaced, everything was laid out. That was all done in the days beforehand, using standard operating procedures [SOPs] that were already established. That is why I always tried to stay in control of where everybody was at and to keep track of everybody for accountability of casualties, medevacs, and everything else."

The bell finally rang at 3 a.m. on November 8—referred to as D+1—when two of Kasal's CAAT sections, dubbed "Carnivore," slipped out the gate at Abu Ghraib. The two pairs of armored Humvees were ordered to confirm whether it was clear to go across the desert shortcut shown in the plan to reach their attack positions.

Carnivore also needed to take the enemy's pulse. If it jumped, deadly projectiles would start whanging off Carnivore's Humvees, a pretty good sign the insurgents were waiting for them. They were to scout out the site that had been preselected for the 81mm mortars to set up.

Kasal went along to make sure his sections were on location when it was time to move. "I was initially traveling out with our first CAAT section, which was commanded by Sergeant Christopher Lopez. I was in a vehicle commanded by Sergeant Die," Kasal recalls. "I needed to be close to a radio to have good comms."

An hour after the first CAAT section departed the FOB another CAAT team mated up with the first serial headed for the jump-off point. (A serial is a group of vehicles that move together on a specific schedule to minimize traffic congestion and facilitate command and control.) Buhl, Major Chris Griffin, the Operations Officer (S-3), and Captain McCormack, the S-2, were in the first serial along with the rest of the Forward Operations Center (FOC). If they were taken out the battalion would be leaderless.

The serial was a stellar group. Griffin, the 2004 winner of the Marine Corps' prestigious Leftwich Award for excellence in leadership and the former CO of A Co., 1st BN, 4th Marines in OIF 1, was the battalion's planner. He was the officer who pulled all the parts together into a cohesive operation. Under his command the FOC kept in touch with the other commands in 1st Marine Division through a sophisticated computer uplink system that passed its communications traffic back and forth between the satellites in geosynchronous orbit thousands of miles in space. Along with the FOC were the Dragon Eye section, a fire support coordinator's vehicle, and a communication truck with all the battalion's high-level radios. Bringing up the rear was Weapons Co.'s Cannonball section and 81mm mortars for close indirect support.

The insurgents could not match the Marines in mobility, but they enjoyed other significant advantages. The jihadists had interior lines of supply that couldn't be easily interdicted. They knew the city. And they had had months of uninterrupted time to turn it into a fortress. They thought that once the Marines entered the city their vaunted mobility would not mean a thing. The Marines would be forced to dismount and walk, covering their vehicles so they would not be destroyed by stay-behind suicide squads trying to take out the heavy weapons.

Marine intelligence had uncovered some alarming truths about the insurgents' defensive plans for Fallujah. The insurgency had placed explosives on bridges and key points of entry and positioned discarded tires and barrels full of fuel around the city—possibly to set on fire to create smoke screens. They also had developed plans to defend Fallujah with coordinated ambushes involving IEDs and small insurgent teams of five to seven men staged in homes at the city's edge. The Marines suspected more than a thousand houses had staged weapons including AK-47s, 7.62mm Russian-designed light machine guns (PKCs), mortars, RPGs, and bombs.

Buhl expected the insurgents "to be highly mobile and prepared to use our ROE against us. Part of their plan was to move unarmed between caches so we wouldn't shoot them."

Also factored into the equation was intelligence that was both unbelievable and dangerously disturbing at the same time. Intelligence had discovered that the insurgents had no intention of fighting the Cav's Abrams and Bradleys for reasons beyond the obvious fact they couldn't compete. The jihadists convinced themselves it was both unmanly and beneath a holy warrior's dignity to engage mechanical devices in mortal combat. To fulfill their spiritual requirements, the insurgents felt honor bound to wait until they could confront the infidel Marines in close quarters shoot-outs.

Buhl found that diabolical. "The insurgents thought it wasn't a fair fight unless we went into a house and went toe-to-toe," he says.

Perhaps the jihadists had searched history for their tactics. Defending the city without the means to escape left them with few options. They could surrender, die, or try to sneak away. Their own intransigence had trapped them in a classic fight that pits a mobile offense against a fixed defense. The last time jihadists had relied on fixed defenses of such a grand scale was during the Crusades. Maybe they were holding out for better luck this time.

Despite the terrible ferocity of the ensuing fight it was a lopsided contest from the start, one the insurgents should never have fought. Genuine soldiers would have pulled out to fight another day, something amateur fanatics armed with medieval logic refused to do. The jihadists were depending on an irrational formula that combined faith and suicidal determination with bad tactics. They started the fight with inferior numbers, inferior weapons, primitive communications, and almost no logistics.

The Marines showed up with enough firepower to turn Fallujah into a rubble pile populated with dead insurgents, but that was not their official intent. To do so would have defeated the Marines' mission to win the hearts and minds of the Sunni population. Division and Regiment didn't want to destroy the city; neither did its commanders or the provisional government. To do so would be political suicide. Unless the Sunni majority in the al-Anbar province was pacified, there would be no lasting peace. The young Marines, on the other hand, just wanted payback. If that meant killing every jihadist in Fallujah, that would have been okay with them.

As incongruent as the multiple points of view seemed, everyone agreed it was time to assert the Coalition's influence. If the Coalition didn't prevail, there would never be a stable government of any kind in Iraq.

Stable governments were far from Kasal's mind as 3/1 rumbled into the northern edge of Fallujah in the false light of dawn on D+3. He was busy monitoring the radios and keeping track of his widely dispersed sections. At the same time he kept an ear tuned to the Weapons Co. frequency to follow what was going on in his company, and he kept an eye on what was happening around Fallujah.

The Coalition had promised free passage to anyone wishing to leave and thousands of people took them up on it. The Iraqi government told the mulish Sunni leadership anyone still in Fallujah after the battle started would be detained or killed. Kasal thought the announcement would make the battle easier for his Marines. On the other hand his CAAT teams had to make sure nobody slipped away from the refugees and attacked 3/1's lines of communication.

"The Iraqis were leaving Fallujah. People were driving out, walking out with their families. I saw kids and old people pushing carts. It was really sad. Many of those people just wanted to live peacefully but they couldn't," Kasal says.

"Once they cleared checkpoints they could leave. The Iraqi police were checking out IDs. They could tell when something was wrong. They knew accents, what people were wearing, their car—if it was wrong—they could do that. We couldn't.

"I don't really know how many people actually left but it was thousands. Probably a lot of insurgents left with them. They were leaving in buses. They knew what was coming by then. The whole thing was in the press and the media were reporting all the bad things happening in al-Anbar province. Everyone was looking for Abu Musab al Zarqawi.

"We were taking Fallujah back from the insurgents. They were Saddam's thugs and murderers. It was a good thing."

CHAPTER 11

THE TRAIN STATION

One of the first objectives of the invasion was to capture a huge train station just north of the city and convert it into a base of operations for the duration of the attack.

Leading the assault on the evening of November 8 was Lieutenant Zachary Iscol, a Cornell graduate commissioned through the Platoon Leader's Course at Quantico during the summers of his junior and senior years. Iscol joined from Long Island, New York. He is now a captain deciding if he wants to stay in the Corps.

AN UNTESTED PROPOSITION

In November 2004 Iscol was a first lieutenant leading 25 Marines from 3/1's ad hoc Combined Action Platoon (CAP) India, a platoon of former Weapons Co. mortarmen assigned to train and advise 50 untried Iraqi National Guard (ING) soldiers.

The mortarmen had been pulled from Weapons Co. for CAP duties because the ROE for the security mission in al-Anbar province prohibited the Marines from using mortar fire except in unusual circumstances—such as for counterbattery fire and for shooting their way out of a jam should they get overrun. Given that it was unlikely they'd be firing mortars during the attack, they were deemed available to advise the Iraqi detachment. That was okay, Buhl says—Marines are trained to improvise, overcome, and adapt.

CAPs, in which U.S. Marines train, advise, and fight side by side with soldiers of the country they're occupying, aren't new. The Marine Corps has been creating CAPs in many guises since Marines fought in the Banana Wars and subdued Haiti, the Dominican Republic, and Nicaragua in the early '20s. Marines in CAPs are always in a tenuous position. They have to rely on making themselves understood to their trainees, often across a wide cultural and linguistic gulf. They also must rely on the loyalty and readiness of those trainees in combat.

In Vietnam Marine CAPs were split into teams of half a dozen men who lived alone and unsupported in isolated villages. They survived on goodwill, good luck, and superb instincts.

The situation in Iraq was somewhat different. The Marines trained and advised the Iraqis who were dependent on the Marines for their welfare, training, and firepower. In turn the Iraqis fought for the new provisional government until the political situation stabilized. It was an untested proposition, Iscol says.

KASAL IMPRESSES THE XO

Eighteen months before Fallujah Iscol was a relatively boot second lieutenant and the brand-new executive officer (XO) of Weapons Co. Kasal was a first sergeant with 20 years of infantry experience. About all that Iscol knew about his first sergeant was that he was indeed a take-charge Marine who had come over from Kilo.

Soon after Iscol arrived he encountered Kasal debriefing Marines after an exercise. Iscol, in the best tradition of second lieutenants, counseled his first sergeant about stepping outside his authority. In Iscol's Marine Corps first sergeants don't debrief line Marines. That was a platoon leader's responsibility.

"Kasal sat down with me and explained he did it for tactical proficiency so he would know how the Marines had done," says Iscol. "He didn't get mad. He wasn't disrespectful—at least not to my face. I probably seemed a little immature then.

"I had another incident with a staff NCO, a very proficient Marine who, after our disagreement, refused to talk to me. First Sergeant Kasal, after a disagreement, would never take offense. His concern was for doing the best job possible. He would explain what would happen if you do it this way and what would happen if you do it that way—he would take the objective approach."

Iscol gained even more respect for Kasal when he saw his first sergeant step in and accept blame for something he could have easily palmed off on the green XO. Buhl wanted a nonregulation guidon, or small flag, in a Kilo Co. picture, and Kasal declined to break it out on Iscol's authority. Buhl took a strip off Iscol's ass as a result.

"I got my ass chewing from the battalion commander for not having the guidon out," Iscol says. "Later I just mentioned it to Kasal. He called the battalion sergeant major right up and told him he had refused to take the guidon out. He is a phenomenal Marine."

Buhl says that was one of the last times he really butted heads with Kasal. Kasal argued it wasn't regulation; a company only rated one guidon. Buhl saw his intransigence as almost tantamount to insubordination so Kasal lost that one.

All of that was buried in the past on the night of November 8, 2004. Like thousands of junior Marine officers before him, Iscol had learned from professionals like Kasal how to share responsibility and accept guidance from others during his training experience at Camp Pendleton.

A critical test in Iscol's career development came when he brought the Iraqis to the jump-off point. Nominally in charge of Company I of the ING was an Iraqi major named Ouda, a former Republican Guard officer. Major Ouda was ordered to lead his unit into the train station using as much stealth and surprise as possible, slay the defenders, then secure the structure until the actual invasion kicked off at 6 a.m. on the 9th. Even with tank support it was a tough assignment for anyone.

"It was the first major objective taken down in Fallujah," Iscol recalls. "It looked enormous. There was a huge platform and warehouses, and we had two platoons of eight to 10 Marines and 20 Iraqis to take it and cover about a kilometer of ground. We had two platoons of tanks with us and the AAVs that transported us behind us."

The Marine Corps tanks supporting Iscol were the same Marines who had taken Buhl, Malay, and Shupp to Fallujah six weeks before. Still under the command of Captain Bodisch they provided security to the Marines and their ING counterparts assaulting the train station.

STORMING THE STATION

At 5 p.m. the combined company moved into position, traveling south from the attack position to the designated release point. There the company would split into two rifle platoons, each supported by a Marine tank platoon.

"We had attached to Lima," Iscol says. "They provided overwatch. The tanks and AAVs with .50-cal and MK-19s [grenade launchers] stayed outside the train station. We wanted to use the MK-19s to set off any IEDs. We dismounted 500 meters north of the train station and moved up using tactical movements."

After establishing a support-by-fire position overlooking Iscol's riflemen, the tankers fired 34 rounds from their 120mm main gun, destroying a number of fortified enemy positions, obstacles, and VBIEDs along key avenues of approach. Iscol could not have been more pleased.

"We were not authorized to fire any preplanned fires," Iscol recalls. "We had to wait until we received fire. Almost immediately we took some fire from the train station. We put down smoke to screen Lima. We called on our FiST [Fire Support Team]; we had FAC [Forward Air Controller] Marines wearing night vision. There was none for the Iraqis. They were dependent on us for fire support.

"This was a big test for our Iraqis. Before the offensive operation in the city, we spent a lot of operational and training time with the Iraqis emphasizing every man is a rifleman, fire and movement, and platoon operator.

"The company commander, Major Ouda, was a great man. The Iraqis were some of the bravest guys you will ever meet. They go home every night to their families. They are getting murdered; their families are getting murdered and kidnapped. The ones that were reliable were the finest soldiers we could hope for."

As soon as the operation began Lima Co.'s FiST began laying down 155mm artillery fire and 81mm mortars on the objective. When they were sure the rounds were hitting their targets, the combined infantry assault began in almost total darkness.

A wall of heavy metal laid down by the gunners kept the insurgents from reinforcing the train station. The insurgents knew the tanks and Bradleys had main guns and coaxial machine guns guided by night vision and thermal imaging equipment that could obliterate them, so for the most part they sat tight and tried to figure out what was going on, Iscol says.

"We had emphasized fire discipline and movement," Iscol says of the training exercises. "The Iraqis listened okay so they understood what we were doing. A lot of them had been soldiers and knew the fundamentals. They were very good with the AKs. They moved quietly, moving in the dark very well. I had night vision and I was impressed how well they moved in almost complete darkness."

Once the Iraqis had cleared the buildings an Explosive Ordinance Demolition (EOD) squad was called for. With two dog teams they began searching and clearing the train station of potential booby traps. Two bombs were discovered and disarmed. As soon as the buildings were cleared the Iraqis set up their command post and waited for orders.

While the EOD team was disabling the bombs, Lima left its overwatch positions on the northeast side of the train station. They started to clear the way for the breach teams who were to break through obstructions the insurgents had built. Iscol thought the entire operation went off like clockwork.

"We could see okay with our night vision. Captain McCormack, the S-2, had really briefed us well. We knew there weren't too many insurgents in the train station. They knew it was isolated. IEDs were the biggest threat," Iscol recalls.

Several hours before dawn, the railroad station belonged to the combined Iraqi-Marine assault company. That meant 3/1 had a good jump-off point for their attack.

OBLITERATING THE OBSTACLES

The next part of the plan was for Marine engineer breach teams from RCT1 and from 3/1's engineer platoon to blow three lanes through the berm immediately to 3/1's south. Each lane was to be wide enough for vehicles to pass through, allowing the invasion to begin en masse.

Unfortunately the exercise didn't begin too well, Buhl recalls. Regimental engineers were a late addition to the plan and their inclusion caused some coordination problems and delays.

But at roughly 3 a.m. the engineers finally got underway. On the way to their breach positions one engineer AAV overturned in a quarry, injuring several Marines and causing another brief delay. Buhl was already getting worked up and the effort had just begun.

"The clock was ticking," Buhl says. "Even with the regimental engineers helping we were barely able to get the work done."

The engineers used mine-clearing line charges, explosives, bulldozers, strong backs, and big balls to break through the insurgents' defense line. During the operation they encountered light small arms fire from the edge of Fallujah, fire that they generally ignored. The incoming fire was suppressed by Weapons Co. gunners, snipers, and Army 120mm mortars—called "Maniac Mortars"—that quickly identified the targets and smothered them with fire.

As soon as the lanes were carved out the Marine engineers and Lima Co. riflemen raced across the railroad yard to take out a high curb that was bad for the tracks and wheeled vehicles scheduled to follow their mad dash to the edge of the city.

On the insurgent side radio and telephone chatter increased tenfold while the jihadists discussed what to do. No doubt some of them wondered which way they were going to die. Would death come on an invisible angel's wings from an almost impervious Abrams tank? From missiles or rockets? Or was death waiting with the Marines who would attack their fortresses with little regard for their fanatical efforts? It would still be a few hours before they found out.

CHAPTER 12

BREAKING OUT

The horrible dangers Kasal and his Marines would soon face still seemed remote when the 1st Marine Division lined up across the northern edge of Fallujah in a mobile wall of brute strength.

Since 3/1 had arrived on the start line the previous morning, targets all over the city were being slammed by the fast movers— aerial artillery spewn from orbiting Air Force AC-130Hs "Spectre" gunships, plus heavy 155mm artillery firing from fixed positions and 81mm mortars.

FIRE IN THE SKY

Huge explosions rocked the night and tracers flashed across the city. It was dangerously beautiful, almost mesmerizing. The big guns would fire, the automatic weapons would rap out a tattoo, and Spectres would rain down automatic cannon and 105mm howitzer fire on what the military calls "targets of opportunity."

Corporal Mitchell remembers November 8 as the day Fallujah came under attack from every heavy weapon in the American arsenal. "They were firing 120mm Army mortars, 155mm guns,

81s, everything. They fired for 24 hours straight," Mitchell says. "They fired a lot of red phosphorous; it looked like red sparklers falling from the sky. The stuff would hit the ground and turn everything red."

Red phosphorus, a variation of the ubiquitous white phosphorus used in other modern conflicts, was used at Fallujah both to create smoke screens and to flush defenders from fortified positions.

LOSE THE SHORTS

Running the air operations at 3/1 was Captain Pat C. Gallogly. "PUC," as he was universally known, was a Huey pilot who had flown more than 100 missions during OIF 1. He volunteered to become a forward air controller (FAC) after his first deployment so he could get some experience with the mud Marines. FACs guide available aviation assets to targets designated by the Grunts. Essentially they are the pilots' eyes on the ground. Marines have championed close air support directed by radio-equipped FACs since its days in the banana republics.

PUC's first conversation with Kasal was a few months before the Fallujah fight when Kasal turned up at the Forward Operations Center (FOC). As usual Kasal was in all his gear—absolutely regulation in every detail. PUC wasn't as well turned out.

"One night a bunch of Marines got hurt by an IED," PUC says. "A Marine comes knocking down my door at about 3 a.m. and says, 'Sir, we got urgent casualties.'

"I put on my pistol over my blue boxers. Other than that I had on my T-shirt and sneakers. I come in, the radios are going, people are all over, and Kasal is in there. He takes a hard look at me and comes up to the side of me and says very quietly, 'Captain. Hey, sir, you better lose those blue shorts.'

"Brad Kasal was a very strict Marine, very formal; he didn't bullshit with officers. He's the kind of Marine that you don't have credibility with until you work with him months and months. He didn't care about your rank. He cared how you did your job."

And in Kasal's Marine Corps officers don't report for duty in their boxers.

Kasal remembers the incident well: "I had just got back off a patrol, and I heard an air medevac come over the radio in the COC [Command Operations Center], so I went there to see who it was and find out what the details were. Captain Gallogly, who was down in his rack sleeping, also got the word, so he came up to direct the helo. He had just woken up and was in a hurry, and he came running up there with just a pair of boxer shorts, a green T-shirt, and combat boots on, and that was it. I think I told him he ought to at least get some shorts on."

The 33-year-old Citadel graduate says he frequently arrived in the COC in his underwear as the nights grew longer and more and more Marines came in requiring urgent care. It was his job to coordinate all the aerial Casualty Evacuations (CASEVACs) for Marines in need of urgent medical care. It was a demanding job that required him to talk every arriving mercy flight into the landing zone (LZ).

AIR OPERATIONS

PUC had other jobs as well. His primary concern was approving the missions and coordinating the efforts of three other FACs spread out among the line companies. He also advised Buhl on the best use of the air assets flying over the city 24 hours a day. A helo pilot himself, PUC had a special affinity for the Huey pilots and the crews of the venerable CH-46 "Sea Knight" helicopters—called "Frogs" by the Marines—who came in low and slow to pick up desperately wounded Marines. Sometimes PUC would recognize the pilot's voices and they would exchange a pleasantry or two, but usually it was all business.

Under the air officer's nominal supervision the pilots and

FACs out with the line companies coordinated air strikes that always changed the momentum of an attack when 500- or 1,000-pound guided bombs arrived through a roof or even a window of a contested structure. The FAC on the ground and the pilot in the sky would share laconic messages in their best Chuck Yeager voices, then buildings would suddenly explode. Each company in 3/1 had its own FAC. That was a departure from the usual three per battalion. Buhl recalls it paid off in spades.

A modern air strike is an awesome display of precision firepower in which a 500-pound bomb can turn a perfectly fine building into a smoking hole in the blink of an eye. For those providing the magic show it was an intense, no-nonsense experience that required close coordination and far more than a modicum of trust between the FACs and aviators flying in lazy circles high over the battlefield. In a lawn chair back home with a can of beer in hand the sights and sounds of D+2 would have been highly entertaining, but not from where PUC stood.

"3/1 was in more serious combat than the other battalions," he says. "They were out there fighting for 12 days. 3/1 had 108 urgents [urgent evacuations] and 276 close support missions during Fallujah. Every bomb that was dropped was a laser or GPS [global positioning satellite] guided bomb. At first I was really worried about the GPS bombs' accuracy. Then we got used to talking them in. The FAC would give the aircraft the coordinates, I would check them, and the pilot would have them. When they were off, they were only 20 meters off. It was a beautiful thing."

THE THIRD STARTS THUNDERING

At 7 a.m. the Thundering Third slipped its restraints. On their right, at the eastern edge of the city, were the 3/5 Marines; next was Kasal's battalion, 3/1, led by Buhl. Tied on their left flank were the 2/7, 1/8, 1/3, and 2/2 Marines in succession.

In front of them was the heavy armor from the U.S. Army's 2d Squadron, 7th Cavalry, with a tradition almost as long as the Marines' and just as proud. The cavalrymen were riding M1A1 Abrams heavy tanks sporting 120mm main guns and Bradley armored fighting vehicles (AFVs) armed with 25mm chain guns that literally eat things up. The Cav's job was to bust through the lines and defeat any expected hard points and IEDs laid out for ambushes along the tightly packed roads. It was a highly mobile force trained to scout and move.

Army doctrine dictates "fire and maneuver," but tanks can't maneuver safely inside cities because of narrow streets and alleys. So the Cav's orders were to smash a path through the city to clear the way for 3/1's rifle companies. Even the Marines had to grant that Cav was brute force's Pro Bowl team at Fallujah.

The first day of al-Fajr, when Weapons Co. was still set up in its firing positions just outside the city, Kasal moved between his sections. When it was time to move out Kasal stayed with Staff Sergeant Lopez's 1st Section, assigned to Kilo Co., a decision that would have far-reaching implications in days to come. Gunnery Sergeant Francis Hurd was his vehicle commander and Lance Corporal Jensen was on the .50-cal in the turret.

"Once the train station was taken we moved into the city through the breach," Kasal says. "As soon as we got into the city I got out of the vehicle and spent pretty much all of my time on foot. We were constantly worried about IEDs and ambushes and things like that.

"As Kilo would clear the buildings our CAAT vehicles would be right up front with them providing overwatch and fire support. I was usually out in the street providing help to whoever needed help, whether it be the Kilo Marines or our own vehicles."

In addition to the frontline punch of Weapons Co. Buhl had been assigned 10 Abrams tanks from C Co., 2d Tank Battalion, the same bunch that had driven Buhl to the train station in late October. This time all the Marines were thrilled to see them.

Still led by Captain Bodisch the Marine tankers' mission was to provide close support to the Marines after the Cav's juggernaut broke through the insurgents' defenses. The Marine tankers' role in the fight was exceptionally perilous because they stayed in the ruins of Fallujah with the mud Marines. Without maneuvering room they had to sit tight while the riflemen dug out the jihadists who hid from the Cav's onslaught. It left the Marines in the Abrams tanks vulnerable to swarming hordes, to shaped charges that could penetrate armor, and to a variety of weapons that could strip off their tanks' external optics and communications, or even kill the men.

Initially 3/1 was assigned a north-to-south axis of attack that followed the Cavalry wrecking ball. The soldiers and Marines expected to achieve early tactical success with that kind of firepower. If the insurgents fought it out they would certainly die. If they ran away they would be seen, and if they hunkered down they would be found.

Weapons Co. was locked and cocked and waiting to go when the order finally came. The plan was for the Marines to follow the Cav "in trace," taking advantage of available cover while letting the Army tanks and armored personnel carriers (APCs) take care of the heavy work. Cavalrymen call the tactic "ass raping."

Kasal was with his CAAT Section providing overwatch and clearing buildings as they crept forward. He felt like he was on a movie set. "When we were entering the city we had Army Psyops [Psychological Operations] with big loudspeakers on their Humvee," he explains. "They were playing the Marine Corps Hymn, Queen's 'We Are the Champions,' things like that. Here we are in combat, kind of like *Apocalypse Now* where they are going into combat with songs playing, you know what I mean? It motivated everybody. Obviously we were already focused on the job on hand, but just the fact that it was typical Marine Corps bravado made us feel more motivated.

'CHARGE SONGS'

"When we saw the enemy we would use all available firepower first. But boots on the ground still have to finish the job with the individual infantryman clearing the area house by house while charge songs are playing."

Between deployments 3/1 had practiced attacking urban settings at training areas on George and March Air Force Bases in California. They learned fundamentals of combat in built-up areas, called Military Operations on Urban Terrain (MOUT) warfare. The training helped but nothing can completely prepare anyone for Iraq, Kasal says. That waited until the Marines arrived in al-Anbar province and did it for real. Kasal says the intense fighting in there was the real training ground to their subsequent success at Fallujah.

Even so. Fallujah was a far tougher nut to crack. In other places they had fought in Iraq the cities teemed with people, cars, kids, dogs, and donkeys. Activity washed back and forth across the streets in mind-numbing progression even while the fighting raged on. Fallujah was a city with its eyes plucked out. All that was there was death.

As battles roared around them the few noncombatants who had stayed in the city seemed pathetic. Trapped, deathly afraid, and without options, they would sometimes welcome the Marines in for tea. Scared, shaking, timorous, the trapped civilians would humbly offer a glass of tea in return for their lives. It made the Marines want to pity them, but it was too late for that. Amid all the crashing noise the Marines would accept a glass from them after searching the premises. If the suspicious searchers found weapons or too many supplies, or more than an AK or two, the residents were hustled off in flex cuffs for delivery to the ING interrogators. By the end of the fight they got hustled off simply for being there. In the end there were no innocents in Fallujah.

What was safe and what was dangerous looked the same. Houses, apartments, and industrial sites rose together in confusing profusion. Every shadow posed a threat. The battle had barely begun and it was already clear to Kasal it was going to be a tough one.

"The insurgents usually let the tanks go by," Kasal explains. "They wouldn't attack them because they knew it was a loser. They would wait until the tanks got in front of us. After a while the tanks got pretty far ahead of us and we were fighting from house to house. We were usually in a MOUT situation."

WAR IN WARP DRIVE

When the Marines found insurgents the war moved into warp drive. The Marines attacked relentlessly and the insurgents resisted fanatically, hoping to kill as many Marines as possible before escaping. Often they got away, but not always. Sometimes it was a fight to the death. Even Kasal grudgingly admits it was good tactics. The Marines had to root them out. They would die and so would Marines. In the insurgents' hopped-up and often drugged-out minds, that was a fair trade, Kasal says.

Countering their suicidal tactics required a combination of force and finesse. Kasal preferred brute force whenever possible. It saved Marine lives at the expense of the insurgents. Every insurgent who died in a massive explosion was one less the Marines would have to kill with their personal weapons. Each opportunity required a different approach, a different set of the tactics that Kasal had been practicing for his entire adult life.

"In MOUT [Military Operations on Urban Terrain], you have to cover everywhere," he explains. "You had a guy pointing in the front, a guy pointing high, guys covering high in other directions, a guy covering the rear. Every MOUT is dangerous. The fire can come from anywhere. It can come from up high, low, down in a sewer. He could be in a window; you have to have everything covered.

"The reason when you look at pictures and see everybody pointing everywhere is because they are in a kill zone. Everywhere is a kill zone. You never know where the fire is coming from. We would see the muzzle flash and light the bastard up but it was always dangerous."

Occasionally the Marines would stop and regroup. Nighttime brought respite from the constant fighting, but the men still had to pull guard duty, patrols, and listening posts.

PUNCHING THEIR WAY THROUGH

During the day movement was potentially deadly all the time, Kasal recalls. Going through doors and gates and over walls was very dangerous. Blasting holes through the sides and backs of houses and walls to avoid exposing themselves was safer. The existing ROE prevented them from arbitrarily destroying the city, so at first they followed the rules. They didn't blow up houses where no resistance was offered, and they didn't shoot unarmed civilians, even those who were highly suspect. But that all changed when the word got around the insurgents were playing the Marines for suckers. By the third day into the battle there were no more rules and the Marines made paths from one fortified structure to another any way they could.

Sometimes the Marines called on Weapons Co.'s tube-launched, optically tracked, wire-guided missiles (TOWs) to punch holes in the buildings or Javelins to level the ones still protecting stay-behind death squads. 3/1 fired hundreds of them at Fallujah. Kasal made sure the mud Marines had all they needed to do the job. "The more shock and firepower you had up front, as quick as possible, the better your chances of success," Kasal says.

On Day 2 the battle sounds around Kilo were from the east and west. Where 2/7 Cav moved it was relatively quiet except for the tremendous booms when the Abrams let loose with their 120mm main guns or the Bradleys digested the contents of a building with a loud burp. The insurgents either had no stomach for fighting the behemoths or they had slipped away to wait for the Marines they knew were following behind.

As usual a few insurgents died in tremendous explosions or tearing roars that shredded their bodies and spattered their remains around the interiors of the buildings they were defending. More important the Cav destroyed a majority of the IED ambushes and obstacles spread all around the city to delay the attackers or channel them into killing zones. Many of the automobiles the unmanned aerial vehicles (UAVs) had photographed exploded with bright orange and black secondaries—proving McCormack's theory that any car left behind more than a few days was a bomb.

When 2/7 Cav reached a map coordinate called Phase Line Cathy, a perky name for a dismal jump-off point, the Thundering Third rumbled into Fallujah. India moved east and Kilo headed west to clear any buildings still containing insurgents that popped up in the rear.

Behind all of them and still led by Iscol were the two Iraqi ING companies under the operational control of Buhl. Their tasks included clearing caches, identifying insurgents, gleaning local intelligence, and backing up the main thrust. Iscol says the Iraqi ING continued to perform admirably.

"We spent the 9th doing patrols north of the train station," Iscol remembers. "I think we went into the city on November 10—the Marines Corps' birthday—but we eventually moved in behind Lima. We found RPGs, weapons, small-arms ammo, detonators, you name it. We found drugs that a few people left behind.

"Lima had been back clearing for Kilo. We took 7-ton trucks down into the city, I think to around Phase Line [PL] Elizabeth, and started pushing west toward the Euphrates. We split up the

Iraqi platoons into reinforced squads and attached one of them to each of the line platoons. It became apparent it was too much for the platoon commanders and squad leaders to worry about an additional 15 guys so Lima Co. gave us our own battle station. The Iraqis did real well."

KILO MOVES IN

India discovered light enemy contact when it moved into the city. Its job was to secure the east flank along PL Henry, a long ink line running south down the map of Fallujah that marked the boundary with 1/8 Marines, Buhl says.

Kilo initially enjoyed the same light resistance as India but that changed quickly when its Marines began encountering stiff resistance from pockets of insurgents firing volleys of RPGs. Two of the C Co. tanks assigned to Kilo were damaged by multiple RPG impacts. The RPGs couldn't penetrate the tough Cobham composite armor, but they could blast away antennae, optics, and other protrusions on the tank turrets.

At the same time the battalion command elements traveling in trace behind Kilo came under indirect fire and heavy, up-close enemy small-arms fire along PL Isaac, nine blocks west of PL Henry. Lima, following behind Kilo, also started taking heavy small-arms fire from around the compass.

Kasal remained with Kilo after it moved into the city. That's unusual: Normally Kasal liked moving among his sections. But for once the enemy had taken away his initiative. He could not safely move between sections without risking being hit. The fire was too intense, too multidirectional, and too accurate to disregard.

Captain Tim Jent, Kilo's CO, was glad to have his old first sergeant around. He considered Kasal and First Sergeant Wayne Miller, Kilo's first sergeant, outstanding NCOs who couldn't help contributing to his mission.

"We had four AAVs and four tanks and plenty of high-backed Humvees when we were moving down [PL] Henry," Jent says. "We were being attacked from the east side of the road. On the other side of the insurgents was 1/8, in eyesight of us. They were so close to the phase line we couldn't shoot. We owned the boundary but they were too close for indirect fire. We had to be very careful even using aimed fire." Jent adds that it was one of the few times the enemy showed good tactical judgment.

"I think the insurgents did it on purpose," he says. "They were attacking us from the buildings along the main road there. It was much more concentrated there; there was a higher concentration of buildings and it was much narrower. It had a slum feel to it. It was all three-, four-, and five-story buildings."

THE BIG GUNS

Whenever possible Jent called for air support to clear a path for Kilo's embattled Marines. Usually he went directly through his company FAC, Captain David "Pork Chop" Smay, an F-18 fighter pilot armed with a computer that shared information with both the Air Officer and the pilots in Fallujah's air space. Captain Gallogly (PUC) says Smay was totally competent to carry out his own strike missions and often did. In addition he was often talking to his former squadron mates in VMFA-242 ("Bats") flying overhead. Before deploying with 3/1 he had piloted an F-18 in that squadron.

PUC preferred the services of the Air Force's deadly Spectre whenever it was available. It only flew at night and was vulnerable to certain kinds of threats, so he had to be careful when he asked for Spectre's support. When he did, Spectre's unique droning engines proclaimed to all that it owned the night.

"We called Basher at night, which was the call sign for the AC-130s," PUC says. "It had a 25mm cannon, a 40mm automatic cannon, and a 105mm gun. The 105 gun camera is really accurate. The next best player was the 2-seater Marine F-18s. That squadron did everything in their power to stay on station. We also had Harriers dropping bombs for us, Super Cobras, and Air Force F-16Cs."

PUC says they didn't spare ordnance. "During Fallujah, we dropped 91 laser-guided 500-pound bombs and 35 GPS 500-pound bombs. We dropped two 1,000-pound GPS bombs on a large complex—they flattened it. We dropped 10 laser Mavericks, called in 119 AC-130 strikes, 21 Hellfires, four TOWs, and nine fixed-wing strafing attacks. 3/1's FACs did not have one incident of fratricide while dropping all that ordnance."

He emphasizes: "The air officer was not just me. We fought as a team. All the battalion's Forward Air Controllers were equally part of the team. I was there to coordinate and help. None of them needed me to call in an air strike."

When air was too much and the CAAT teams not quite enough, Kilo called for Marine tank support. With all the Abrams grinding around Fallujah it would seem there would be plenty of them to go around. Unfortunately that wasn't the case. Tanks are high maintenance and require plenty of attention to give up their wares, and 3/1's companies and sister battalions all needed tank support, so they were in high demand. Buhl remembers that getting tanks was never easy, especially after battle damage began degrading them and they were taken out of battle for repairs.

"We couldn't touch the tactical integrity of the tanks," Buhl explains. "They were loaned to us from Regiment and were part of RCT1. Each of the infantry battalions had a company of tanks. A company sounds like a lot of tanks—three platoons of four tanks and the commander and XO—but with two up and two back for rearming and refueling, and sometimes maintenance that took them out, we never had too many at once."

The next best thing to tanks was Weapons Co.'s own weapons. It could provide Mark-19s that knocked the buildings down chunk by chunk, TOWs that could flatten them or kill everyone inside, Javelins that were deadly accurate and almost as destructive as the TOWs, and Ma Deuce, the .50-cal weapon they could always count on to ruin an insurgent's day. When Ma got done talking most of what had been in front of her was blasted to oblivion.

Occasionally the Marines simply bashed their way through strongpoints using satchel charges made from C-5 plastic explosives and sledgehammers—whatever it took to make a hole. Later on, after casualties mounted and the fight grew personal and bitter, they simply blew houses to pieces without going inside. According to Lieutenant Grapes, the rule was "Never enter a house without throwing into it something that explodes."

MITCHELL'S MEMORIES

One of the Marines who wholeheartedly believed in following Grape's rule was R. J. Mitchell. The self-assured sergeant with Hollywood good looks believed in never giving the insurgents a chance. His ability to think under fire earned him a meritorious promotion to Sergeant at Fallujah, but he was too shot up to know about it until he got out of the hospital a month later. Mitchell was awarded the Navy Cross in July 2006, the Marine Corps' second-highest honor, second only to the Medal of Honor, for bravery for his actions with Kasal at Fallujah. Kasal considers Mitchell's small-unit leadership skills impeccable and his warrior spirit unquenchable. Grapes says Mitchell never flinched until he was wounded for a fourth time and finally yielded to his pain.

Mitchell is a civilian now, a new dad, and a serious student studying Harley-Davidson motorcycle technology in Phoenix. He has a son named "R. J." whom he adores, a wife he loves, and a lot of memories from Fallujah.

For the moment Mitchell is sharing his home with former squad member Alex Nicoll, down from his home in northern California to go to the same motorcycle school. Still spirited and rambunctious despite terrible wounds, Nicoll has welded a metal bolt to his prosthetic leg so he can use the stock foot controls on his Harley. Both men share many of the same memories from Fallujah, many of them ugly.

Mitchell is getting VA disability now and deserves more, he thinks. Even so, he is content with life. He is glad Phoenix is a long way from the frozen winters of his Nebraska youth even if it does hit 135 degrees in the summer. It was even hotter when 3d Squad, Kilo Co. crossed through the breach in the berm at Fallujah and went on the attack in November of '04.

Mitchell remembers the places where he fought in Fallujah were jammed together with courtyards and walls creating natural fortresses that demanded a grenade or a satchel charge before they were entered. The buildings were constructed from brick and mortar, thick and strong to keep out the heat, but equally efficient at keeping out Marines. The architecture forced the Marines to work their way room by room across the gut of Fallujah, killing and dying in their relentless pursuit of the stubborn insurgent Iraqis.

"I really don't know how or where to start," he says now. "And I wouldn't pretend to remember everything from the first day that we went into Fallujah. I remember getting into the city with relative ease. 1st Squad, led by Sergeant Chris Heflin and my good buddy Corporal John Arzola, led the way into the city to our squad release point. At that point my squad broke away and started our advance south while 1st Squad pushed one more block to the east before beginning their advance to the south. 3d Squad was to follow behind mine and catch whatever we had to pass up or got by us, as well as act as the casualty evac detail."

When the 2/7 Cav began their drive into the city, Mitchell says, "it was one hell of a sound and light show."

THE VIEW FROM THE TOP

From time to time Mitchell would see Buhl come up for a look. The fighting was intensifying and bullets were whizzing in all directions. Buhl tried ignoring the fire while he conferred with Jent and Miller. When it got too hot he would hole up in a building with his Marines. If a squad was kicked back he would come over for a chat.

Whenever he would see Kasal he would stop for a word.

"A few days before Kasal was hit I saw him," says Buhl. "I think it was either at our attack position or when we first got inside Fallujah. I asked him what he was doing. When we got done talking I told him to stay out of trouble."

That simply wasn't going to be possible.

It had taken the men in 3/1 a while to get used to Buhl when he took over command from his more reserved predecessor. He would stick out a hand to the junior Marines and introduce himself as "Willy Buhl, your new battalion commander." The men couldn't have been more surprised than if they woke up with their heads sewn to the floor.

Sometimes Buhl would spend hours riding in his Humvee, listening to the war on the radio while he moved between units. Other times he sat through long brainstorming sessions. Most of the time he was on his feet, dashing from one position to the next during a fight. He says he likes it there. Commanding from the front allowed Buhl to watch his companies, evaluate their performance, and determine what needed to be fixed.

Fatigue numbed both bodies and minds and part of Buhl's job was figuring out when people were too tired to perform. At the same time Sax and the company first sergeants were watching their commanders for the same symptoms. Keeping each other from getting loopy was more of a mutual aid effort than anything else. They all spent their time worrying about everybody else while they all sank into a fog of exhaustion.

Buhl's vantage also allowed him to measure the battalion's company commanders, ordering changes when his Marines started making too many mistakes. He says it is a tough job when the commander has to interfere with his subordinates because it sows self-doubts in them that they don't necessarily deserve.

"Command is just knowing your people, employing your units within their capabilities," Buhl says. "It may sound boring and flat but it's knowing your people—putting the right resources to whatever needs to be done. Sometimes you don't have a choice. You just have to tell people, 'Hey, I need you to do this.' It may not be your first choice but, because of circumstances or time, you do it.

"I had to pull companies off the line for fatigue just like Sergeant Major-select Ruff had to tell me, 'Sir, you need some rest.' You can't run somebody continuously every day without mistakes. You had to plug different companies in.

"Sometimes you quickly realized specific units weren't suited for that task you just gave them. They would be taking excessive casualties and you would have to pull them off. You go up and have a look yourself to see."

Doing so was essential to spot mistakes.

"When things aren't going well," Buhl says, "you see Marines putting people in danger areas, not employing all their combined arms at their disposal, doing things the hard way, insisting on taking down houses the hard way, using a satchel charge that requires an approach—that requires the physical emplacement of a charge vis-à-vis an air strike—or using the combination of tanks and bulldozers. These are just simple examples."

Meanwhile the enemy was everywhere and nowhere until they wanted to be cornered—and then it was a fight to the death.

Mitchell's squad took its first casualty almost as soon as they slipped into the city.

"No more than 15 minutes after my squad started its push south from the squad release point we had our first causality," Mitchell says. "Corporal Korey Kaufman, my First Team leader, had a malfunction with the breach of his M203. First the damn thing didn't fire and he and I both tried to pull it open.

"I didn't see it happen but I guess out of frustration he slammed the butt of the weapon on the ground causing it to either fire and graze his hand or blow up inside the breach and somehow fuck his hand up that way. However it happened the injury resulted in Kaufman being medevac'd away from the fight.

"It was probably five or 10 minutes after Korey left that we started taking fire. It was coming from some kind of bunker on a rooftop of a house between the street that my squad was operating on and the street block to our west.

"I made the decision to have a team clear a nearby house to see if they could take out the bunker from there, and I took the advice from my assistant patrol leader, Corporal [Francis] Wolf, to have 3d Squad flank from the west."

The consequences of that decision will stick with Mitchell forever because it cost the life of a dear friend.

"That was when Segura got killed," he says slowly, recalling Lance Corporal Juan E. Segura. "I still don't know exactly how it happened. I guess his squad started flanking but got hit from the flank as they did. He was one of my best friends for over 3½ years and will never be forgotten."

Segura's loss also bit deeply into Kasal who considered Segura one of "his" Marines. When Kasal was the Kilo Co. first sergeant from 2001 through 2003, Segura was one of his young Marines.

"By 2004 he was a pretty seasoned Marine; he was a team leader," Kasal says. "When we were staged at Abu Ghraib right before we motored up and headed out, I saw him. I told him to keep his head down and that I would be watching out for him while we were out there.

"He said, 'Roger that, First Sergeant, you take care too,' and then we left our different ways. Then the first day of the assault, I got a report over the radio that he was killed by small-arms fire that hit him in between the strike plates on his body armor while he was clearing a house."

Kasal adds: "That kind of hit me hard. Just the day before I had told him I would be watching out for him. Then the next thing I know, on the next street over from me, he ended up getting killed. So I was pretty sad about that."

Mitchell says the attitude of the Marines around him changed after Segura's death. He was a popular Marine who was thought to be both salty and savvy. If he could die, so could any of them. His death got their blood up, and they were even more ready to fight.

"As soon as that happened, we all started killing people," Mitchell says. "I know at least four fighting-age males died when 3d Squad put a large shaped charge on a wall in front of them. There were four or five in a house. They were at the wrong place at the wrong time."

In 24 hours the battle had evolved into a contest of extermination. There would be no quarter asked and none given. The only prisoners taken were the ones who wisely surrendered before the fighting began. After that it was too late.

The first page in a new chapter of Marine Corps history had just been written.

CHAPTER 13

CLOSING IN

On D+4 the battalion pivoted east from its southern direction and attacked toward the Euphrates River. The area was densely built up, old, and poor. It was in the oldest part of the city, the inner sanctum of conservative Islamic thought. Many of the Marines were on their second and third days without decent sleep. The air was hot, smoky, and filled with the echoing sounds of war erupting all around them. The only rest they earned was in their night defensive positions when they got to pull half watches and every other man was allowed to sleep for two hours between stints of guard duty.

The Marines were scheduled to jump off the morning of November 10 into the "Byzantine" quarter of Fallujah. It was an ancient labyrinth of streets and alleyways that connected the jihadist warrens. 3/1's objective was Regimental Objective D, the Al Jamah Kabir mosque along the Euphrates. The regiment called it "the heart of the insurgency" because of its importance to the jihadists' control of the city. They expected to find weapons, supplies, and insurgents prepared to fight to the death.

The new direction took Kilo south of PL Cathy. Meanwhile 2/7 had slipped behind them to guard the battalion's rear and disrupt any jihadist reinforcements attempting to get into the area. The preceding day the cavalrymen had taken Regimental Objective I—dreaded Jolan Park—a huge open space in the center of the city that was the reported spiritual center of the uprising. For the moment the cavalrymen owned the ground they occupied and little else. Protecting the Cav's left flank from the west side of PL Henry were hard-pressed 1/8 Marines. Between the two American forces the insurgents holed up in thick-walled houses. The Marines called the situation a "shit sandwich."

BUHL'S DILEMMA

The enemy's intransigence since D-day forced Buhl to make some adjustments in 3/1's fighting style. Marines are trained to find gaps in enemy lines—areas that the enemy isn't defending—and attack. But at Fallujah the Marines were attacking regardless of circumstance and smashing headlong into the enemy, resulting in too many casualties. Buhl had to find some way to slow his Marines down. Instead of immediately attacking whenever his Marines encountered the enemy, he told them to wait for reinforcements to ensure an overwhelming advantage.

"One of the things we had to adjust to quickly was to reinforce contacts," Buhl says. "Because we had all the advantages of combined arms and firepower—and, thank God, we had authorization up the chain of command to employ whatever means were required—we could act quickly.

"Our young men are trained to run through walls, so we had to teach them that when they got bad guys in a house, not to just send in people. The minute you get into contact back away, cordon, coordinate, and drop it. Try to get them to come out and surrender. In our case at Fallujah they didn't—or did so very rarely—so the alternative was to take the structure down."

Buhl insists: "We were not there to destroy Iraq. We came to rebuild Iraq. But if you have people's lives on the line, you use what means you need to save lives. Destroying buildings might not have been a goal, but to preserve lives it was often necessary.

"Eventually we got the word down to the small-unit leaders," the commander recalls. From then on most of the Marine casualties "happened in extremis, when a man was wounded, when men got hurt, couldn't get themselves out of contact, and the mission became a rescue effort. This is where we found we had most of our casualties—when it was 'no buddy left behind.'"

At night the Marines holed up somewhere relatively safe, posted sentries and observation posts, and tried to get some sleep. The FACs kept busy and so did the men manning the observation posts (OPs). Only the snipers and Special Forces snatch teams were on the prowl.

That didn't mean nighttime brought solace to the insurgents. American night-vision technology owned the darkness. Long after the sun went down Basher's unblinking eye could detect the heat of an insurgent's body against the background of a cooling building or the darkest street. On the operator's targeting screens the insurgents looked like ghosts slinking across the dark terrain. The discovery brought their almost immediate destruction.

The jihadists called Basher the "Finger of God." During negotiations with the Coalition during the first Fallujah fight, one of the insurgency's non-negotiable demands was to end the AC130 overflights. Once night fell the jihadists were locked into a fixed position for the duration of the darkness unless they wanted to risk obliteration.

Some, however, were willing to take the risk and Marines in OPs around the battalion area observed movement as the insurgents tried to regroup. PUC Gallogly and the other FACs were especially busy on D+3, calling in 14 AC-130 air strikes against targets the battalion was assigned to take out the next day.

FROM TRAIN STATION TO HOSPITAL

November 10 was also the first night Landing Zone North Penn Station, located with the battalion Forward Command Operations Center (COC) at the train station, opened for business.

PUC spent a lot of time in his blue boxers over the next four nights; Kasal would not have been amused. The casualty rate was soaring as the Marines encountered stiffer and stiffer resistance, and PUC often didn't have time to get into his pants.

"We had urgent Casualty Evacuations [CASEVACs] coming in frequently," PUC remembers. The Marines used CH-46 "Sea Knight" twin-rotor helicopters and occasionally smaller Hueys to fly their wounded from the battlefield. For the next four days any bird going in to pick up an urgent casualty flew through a gauntlet of enemy fire from the northern portion of the city.

"The Hueys and Cobras would escort them in," PUC says. "I would hear that we had urgent casualties being rushed to the BAS [Battalion Aid Station] in a Humvee or an M-113 armored ambulance the 2/7 Cav had loaned us. I will never forget seeing a 113 [M-113 armored personnel carrier] driving about 55 miles per hour flying into the train station. It would come sliding into the station on the concrete and drop its ramp.

"We never allowed one of these casualties to wait. As soon as we heard of an urgent there was a marriage between the arriving helicopter and the casualty. At the BAS they would try to stabilize the injured Marine. CPO [Chief Petty Officer] Frank Dominguez, the senior Navy corpsman, saved dozens and dozens of lives. He was phenomenal!"

Nonetheless, PUC says, "Some of the urgents would die. It was heartbreaking sometimes."

TWO KINDS OF ENEMY

Back in the streets, alleys, courtyards, and houses of Fallujah, the Marines were encountering two kinds of enemy, Kasal recalls.

The first kind were classic guerilla warriors taking a page from Mao and Geronimo, Giap and Crazy Horse. They tried to engage the Marines at a time and place of their choosing, then slip away.

Most of these were local Iraqis. Almost chimerically they would disappear from sight through the maze of strongpoints into bleak warrens of refuge in the rubble or underground into craftily hidden tunnels. Then they would pop up out of nowhere, pray and spray down the street, and disappear into another hole.

The second kind of enemy was scarier: self-anointed martyrs who wanted to die at the hands of Marines after a long, slow digging-out process. Their aim was to find a strong position where they could kill as many Marines as possible before they died. They were reminiscent of the Japanese at Iwo Jima and Saipan, or more recently the Afghan and Chechen guerilla mujahedin who badly abused the Russians in Afghanistan and Grozny, the capital of the Republic of Chechnya.

These suicide fighters waited in barricaded homes, shops, and factories that they had prepared for their final stands. Negotiations were pointless and seldom sought in the no-quarter life-or-death struggle in which the young men of the Thundering Third found themselves. It quickly became obvious that the martyrs had no intention of surrendering, intending to fight until they were dead. Kasal says it didn't take any longer for the young Marines to discover they were in the fight of their lives.

In the narrow confines of the old section of Fallujah MK-19s and TOWs were hard to use because they needed space to arm and safely deploy. The fighting was close—sometimes only 15 or 20 meters separated antagonists firing RPGs, hand grenades, emplaced machine guns, and automatic weapons from one another. Sometimes the fighting was so close that blood from both sides mingled on the floors and walls. Victors and vanquished would be covered in each other's blood. There have been few fights like it in the annals of the Corps.

Occasionally a self-declared Iraqi martyr would surrender, but Kasal says the foreign fighters almost never did. Among them were Saudis, Syrians, Georgians, Pakistanis, and Afghans. Before it was over the Marines captured insurgents from 16 countries.

There were clues that Chechens were also there. Kasal remembers seeing a knitted, multicolored beanie that Chechens liked to wear lying on the ground outside a house that had been flattened. Other Marines reported similar finds. Whoever they were, the light-skinned jihadists inside the buildings didn't quit until they were exterminated. Even then they sometimes had the temerity to toss out a grenade with their last gasp.

Although the insurgents did not deploy tube artillery in Fallujah they made liberal use of free-flight rockets, mortars, and RPGs. They lobbed these at the attacking Marines in much the same way mortars and artillery shells are launched. The Marines retaliated with air strikes, helicopter assaults, and precision-guided munitions that picked out strongpoints and obliterated them and anyone inside.

BRINGING DOWN THE HOUSE

One of the Marines' favorite methods of announcing themselves to insurgents hiding in a structure was to "keyhole" the house before making their entrance. They did it using two Shoulder-launched multipurpose assault weapon (SMAW) rockets. The first one, containing a conventional warhead, would blow a small hole in the wall. It was followed by a second thermobaric SMAW round, correctly identified as the shoulder-launched multipurpose assault weapon–novel explosive (SMAW-NE), intended to kill anybody inside and collapse the roof on the rare survivor.

Thermobaric weapons distinguish themselves from more conventional weapons by their mind-boggling explosions, created using atmospheric oxygen instead of carrying an oxidizer in their explosives. In laymen's terms the warhead uses all the available oxygen in the area to enhance the explosion. The largest variant of the warhead in the U.S. inventory is the fearsome GBU-43/B massive ordnance air blast bomb (MOAB), a 21,000-pound GPS-guided bomb nicknamed the "Mother Of All Bombs."

The young Marines in 3/1 delighted in calling the SMAW-NE a "mini-nuke" because it could flatten the building the enemy was in, eliminating the need for the Marines to dig them out. As Gunner Wade says, they "worked quite satisfactorily."

The gunners in the line companies eventually used up the battalion's supply of SMAW-NE and had to rely on ordinary high-explosive rounds to clear rooms. After the roof crashed in riflemen would summon the Marines' Israeli-built armored bulldozers to mash the structure into the ground.

Keyholing was not exactly what higher headquarters had in mind when it promulgated the ROE for Fallujah, Buhl acknowledges. According to its tenets someone inside a building had to display hostile intent before the Marines could engage him.

When the rules were followed precisely they often put the young Marines taking the risks at a significant disadvantage, so they were quietly ignored. Once the fighting began in earnest, Mitchell says, the Marines preferred facing disciplinary action to getting shot in the face while looking around corners for the enemy.

Whenever the Marines suspected an insurgent was holed up in a house they initiated their visit with a SMAW, a satchel charge, or a grenade. Buhl says he was well aware of the challenges imposed by the ROE, and in this tactical situation he considered them a guide rather than a mandate. Buhl even invited the Regimental Judge Advocate up to the front lines to get a first-hand look at the tactics the enemy was using and how the Marines had adapted to defeat them.

"The correct criterion is that you confirm you have an enemy presence in a structure either by physical observation or by receiving fire—troops in contact," Buhl explains. "Well, it is impossible when people are waiting for you quietly. They did not give their positions away in most cases. They waited until Marines physically entered a structure before they would fire on them.

"At this point, we were able to use all of the powerful combined arms at our disposal with only enemy to our front. This is when the Thundering Third became the most lethal infantry battalion on the earth. We tried to do it carefully. But from commanders right down to that small-unit leader, that young corporal or lance corporal leading a fire team who thought he needed to throw a grenade into a room before he entered or fire weapons through a house before he sent his people in—that was his prerogative."

It truly was a dirty war and Weapons Co. Marines were in the thick of it. They fired more than 200 TOWs and dozens of Javelins before the fight concluded. Both weapons are very expensive and always in short supply so shooting them randomly was not an option. The Marines had to wait for permission before they let one rip.

"The Marines on the ground would request to shoot from the local commander," Kasal says. "Now if it was a target of opportunity—an Iraqi tank pops out of nowhere—the TOW gunner is going to shoot automatically. But if it were a building or something like that the local commander would give the authorization to fire."

That authorization could come from one of the section leaders, the platoon commander, or the company commander responsible for the TOW, Kasal says. Someone had to determine whether there were soldiers or Marines on the ground nearby and if a particular building was a safe target.

"When you shoot a building with an M16 it isn't going to hurt anything," Kasal explains. "When you shoot a building with a TOW you are going to hurt a lot of people. So you had to be real careful and make sure there were no friendlies inside."

EYE IN THE SKY

One weapon the jihadists never seemed to get a handle on was the Marines' Dragon Eye unmanned aerial vehicle (UAV), a $10,000 flying camera that instantly fed live pictures back to the COC. The battalion had six of them, giving the CO and Major Griffin (S-3) an unprecedented view of their enemy's dispositions.

The intel Marines could store single pictures or watch events unfold in real time from downloaded computer images. The UAV's optics were capable of taking a close look at an insurgent strongpoint. The UAV operators could occasionally even coerce the insurgents into taking a shot at the flying cameras. Then Marines could confirm the enemy's position. It was costly in airplanes and after a while the practice ceased; but the video was amazing, Buhl recalls.

Often the Marines used the intelligence gleaned from a Dragon Eye to direct air strikes onto targets. PUC says a good formula was two 500-pound bombs on a two-story structure equaled a collapsed pile of rubble.

In one recorded scene an insurgent was videotaped shooting at a 3/1 UAV with his machine gun. A few moments later the insurgent, his house, and the threat he posed were erased by a 500-pound bomb. It truly was death from above.

In another incident in the Jolan district on November 11, a Dragon Eye cruising at 291 feet at a sedate 31 mph was used to coordinate an air strike on a jihadist strongpoint. At 11:47 a.m. local time its pictures were used to direct a fighter bomber onto the target. At 11:58 a.m., cruising at 318 feet and 22 mph, it returned to film the bomb damage assessment (BDA). It was almost instantly determined that the target was destroyed.

The little plane could be flown from wherever the Marines needed a look. Dragon Eye operators would pick a roof for flight ops, put the little airplanes together, and launch them exactly like radio-controlled model airplanes. With a wingspan of only 45 inches, a length of about 3 feet, and weighing 5 pounds, it cruised at about 40 mph and could stay in the air up to an hour at altitudes between 300 and 500 feet.

3/1's leadership credits the little planes with identifying many strongpoints and possible ambush sites that were neutralized without any loss of friendly life. But even with all the eyes in the sky and armor on the ground most of the time Fallujah remained the same dirty, debilitating site of combat stress for Marines who faced deadly risks from grenades, RPGs, snipers, and ambushes.

ON THE MOVE

At 10:00, Kilo moved out to seize Regimental Objective D, the mosque. At the same time Lima was to conduct a surprise attack on the city's water treatment plant just to the north of the mosque, and India was to seize the dominant terrain along the river.

Prior to the attack the mosque had been prepped with multiple GBU-12 guided 500-pound bombs directed by Captain Smay. Additionally all three companies were supported during their attacks by a rolling barrage from 155mm howitzers and 120mm mortars reminiscent of the Great War. The barrage moved forward at a stately walking pace striking targets just in front of the battalion's line of attack.

The strategy played out almost like clockwork: The Thundering Third captured all three objectives in less than four hours.

The next day, November 11, Kilo was involved in a series of running fights with insurgents holed up in strongpoints and supported by indirect fire from mortars and RPGs lobbed onto them from nearby buildings. Along with India, Kilo attacked abreast from south to north to clear out the insurgents still shooting up the train station. Kasal recalls that mortars rained on Kilo and RPGs sizzled into their positions from every direction.

At nightfall the company again went firm, establishing static OPs and attacking by fire any enemy forward of their positions. Throughout the night all three company FACs and the air officer conducted continuous air strikes using fast movers and two AC-130 gunships.

By now Corporal Mitchell was on a holy mission of his own, he says, to kill every insurgent he found until the battle ended. "With me personally, it was kind of a religious thing. These guys were trying to kill me. I wanted to kill them. I wanted to get a big white flag like the Crusaders had. It was my fucking Crusade. I knew that it would make them angry. I was all into taking down the Islamists. I hated them; I was passionate about it. A lot of it was about revenge."

KILLER QUEENS

On D+5 3/1 attacked the southernmost part of Fallujah, nicknamed "Queens" by the Marines. It was November 12, but most of the Marines didn't know that. They didn't need to know that so they didn't bother remembering. They had bigger things to worry about.

Queens was the most dangerous part of Fallujah. In this district the most capable and best-equipped insurgents had dug themselves in. Most were foreign fighters who positioned themselves there early on when they still believed the Marines' main attack would come from the south.

The move is vivid in Kasal's memory: "We started entering the Queens and all that morning it was heavy fighting—building by building—the whole way down the streets.

"I was on the street outside of houses, or on the radio all morning long doing different firefights, different controlling procedures, whatever. The next thing I know we were moving out. That's when Lieutenant Grapes [3d Platoon Leader, Kilo Co.] asked if I had any extra people to help out the fire team in our building to the left."

Kasal's answer was a resounding yes. It was the toughest fight he had been in and his account gives a moment-by-moment picture of what the battle of Fallujah was like:

"Sergeant Mitchell, Lance Corporal Nicoll, Corporal Wolf, and Lance Corporal [Samuel] Severtsgard and me got together. We ended up getting pinned down in this building. We were trying to clear a building full of enemy, and while we were in one room an enemy sniper shot Sergeant Mitchell through the back of the arm."

Fortunately, the sniper's bullet tore through flesh but missed the bone. "It went through the back triceps, the meaty portion of the arm," Kasal says.

"Corporal Wolf and I bandaged him up and then we formed a plan to clear this building. I said, 'First, let's try to go through the front.' So Sergeant Mitchell sends Marines up on the roof to do overwatch that suppressed the street, the alley, and anyone they could see in the building. Then me, Mitchell, Nicoll, and Severtsgard stayed down on the bottom. I said to Sergeant Mitchell, 'Let's punch a hole through the building and go through.'

"I told Mitchell I had a TOW out there, so let me just go tell Corporal Hurd to fire a TOW through that building. So I ran back out in the street and small-arms fire started to shoot around us. I ran out there anyway and told Corporal Hurd to pull up into position to shoot that building with a TOW, hoping that we could blow a big enough hole so that we could make our own entrance and that it would also kill everybody in the immediate area inside the building."

It was a good idea and probably the safest approach given the weapons they had at their disposal, but this proved to be a particularly robust building. Powerful as the TOW is it only managed to punch a 12-inch hole in the wall—too small for anyone to squeeze through. It was time for Plan B, which was considerably more dangerous—running right up to the building and trying to force open a door. That didn't work either. "It was a big metal door," Kasal recalls. In addition to exposing the men to enemy fire it created another danger in their midst.

Before entering the house Severtsgard had armed a grenade. When they couldn't get the door open Severtsgard was essentially a walking explosion, with only his handgrip on the grenade preventing it from going off and blowing up the four men. Simply giving it a heave wasn't an option as the four couldn't be sure there weren't friendlies around. Such a move could be deadly to their comrades.

"So now we can't get the door open; so there is nowhere for Severtsgard to throw the grenade," continues Kasal. "For the next 15 or 20 minutes while we are still in this firefight he is running around with the pin pulled on a grenade. Finally when we realized there was nobody else around, he was able to throw that grenade into the back part of the house and get rid of it."

The men retreated into the adjacent house again where Kasal came up with Plan C. "Now I say, 'Okay, we will go through an alley that parallels the house and come around and try and enter the back side.' Me and Nicoll were in front, Mitchell was third, and Severtsgard was fourth. I helped Nicoll get over a wall leading into the alley. Then I jumped over the wall and Sergeant

Mitchell and Severtsgard did overwatch while me and Nicoll started moving down the alley."

Unfortunately this was just the opportunity for which the entrenched enemy had been lying in wait. "We got about halfway down the alley when all of a sudden small-arms fire started hitting all around us, just barely missing us," Kasal says. "Then a couple of hand grenades landed right at our feet.

"Luckily there was a 3- or 4-foot wall right next to us and we were able to jump over that wall and avoid the blast of the hand grenades. So then we knew that wasn't an option anymore; the enemy had that completely covered by fire.

"We just barely escaped. We got lucky. We got lucky as hell! There was probably a 20-round burst and all 20 rounds came within inches of us."

Plan D involved calling in the heavy artillery. "I had Sergeant Mitchell call Lieutenant Grapes and see if they could get tank support—81s or some other kind of fire support—to bear onto the building and level the whole thing."

Unfortunately given the close-quarter fighting that was going on all around them, that option wouldn't work either—and for the same reason it took Severtsgard so long to dispose of his grenade.

"We got word back that we couldn't because of adjacent units being too close," Kasal says. "Then we got word to move out and give up the building altogether. We marked it with a grid and sent it over the radio up to higher so higher knew that the building had not been cleared yet and was full of enemy activity. There was another battalion on the next street over— I think it was 1/8—so we marked the building for them, hoping they would have better luck coming from another direction, or after we moved out level it with some kind of fire support."

Much later when he had time to reflect Kasal decided his close calls on the 12th were a true test of his warrior skills. For him it was an intense exercise in correctly implementing tried-and-true infantry tactics in close-quarters combat. The correct solution was to probe the enemy, make him react to reveal his location, then find a place to flank him and get the upper hand. The ultimate goal was to counterattack and destroy the insurgents as quickly and efficiently as possible.

"To me a firefight is like a chess game," Kasal says. "It's a fight between me and him and I am trying to outwit him. When he fires at me, in my brain housing group [a Kasalism for 'head'], I am trying to figure out a way to counter him."

Irrepressible Nicoll had a much less intellectual reaction. He talks about it as though it were a grand adventure: "The day before we got hurt was probably crazier than the day we got hurt. Anytime there would be something, First Sergeant would be there. He was the only one [senior NCO] I ever saw out there. For the last two days we had been walking side by side. First Sergeant called me up and wanted me to go point for him. We were between two houses and a fence.

"There was about 2 feet between the houses. We jumped over the fence. Him and me were the only ones who had gotten over. Me and him were taking fire; we were wide open. I got shot in the shin," Nicoll says. "It barely broke the skin."

Almost immediately after Kasal's intense fight, while moving south along PL Henry, Kilo was ambushed from both the east and west flanks by a skilled group of foreign fighters with good equipment and excellent discipline. The foreigners used booby traps and other obstacles to halt the column in an almost inescapable kill zone. The insurgents' craftily laid explosives channeled the Marines into killing zones that made them easy targets. Kilo's Marines were forced to root them out in the face of heavy RPG fire, small-arms fire, and sniper fire, much of which originated from 1/8's zone.

In a rare display of very close air support Kilo's FAC directed nine strafing attacks by Marine Corps F-18s using 20mm cannon fire because rockets and bombs were a "danger to adjacent friendly units," Smay recalls.

By late afternoon, about 5:30 p.m., Kilo's Marines had broken through the insurgent ambush with brute force, but not before they had fired every weapon in their inventory. Smay's precision air strikes allowed the mud Marines to continue their advance to the intersection of PL Henry and PL Isabel.

In a final effort Kilo called in four more air strikes that made use of four precision-guided 500-pound bombs to neutralize an active sniper position on top of a mosque minaret. When the smoke cleared the sniper was gone, and so was the minaret, Smay says. Meanwhile, India reached the city's southern edge.

Optimism was high back in the rear, Buhl recalls.

THE VIPERS' NEST

Smay's last mission brought the day's intense fighting to an end, allowing Kilo to set up a firm base for the night. They picked a huge house, a building photographer Lucian Read would later describe as "almost a palace." Mitchell thought it was the mayor's house. Whatever it was, the house was an imposing structure that gave the Marines plenty of room and plenty of cover. As soon as they settled into the debris-filled rooms they posted sentries and put out observation posts (OPs). Queens was no place to let their guard down.

By nightfall the shooting quieted down except for the AC-130Hs working out in the neighborhood, providing night music that ebbed and flowed with the movements of the insurgents. Basher was busy all night reporting small elements of insurgents darting from building to building and point to point around Kilo, while the OPs called in movement from around the compass.

The foreign fighters were smarter now and they didn't give the Finger of God a lot of time to strike them dead.

Basher's syncopated symphony was accompanied by odd bursts of automatic weapons fire that ripped down alleys and boulevards. Sometimes green tracers would arch into the night sky and sometimes the bullet swarms were red. An occasional series of unexplained booms echoed across the city. Now and then a fast mover opened the sky when it climbed out after a pass, or a chopper settled into the LZ at the train station. Occasionally mortars coughed or the artillery on the eastern edge of the city cleared its throat, but compared to the daylight hours it was almost peaceful.

The Marines off watch settled onto floors, abandoned furniture, and nooks and crannies where they could chow down on some MREs and bottled water before stretching out for two or three hours. But that night nobody got much sleep.

Given all the movement they detected, it didn't take long for Jent and Buhl to deduce that Kilo had settled in for the night in a viper pit. Foreign fighters appeared all around Kilo's firm base preparing for Round Two. The Marines believed getting into the next day's fight was going to be easy. All Kilo had to do was try to move.

CHAPTER 14

THE
HOUSE OF HELL

After the intense fighting the day before, the morning of the 13th broke with an eerie calm. Kilo's Marines were slightly west of PL Henry, still in the old quarter of the city the foreign jihadists had staked out as their own. Kilo's orders were to push west toward the Euphrates conducting a systematic pattern of search-and-attack maneuvers to clear the foreign fighters that were reportedly all around them.

Lima was to the north of them clearing stay-behind insurgents. India had pushed down to the southern boundary of Fallujah and was to clear the heavily fortified part of the city by advancing slightly north and west along PL Isabel. Both companies expected another day of fierce resistance.

Most of the platoon didn't know it was Saturday, D+6. The days and nights blurred together. For five days the sounds of battle rose with the sunrise, stuttering first, then growing into a roar that filled the day. That roar had not yet happened on this day, so Kasal used the respite to look after his CAAT teams and talk to his far-flung company on the radio.

Mitchell prepared his Marines for another hard day of fighting, making sure they had all the gear and ammo they needed. Most of the equipment the men carried on their backs in Fallujah was for hunting insurgents. They usually carried six or seven 30-round magazines for their M16s, grenades, satchel charges, SMAWs, squad automatic weapons (SAWs), M203s, and an occasional M240G, the 7.62mm adaptation of the Vietnam-era M60 machine gun. In addition they carried water, ballistic sunglasses, knives, and personal favorites for killing. The rest of their personal gear was stowed in their rucks, currently attached to the AAVs that followed them into the city. Like most mornings in Fallujah the AAVs were parked outside the firm base under guard. This time it was at the fancy residence in a courtyard of sorts.

It didn't take long for the Marines to roll up their poncho liners and fall out. It wasn't as if the men needed time out for a shower. At best they got to brush their teeth, shave, and wash the crud off their hands and faces. As soon as the morning brief and equipment check were over, the Marines prepared to move out.

"NEVER QUITTING"

In Grapes' mind 3d Platoon was the saltiest platoon in the company. Grapes had joined the Marines Corps after 9/11 to defend his country and he was exactly where he wanted to be.

"For two and a half years I commanded the same platoon," Grapes says. "We had 43 Marines and two corpsmen. After the battalion returned to Pendleton after our first deployment, I got to retain about eight guys, most of them NCOs. Sergeant Pruitt and I got to build our platoon from the bottom up. Pruitt was a fine NCO and a master tactician—the best in the company. Mitchell was a good NCO, very bright. Nicoll was a good Marine and definitely the most popular Marine in our company and possibly the most popular Marine in our battalion."

At Fallujah Grapes had the added advantage of having Kasal

along. Coincidence found Kasal with Corporal Hurd, a Weapons Co. CAAT section leader supporting 3d Platoon including Mitchell's squad. It was typical of Kasal, Nicoll says, to be out in the field with the troops.

"Kasal is the toughest human being I will ever meet in my life," Nicoll adds. "His idea of being a leader was never quitting."

Mitchell says that he, Nicoll, and Kasal "always seemed to run to the sound of the guns. Kasal liked to be where there was shit going on."

Although Kasal liked working with Mitchell's platoon—after all he knew every man in it—he would have preferred spending time with his other CAAT sections that were spread out all over Fallujah, but the war was in the way. In Queens it was simply too dangerous to move around solo: Insurgents filled in behind the advancing Marines in small detachments of four to eight men— easily enough men to take out a lone Humvee.

"I just couldn't get over to the other two sections," Kasal recalls. "My intent, and I tried it every night, was to get on the radio and run over and join India or Lima, but I wasn't able to make it over to their positions. We were separated too far."

Whatever the mixture of choice, chance, and fate, Kasal found his CAAT section supporting perhaps the most experienced and aggressive squad around, in the heart of the battle for Fallujah as it entered its fourth day. It was to be one of the most intense days of combat Marines of his generation had ever faced.

HITTING THE STREETS

At about 8 a.m. Kilo moved onto the street. Grape's 3d Platoon pushed off first. Each squad in the platoon was assigned a sector to search. 3d Squad took a route that first sent them west, then south. 1st Squad went south. Staff Sergeant Lopez and half of 1st Section of Weapons Co. went with them. Grapes remembers that 1st and 2d Platoons had tanks assigned to work with them.

Kasal was in Corporal Hurd's Humvee, which belonged to Staff Sergeant Lopez' section. Nicoll was up front on point. In back was Hurd's squad along with his Humvee. The little column slowly snaked its way down the battered street. The air was filled with the smell of smoke from fires still smoldering along PL Henry in the aftermath of the previous day's fighting.

The scene was one of devastation and despair. Dusty roads were filled with debris, corpses, blown-up cars, pieces of furniture, and Marines very cautiously moving from house to house, methodically looking for combatants.

Lopez and his team stayed with Grapes and 1st Squad providing overwatch while the Marines searched for the insurgents. Lopez remembers the streets were narrow with poor fields of fire. His Humvee was armed with a TOW, which needs room to arm. Everything was too close for the heavy weapons to deploy effectively, but they were still intimidating, Lopez says. Lopez meanwhile kept his ear tuned to the radio listening for Hurd's team. He knew that two blocks away Kasal was walking alongside Hurd's Humvee providing flank security.

Elsewhere Weapons Co. Marines were providing the same kind of support and cover for India, which had been deep in the fight since the battalion jumped off. Lt Iscol's advisory team of former mortarmen and the Iraqi soldiers had their own sector. For five days they had been finding and destroying enemy supply and weapons caches spread all over the battalion's AO. North of Iscol's team Lima Co. was clearing out the deadly backfill of bypassed insurgents who had a nasty habit of reemerging behind the 3/1 Marines pushing south and west. Weapons Co. Marines gave 3/1 the edge in firepower the insurgents found irresistible.

"Weapons Co. Marines were in every fight in Fallujah because we had CAAT sections with every company," Kasal says.

Kasal's other sections were always on his mind. He didn't like being out of touch with his own men. The radio kept him informed of the big events, but it didn't allow him to see for himself.

"Being the first sergeant of Weapons Co. was different than being the first sergeant of Kilo because it is so spread out," Kasal says. "I had 170 Marines doing all sorts of things. They were with the rifle companies; I had mortar guys with Lieutenant Iscol and the ING behind us; and I had Marines securing roads and providing security. And the CO was somewhere coordinating everything. I really wanted to be with my other Marines."

Kasal kept waiting for a chance to move through the lines to his other sections but the enemy–infested city made it difficult.

"We were separated," he says. "I thought I might be able to jump out of my vehicle, or out of formation with Kilo, and join SSgt Mortimer, who was attached to India, or Sgt Como's section, who was attached to Lima, or even possibly join Lt. Iscol's group with the 81s and the ING. However, because of the fighting we were unable to get to other units so I stayed with Kilo."

Lopez says Kasal liked to stay on his feet providing flank security for his CAAT teams when they were on the move.

"Kasal was different than a lot of other first sergeants," Lopez says. "If you were the patrol leader he would not try to take over your patrol every time we would stop. He would do the 5- and 20-checks. When the vehicle stops the GIBS gets out for security. As soon as he gets about 5 meters out he checks for anything dangerous, and then he goes out 20 meters and does the same thing. Every lance corporal knows to do that. When Kasal was done, he would take cover. He was serving as just another lance corporal, a rifleman.

"When we came back, if he had a question he would ask you why you did something," Lopez recalls. "If he made a correction he would make it more like a suggestion. He would ask you why—very professionally, very polite. Kasal was like that all the time."

DISCOVERING THE CACHE

The unexpectedly quiet morning did nothing to calm the entire CAAT section's jumpiness. There was good reason to be on edge. Kilo had been searching houses for about an hour or so when 1st Squad discovered a huge cache of weapons and unexploded ordnance. That meant the enemy wasn't too far away. Everything came to a halt until the cache was secured.

Upon examination the cache proved to be big enough to wipe out a good chunk of the platoon—and to get the attention of 3/1's XO, Major Watson, who also headed an intelligence team called Bravo Command.

Watson's team collected data on recovered ordnance and weapons, as well as the torture chambers, death houses, IED factories, and other infernal services the jihadists provided in Fallujah. His team had provided the world the evidence of the grisly beheading of 62-year-old British civil engineer Kenneth Bigley, who was murdered 22 days after being kidnapped in Baghdad.

When Watson heard about the cache, he sent McCormack and his intelligence-gathering section from Bravo Command to record the jihadist hardware using digital cameras. McCormack describes the cache as huge. "It included an unexploded 500-pound bomb," he says. "We used satchel charges and time fuses to destroy it."

Lopez's CAAT provided overwatch while 1st Platoon prepared the cache for demolition. After the charges were set the Marines would back off a safe distance until after the ordnance was destroyed. On the way to the cache McCormack remembers seeing Mitchell walking down the road with one sleeve of his shirt missing, replaced by white bandages that covered a wound.

"I see this Marine; it's Mitchell. He's got the sleeve ripped off of his cammie blouse and he's got white bandages around his arm. I remember I grabbed the platoon commander and I said, 'Hey, is that Marine all right? Does he need to get back?' Grapes said, 'He's all right, he just got shot through the arm.'"

Mitchell was oblivious of the wound, he says: "It happened so fast I hardly felt it. It stung but it didn't even bleed. The bullet cauterized the hole as it went through. I was stiff and it hurt some to move it, but it wasn't bad."

Mitchell wasn't thinking about his arm when McCormack spotted him on the road. He was wondering what lay ahead. All the Marines were tense and somewhat numb from the day before. Mitchell was glad to see 3d Squad moved slowly, cautiously, well aware that the foreign fighters were lurking somewhere watching them move ever closer.

"When we pulled out of the firm base we hadn't gone too far when we stopped. I think we had gone west for a block and were now heading south just checking out houses," Mitchell says. "1st Squad was exploding some ordnance they had found so we stopped. Before that we had been searching the houses on both sides of the street, going into each one. The only thing that seemed like it was going on was 1st Squad getting ready to blow the UXO [unexploded ordnance] in place. I don't remember any shooting. Kasal was with us. His CAAT section was right behind me. He was just hanging out with us."

THE BUZZ SAW KICKS IN

Little did Kasal or any of them know, but only a moment later their lives would change forever. Suddenly, inexplicably, the essential elements that propel the average moment into history and history into legend came into place. Capturing that ordinary moment in an extraordinary time might not have happened at all had photographer Lucian Read not been on that particular street in Fallujah when the moment arrived. He was sitting in one of the Kilo Co. Humvees talking to the Marines manning it. Read was a regular among the Marines of 3/1. In fact he was almost one of them—to the extent a civilian puke can hope to be a Marine.

All around him the Marines of Kilo were making war in the dispassionate, careful way of routine combat operations. Each man was as taut as a drawn bowstring waiting to run its course. Kasal was standing alone and aloof as was his way, taking counsel with no one. Later he would say the moment had no particular significance to him.

Mitchell felt something would happen before the morning ran out. So did Nicoll. Two blocks from the epicenter of the moment Grapes and 1st Squad were standing around a cache of weapons preparing them for demolition. Up the street from Mitchell, Pruitt and his men were going through the cautious motions of checking out yet another house, knowing full well that eventually they were going to find something.

Seventeen months later Read recounted his observations in an interview with Joseph Shapiro on National Public Radio. Read said the fight came as a complete surprise to him. He had been following 3d Platoon all morning while they searched the houses lining the street. Marines were all around him—clearing buildings, smoking, providing cover, and just milling about.

They were finding nothing so Read decided to take a break while Kilo's Marines checked out the last house on the block. He moved over to one of the Weapons Co. Humvees to talk to the Marines inside when the buzz saw kicked on. He told Shapiro: "The house that the fighting ended up in was pretty much the last house," he says. "I had decided to sit that one out and it turned out there was six guys in there waiting for the Marines to come through the door."

After that Read remembers pistol fire, rifle fire, grenades, and Kasal passing by, heading for the sound of the guns. Next to Kasal was Hurd's CAAT. Read thought that seeing Kasal heading to the fight was extraordinary.

"It is not unusual for a first sergeant to be in the fight, to be present," Read says in the NPR interview. "But it is unusual for a first sergeant to put himself on the line like that, to go to a house like that, and to further push on risking injury. It was sort of a mark of the seriousness of that moment that the senior enlisted man—whose job usually would be to coordinate things through the officers for the men—felt it necessary that he was going to have to go in there and do what needed to be done. It speaks to the danger and confusion of that moment."

What Read couldn't know at the time, of course, was that Kasal had learned Marines were pinned down. "The first thought in my mind was that there were three fellow Marines trapped inside a house with the enemy and time was critical," Kasal recalls.

"All I could think of was the possibility of Marines being captured later appearing on TV being beheaded," Kasal explains. "My rank was irrelevant. Three Marines needed help and every second counted. That's the reason I ran to the house."

Kasal wasn't the only Marine heading to the sound of the guns. Staff Sergeant Jon Chandler, the new 3d Platoon sergeant, Severtsgard, Mitchell, Nicoll, and several more 3d Squad Marines went by with Read and Hurd's CAAT in hot pursuit; Jensen was still on the .50 cal. "Suddenly a hail of gunfire erupted out of nowhere," Mitchell recalls. "We all went down to where all the shooting was to secure the area around the gunfire. Kasal and the CAAT section were moving with us."

Pruitt, the 3d Platoon guide, was the mission commander at the firefight Mitchell was racing toward. He had attached himself to Corporal Ryan Weemer's fire team along with Sergeant James Eldridge, a machine gunner off one of the company Humvees looking for some action. Weemer was carrying an M16 with an M203 grenade launcher; the two others on his team were Lance Corporal Cory Carlisle, armed with an M16, and Lance Corporal James Prentice, carrying a SAW.

ENCOUNTERING THE HOUSE OF HELL

At first the Marines were merely curious about Pruitt's find. Behind the modest home's gated courtyard wall, the house seemed to be an ordinary Iraqi dwelling with a rooftop patio. The patio was surrounded by a wall. Near the front gate was an outhouse common to many Iraqi homes. Ten or 15 feet in front of the outhouse was the main entrance to the home.

Pruitt's five-man patrol was about 100 meters beyond the rest of 3d Platoon's position when they encountered the house for the first time. The team began their search by unsuccessfully trying to break into the back of the house. Despite their best efforts they couldn't batter their way through the steel back door. And until they got a door open they couldn't throw a grenade or satchel charge inside to clear the room.

Pruitt walked around to the front of the house to see if they could get in there. Immediately he noticed the gate was open. Pruitt ran back to Weemer's fire team and reported his find. He had already seen plenty of signs that insurgents were somewhere in the neighborhood, and the house on the corner looked like it might be the place. Pruitt couldn't put his finger on why he knew, but his instincts were telling him it was so. He told the Marines to saddle up and get prepared.

"I could see holes knocked out in the walls where they can egress," he says. "Somebody had knocked those holes out to move around. Every few houses we would find fresh water. We found training gas masks, plywood boards with instructions on how to use gas masks, all kinds of weapons. We had found drugs—adrenaline or amphetamines, I am not sure which—and syringes. We also found 55-gallon drums of oil where the insurgents were hiding weapons. When we poured the oil out of the barrels, inside would be all kinds of guns—AKs, old grease guns, you name it. They were around us."

Weemer, 23, from Hindboro, Illinois, was smoking a cigarette on the curb outside the back door when Pruitt ordered him to bring his team around to the front. "Pruitt looks around the corner and tells me to grab my guys, get my team," he says. "He said there was an open gate and a door he thought we could get through. He thought there were insurgents in the building. Pruitt said that from the very beginning."

The insurgents who chose the nondescript light yellow house on the corner knew exactly what they were doing. Because of the wall around the rooftop patio and a circular skylight built into the roof, a crafty shooter could stay on the roof all day covering the approaches to the house and the interior of the house (through the skylight) at the same time. Later a scout-sniper would apologize to Mitchell for never taking a shot at the insurgents on the roof covering the stairs and central room in the house. He never had a target.

Inside, the house was as much a fortress as a dwelling. In the main room was a stairway leading to a small vestibule. The vestibule had a catwalk that marched around the inside walls. The catwalk gave the defenders an unobstructed field of fire into the room below. Anyone topside had space to fire from cover without exposing himself to immediate danger—an almost perfect field of fire. Anyone entering the main room was at the mercy of the jihadists unless he could bring his weapon to bear before the jihadists got off a burst. Behind the main room was a rear doorway leading to still more rooms, including a kitchen. Off to the left of the main room was a small room—perhaps a crude bathroom.

The smell of fresh feces was the first thing to alert Pruitt. He followed his nose into the outhouse and saw a fresh pile of crap on the floor by the hole that passed for a toilet. "After I seen the shit I told Weemer there were insurgents in the house," he says.

After formulating a brief plan they moved in to clear them out. Pruitt told Eldridge, armed with an M16, to cover the right flank.

Weemer told Prentice to cover the left flank with his SAW. In the back of Pruitt's mind was the current ROE. He didn't want his men simply shooting up everything and everybody in sight.

"The ROE was given to us as a guideline," Pruitt would say later. "We used our best judgment. I trained these Marines for a long time. I told them they had to know when to turn on their kill switch, they had to know how to turn it on and turn it off." They turned the switch on.

It took only a few seconds to reach the front door after they passed the outhouse. When they got there Pruitt, Weemer, and Carlisle took a deep breath and got ready to move inside. Pruitt was bringing up the rear of their three-man stack. To make the stack the three men closed together into a bristling porcupine of pressed bodies with weapons pointing out in every direction.

"I am standing in front of the house. It's Weemer, Carlisle, and me," Pruitt remembers. "We got into a combat stack and went up to the door. Weemer pushed open the door and we saw the first motherfucker inside the house, squatting down in the front room with his weapon. He was probably high on something because he didn't shoot."

Weemer said he went to the door with his M16 hanging on its sling as he preferred his pistol in a close fight. He had come to 3/1 from Fleet Anti-Terrorism Security Team (FAST) company where he had endlessly trained, dropping his rifle to go to his pistol when the circumstances called for it.

"I started off with my pistol pulled," he says. "The house had saloon-style doors that opened inward. They were like saloon doors except they were full length doors. I pushed in the one on the left and went through the door.

"I was sweeping left with my pistol when I saw the insurgent. The guy froze up; he was down in the far left corner on one knee. He didn't shoot. I started shooting. As I was shooting Carlisle was coming in. He saw the guy and froze. That is when Pruitt pushed him [Carlisle] and he engaged, shot several rounds, and then stopped and then fired several more rounds," Weemer says.

"I gave him three rounds in the chest. Carlisle was still shooting. I had to yell at him and tell him the guy was dead," Weemer adds.

Pruitt says the jihadist who died must have been too high on drugs to react to the sight of three Marines busting through the door—too drugged or too scared. Either way he never got off a shot. He died where he squatted. The stack continued forward into the next room.

AMBUSHED!

"Then we moved through the next doorway that was directly in front of us," Pruitt says. "I saw a guy directly to my front. An insurgent came out from the left side of the room and started shooting at Weemer and Carlisle. He fired 10 or 15 rounds and missed. The guy in front of me was on my right side. I fired at him and he opened up on me. He had an AK. He was a big guy with a full beard. He wasn't an Iraqi. I don't know what he was, maybe a Chechen, but he wasn't an Iraqi. He shot me through my right leg and right wrist. The fire that hit me all came from the right side. I don't know if I hit the guy shooting at me; I can't say if I did or didn't. I spun around and dropped my weapon. As soon as that happened I knew we were in a shit sandwich."

Unarmed and incapable of fighting, Pruitt decided to go back out and bring in Eldridge and Prentice. Both Marines were still outside guarding the flanks.

Inside Weemer and Carlisle were still engaged. Weemer couldn't believe the guy he was shooting at wouldn't go down.

"Carlisle was stacked to the left. Prentice was covering the front door facing outboard. That is where he stayed. I didn't know what happened to Pruitt. I never saw him again until we got medevac'd.

"While that is all going on we were still in the second room in contact with the enemy. I unloaded a whole pistol mag into the guy. He was just spraying. The only reason I could see him was his muzzle flash; it lit up his face. I shot him so many times his gear was on fire.

"Somehow neither one of us gets hit by this guy. By then I am real low on ammo for my pistol. I pushed Carlisle back through that door; now we are back in the first room reloading. I haven't seen anyone shooting; as far as we know there is one guy. As we reload I put my pistol away and pull out my M16 again. The pistol wasn't doing the job.

"When we go back I see [another] insurgent. He looks hurt but he is still coming toward us. We're almost positive he was drugged up on adrenaline. He was a Chechen; he had on a colored beanie. I shot him in the legs and when he went down in the doorway—dropped his weapon when he fell—I shot him in the face. His chest rig was still on fire so I could see his face."

In the time it took Weemer to kill the second insurgent Pruitt made it outside. He was reeling from the wound to his hand. It was hurting now and his hand was turning blue. All Pruitt was thinking about was bringing Eldridge and Prentice into the fight.

TAKING IT OUTSIDE

"Eldridge got shot while he was still outside," Pruitt says. "The guy on the roof got him. Eldridge got shot from behind or above. The bullet hit the back of his shoulder. It missed the SAPI [small arms protective insert] plate and went into his shoulder or back. He still tried to come in after being shot. He came in the house and was shot again.

"My sole intent before he got hit was to grab him and Prentice and go back in. I knew somebody was shot. I thought it was Carlisle. I later found out he was shot in the leg and it was fractured from his hip to his knee. I couldn't hold a weapon but I could still do something to help. Prentice had the SAW so I figured we could use him inside. When I went outside I could see he was covered by an overhang. Then the son of a bitch started shooting at me from the roof. I got to the gate and then I guess I fell again, or that is when I got shot in the back. When I fell I was hit in the back of my SAPI plate. I didn't feel it then. I got two big bruises on my back. That was in addition to the one that hit me in the wrist. That bullet broke the bone, hit the ligaments; my hand was just hanging down. I didn't want to look at it. I didn't look at it until I was in the hospital. I also was hit in the leg."

REINFORCEMENTS ARRIVE

"I remember being outside the wall low-crawling; and then I saw Kasal coming," Pruitt says. "When I saw Kasal I headed straight to him. I got up and started jogging down the street. He was walking security next to the CAAT vehicle. Kasal said I was walking. I didn't want to talk to anyone else."

Kasal and the other approaching Marines still didn't know what was going on when Pruitt suddenly staggered into the street in front of them. Kasal and Mitchell both saw Pruitt at the same time and headed toward him.

"He was wounded in the arm and leg," Mitchell says. "I think he got shot in the leg when he came stumbling out of the house."

Pruitt remembers seeing Nicoll first. "I could see Nicoll 60 or 80 yards away from me—he was point. His eyes were all big. He was trying to figure out what was going on. Mitchell, Chandler, Severtsgard, and the other Marines were behind him. I got to Kasal first. He moved me out of the fire.

"He said, 'Come here, Sergeant Pruitt. Come over here and sit down.' We moved maybe two or three times before I sat down. I think we were behind a wall. I knew exactly what was going on. I was pissed I couldn't do anything about it." Mitchell came up, and both men started giving first aid. Kasal was putting a bandage on Pruitt's wrist as Mitchell was working on his leg.

Inside the house Weemer and Carlisle took a break. They still didn't know there were more insurgents in the house. They didn't know where Pruitt had gone, and Weemer didn't know Eldridge was even part of the plan.

"I told Carlisle to hold the door to the main room and went outside. I saw guys coming up. It was Severtsgard and Chandler. They were the first two in. They were on the street with Mitchell's squad," Weemer says. "Prentice was still outside providing security. He apparently wasn't sure what had happened. I pulled them to me and got Prentice. Prentice didn't tell me Eldridge was shot and that Pruitt was wounded.

The initial burst of fire that wounded Pruitt and Eldridge was drawing Marines to the yellow house like moths to a flame. Within a few minutes more 3d Platoon Marines showed up, including Chandler, Corporals Tyler Farmer and Jose Sanchez, and Lance Corporal Morgan McCowan. Still more Marines were pounding down the street toward them.

Two blocks away Lopez and his team were still idling on the street, relaxed but alert to any changes in the electrified air. The Weapons Co. Marines spent long hours waiting to be needed. It was especially true for the TOW gunners because their weapons were so powerful and expensive, Lopez said. He didn't just shoot it because somebody started firing. The same was true for the Mk-19 grenade launchers and Ma Deuce. The big .50 cal Browning machine gun can eat concrete walls and light up enemy vehicles with its incendiary bullets. But it wasn't something a gunner just let fly. Sitting and waiting in a firefight takes a tremendous amount of discipline.

In the meantime the CAAT sections had to stay alert and ready to turn a weapon in the right direction and start laying down fire instantly.

"My Weapons Co. Marines were essential to the mission," Kasal recalls. "Even though I was with Kilo the sections were spread out all over the city fighting. I had to depend on my NCOs to do the right job. I wasn't there but I knew their training would kick in. They were perfectly capable of doing their jobs. Gunny Wade was always around trouble, and I knew I could count absolutely on my other sergeants and young Marines because we had trained together. Weapons Co. was as well trained a unit as I had ever served in."

The riflemen were almost completely dependent of the CAAT sections for heavy firepower inside Fallujah, Buhl says. The steel wall the 2/7 Cav provided the first days of Fallujah had dissipated by the fifth straight day of combat and the Marines' tanks were spread all over the city. The Army was still around in their Bradleys and tanks, Kasal says, but they stayed buttoned up. The CAAT Marines always kept one eye peeled for the Army cavalrymen because of their fighting methods, Kasal says.

At one point, the Marines placed a sniper team on the top floor of a building to provide security for a group of men resting downstairs. When Army Bradleys saw movement at the top of the building, they presumed it was an insurgent stronghold and cut loose with a TOW missile and cannon fire. "Luckily," Kasal recalls, "the TOW was a dud and the cannon fire missed.

"The Army idea of clearing buildings was driving along in their buttoned-up tanks and Bradleys, shooting at the buildings and then driving on." In contrast, he says, "the Marines cleared each building on foot, house by house and street by street, by the individual riflemen and supported by firepower from Weapons Company CAAT and mortar teams.

"Weapons Co. was always with the riflemen. They had to know where the other Marines were. A TOW can go through two or three buildings and do a lot of damage. A lot of times my Marines would get off [their vehicles] and help clear buildings, or put out security on the buildings being cleared. It wasn't like they were just waiting for some insurgent to start shooting at them. Marines are always engaged. We train to take the fight to the enemy."

STACK AND STORM

Inside the house of Hell, Marines were doing exactly that:

"We stacked up again," Weemer says. "Severtsgard pulls out a grenade. The stack was Carlisle, me, and Chandler. Severtsgard is to the side of me. Behind us are Tyler, Farmer, and Sanchez. We go back through the door and Severtsgard steps up and throws the grenade. I couldn't hear shit after that grenade went off.

"Chandler, Farmer, Sanchez, and Prentice were in the first room. I thought Prentice was with us. I didn't know until later that Chandler had told him to stop. I go left this time and Carlisle goes right. I had to push Carlisle over the body. I had my hand on his back pushing him forward.

"My mindset was 'just go.' We had no one shooting at us from up. I told Severtsgard to throw the grenade. It was pitch black; the air is full of dust smoke and lead from the grenade. I literally ran into the set of stairs that go to the second story. I could hardly see it.

"As the smoke clears I am moving my weapons with my eyes. In my mind things were going very slowly. Once I could see up on top, I could see a guy up there and he shot down at me. I shot four or five rounds when I felt something hit me in the leg and then I felt something hit me in the forehead.

"I remember seeing a guy with his head almost gone. The day before my squad leader had shot a guy twice in the forehead and the whole back of his head was gone. I thought that had happened to me, that the bullet had severed the nerves in my head and I couldn't feel it."

Carlisle had been shot as well although Weemer didn't know it at the time. The insurgent who wounded Weemer probably hit Carlisle in the same exchange of fire. For a long time Carlisle lay on the floor screaming. The jihadists left him alive for bait. Carlisle couldn't move out of the line of fire because his leg was fractured from his hip to his knee. Weemer staggered out without realizing how badly he was hit.

"I turned around to go back into that first room," Weemer says. "Then I went back outside and sat down. Prentice is sitting next to me. He was supposed to be going with Chandler. I remembered putting him in the stack. I didn't find out until way after the fact that Chandler had stopped Prentice at the door.

"I had been shot three times in my right leg. Two rounds lodged below my knee in the bone. One had gone around the major tendon in my knee. I was more worried about my head. When I went outside I asked Prentice what was wrong with my face. He said it was just a scratch."

With Weemer out of the picture Chandler took the lead. He told his team they would have to flood the room to rescue Carlisle. He ordered them to shoot into the ceiling around the top of the stairs while he grabbed Carlisle. After a few more seconds of discussion he kneed Sanchez in the back and yelled, "Go!"

Chandler and Severtsgard went to their right. Farmer had just cleared the door behind them when a grenade dropped on the floor and exploded in a huge cloud of dust and debris. The noise was deafening. Farmer went flying into the foyer he had just come from and Severtsgard and Chandler were sprayed with shrapnel. The insurgent who threw the grenade followed up with a long burst of automatic weapons fire that struck Chandler three times in the leg. Although wounded, Severtsgard used one hand to drag Chandler into the back of the house where the kitchen was located. They would remain there until the end of the fight. Farmer, his hand shredded by shrapnel, could do nothing but scream curses at the insurgents.

As Chandler's group was fighting for their lives inside the house more Marines arrived on the scene. Private Rene Rodriguez and

Lance Corporal Michael Vanhove had seen Weemer come out yelling for reinforcements. The two men rushed in looking for Sanchez, their fire team leader.

They found Sanchez in the back of the building putting a pressure bandage on Carlisle's grotesquely twisted leg. With nothing else to do, they hunkered down to provide security. Meanwhile, insurgents sprayed the doorway to their front with fire. There was no way out except back through the gauntlet they had just survived. For the moment they were trapped and useless.

Weemer didn't know what was happening inside. He was agonizing over what to do when more help arrived.

"Grapes and Wolf showed up," he says. "I saw Grapes and I told him Carlisle was still in there and so was Chandler. I wasn't sure who else was until later. I told him, 'I am ready to go back in there.' Grapes told me to stay there and let Jensen work on me. He tells me, 'Jensen is giving you first aid; you need to let him give you first aid.' He probably told me five times not to go back in there. It was all I could think about. I wanted to go back because my team was in there. From what I saw in that house I thought they were dead. Jensen kept holding me back. I think that was when Kasal and Nicoll showed up."

Kasal first saw Pruitt staggering up the street toward him covered with blood. He still didn't know anything about the fate of Pruitt's team. Behind Pruitt the noise of automatic weapons fire and exploding grenades was still coming from the house.

"I noticed Pruitt walking toward me," Kasal says. "He appeared to be in a state of shock and I quickly noticed he had wounds to his hand and lower leg."

Kasal ran to Pruitt and pulled him in between two buildings for cover. There Pruitt explained how he had gotten out but that the other three were trapped in the house wounded or possibly dead.

"The first thing that came across my mind was getting to those three wounded Marines as quickly as possible because I knew the enemy would give no quarter to a wounded Marine," Kasal says. "I was particularly concerned they would be captured and later tortured or beheaded. So I grabbed a nearby Marine and directed him to treat Pruitt's wounds and provide security for him while I headed directly for the house."

TRAPPED AND WOUNDED

Mitchell remembers how clearly and concisely Pruitt gave his report to Kasal despite being shot in the leg and wrist. "He kept his composure," Mitchell says. Mitchell was trying to administer first aid but Pruitt was still in the fight. "Even though he was wounded Pruitt still had his head on a brass swivel. He knew exactly what was going on. Outside of First Sergeant Kasal, Pruitt is the epitome of the Marine Corps."

Mitchell radioed Grapes the information he obtained from Pruitt informing him they were in contact and had wounded Marines trapped in the house. 2d Platoon, the designated Quick Reaction Force (QRF), also headed to the scene. The report immediately burned its way through the ether to battalion. Hell House was suddenly the center of attention.

Lopez heard the gunfire break out but didn't pay too much attention to it until he heard Mitchell's call to Grapes on the radio in his CAAT vehicle. His attention was focused on watching over 1st Squad while they prepared the unexploded ordnance for demolition.

"We were hearing gunfire. We were always hearing gunfire," Lopez says. "Then we got the call. We had some casualties inside the building. Each vehicle has a VRC-99 radio so we always had comm with each vehicle. Grapes left a few men from 1st Squad with the cache and we headed for the contact.

"We had to make a left turn down the next block. The rest of 1st Squad came with us. I was driving alongside them, going about as fast as they could go. They were jogging, still providing bounding and overwatch. It took us just a couple of minutes."

When Lopez arrived with Grapes to help out he discovered he didn't have a way to help. There was no way to use the TOW because of the Marines inside the building, and he didn't have a target for anything else. In the next 90 minutes Grapes and Lopez would try several avenues of approach to the house without being able to bring a weapon to bear. Although the TOW on his CAAT was too big to use without endangering the Marines inside, the M240G was just right, Lopez says, but he had to have something to shoot at. Lopez left the rest of his section facing outboard, securing the building's perimeter while he and Grapes tried to find a place to bring fire.

Lopez thought the jihadists were smart to have picked that house. Nothing about its innocuous appearance suggested it was part of the great deception they had waiting for the Marines. Pruitt agrees. He thought the jihadists who picked that particular house were trained soldiers who knew exactly what they were doing. "They were all trained soldiers in that house, good soldiers except for the first one," he says.

FIGHTING FOR THEIR LIVES

The fighting inside the house was still going on. Somebody was screaming. Then a grenade exploded. The whole street was suddenly alive as Marines up and down the road took up firing positions while trying to get a grip on what was suddenly happening. Word that Marines were trapped in the house was traveling fast.

Mitchell and his fire team rushed to the same gate Pruitt had stumbled through to get away. Mitchell says they almost instinctively pulled together to formulate an attack. Surprisingly there was no fire coming at them. For a moment it was very quiet.

"We guided in between the walls," Mitchell says. "We had a four-man stack. The first two guys were Nicoll and Kasal. Nicoll had Kasal's back. I was with McCowan. We went in and sort of staged for a second in this little room. There was a dead insurgent lying there. We knew there was a casualty and we had to go in there and get him. I could see two doors and a stairwell. Beyond the second doorway I could see a Marine's boots. Then we just headed inside."

Before Kasal went into the house he grabbed two passing Marines he didn't know and told them to cover the doorway. Then Kasal, with Nicoll covering his back, moved into the house.

KASAL STORMS IN

Kasal quickly sized up the situation after storming the door and entering the first room—one dead insurgent, the floor covered in blood, and a pair of doors straight in front of him leading to two other rooms. "In the room on the right I saw one of the wounded Marines lying on the floor," Kasal says. "In the door on the left there was a second dead insurgent." He noticed a ladder well to the left, which would be to their rear as Kasal's team entered the room. Immediately the Marines with Kasal started fanning out through the house.

"I quickly noticed in the far right corner a room by itself that was bypassed by all the Marines," Kasal says. "I recognized that as being uncleared and thus a danger area, so I grabbed Nicoll, the Marine nearest to me, and told him to help me clear that room. I also realized the stairwell was now to our rear and also uncleared, making it a danger area to myself and all the Marines inside the building. To protect our rear I grabbed two unidentified young Marines and directed them to lay security on the stairwell and keep it secure. I then moved across the room to the far doorway with Nicoll on my heels."

Before Kasal entered the overlooked little room he paused outside the door and took a careful look, using a technique called "pieing," mentally divides the room into pie-shape slices and visually searches one "slice" at a time.

"All of a sudden no more then two feet from me there was an enemy insurgent with his AK-47 barrel pointed right at me," Kasal says. "By pieing off the room and exposing only a little of my body at a time I was able to avoid him getting a good aim at me until we were so close we could have shook hands.

"He brought his weapon up to fire and at the same time I moved back a step and brought my barrel to bear on him. He was too close to aim directly as my rifle was longer than the distance between us, so as he fired a short burst, the rounds were skimming in front of my chest and impacting to my right.

"I placed my weapon over the top of his rifle and stuck my barrel straight into his chest and pulled the trigger," Kasal says. "I emptied eight to 10 rounds into his chest before he went down. And as he fell to the floor I noticed him still moving, so I placed two more well-aimed shots into his forehead to make sure. Even after this he was still moving around but I was convinced he was dead. I directed my attention to deeper inside the room, which by now was dark and dusty—filled with the smoke and dust caused by the firing from our weapons in such a small space.

"I had my weapon trained on the darkness to my direct front when all of a sudden I remembered the stairwell to our rear and became nervous because it was a real danger area. Not wanting to take my eyes off my front, I yelled behind me to the two Marines I placed as security on the stairwell.

"I got no answer and so I yelled again. Then, out of nowhere, all hell broke loose from my direct rear."

★ ★ ★

CHAPTER 15

FIGHTING FOR LIFE

When Kasal and Nicoll turned, Mitchell and McCowan went straight ahead into a room where they could see Carlisle. For some reason the insurgents on the roof did not immediately fire at them when they ran through the main room to get to the wounded man. When Mitchell got there he discovered several Marines already crowded inside.

"I went into that first room where Carlisle was," Mitchell says. "Nicoll and Kasal had gone to the left. Chandler and a few more of us went in that back room. I think Farmer and Severtsgard were there. Carlisle was lying face down on the floor bleeding from his leg. I started to apply direct pressure to stop the bleeding. I felt his bones shift. He screamed and I stopped. I was afraid I would do more damage and cause him more pain.

"That is when I think I heard Nicoll and First Sergeant get hit. Shooting was going on everywhere. Somebody fired an AK and I heard a scream. I think it was Nicoll screaming in pain although I am not sure. There was noise, explosions, shooting, and screaming. I decided to go back to where Kasal and Nicoll were. I didn't know for sure they were down, but I knew they were getting shot at."

Kasal and Nicoll were still looking forward when shots rang out behind them. The room was dark, filled with smoke and dust. Kasal still doesn't know what happened to the pair of Marines he had posted to protect their rear. They may have been called away by their squad leader, or perhaps they were ordered to some other urgent duty—but for whatever reason they left, the repercussions were profound.

SHOT FROM BEHIND

"I never saw it coming or even where it came from," Kasal says. "I just heard automatic weapons fire and then what felt like someone hitting me in the lower leg with a sledgehammer as my legs crumpled from beneath me; I fell to the floor. I heard Nicoll yell in pain behind me and immediately knew he was also hit.

"Rounds were still impacting all around as I lay there. I started crawling inside of the room I just cleared in order to find some cover. However the enemy insurgent I just shot was blocking the doorway, so I had to push him out of the way and get around him. Nicoll then fell inside the doorway. I looked back and saw rounds still impacting around him, and then he winced and grabbed his stomach, and I saw blood coming from between his fingers.

"Realizing he was still in danger, I crawled back out into the doorway. The enemy started shooting at me again and I grabbed Nicoll to try to pull him to cover. As I was doing so I felt a round hit me directly in the buttock and the sharp pain that followed. Rounds were still coming and I felt like a duck during hunting season. But I was able to grab Nicoll and pull him into the room. I rolled him over the top of me so that I was between him and the enemy with the door to my immediate right."

The room was so small that Kasal was lying partially on top of a dead enemy combatant. "His system was still kicking from all the drugs the insurgents would take so they could keep fighting until the end," Kasal says. "They would take huge amounts of different drugs so that they could take pain and multiple wounds and still stay alive to, hopefully, take one more Marine with him before he died."

Pictures of dead insurgents with drug-filled syringes found on or near their bodies were taken in grisly monotony by Marine intel specialists at Fallujah. During the fighting the Marines found large caches of amphetamines, adrenaline, and painkillers with their attendant syringes donated by humanitarian aid organizations in Europe and the United States. The drugs were intended to treat innocent wounded civilians, but they ended up being used to hype-up insurgent killers so they could kill more.

KASAL DECIDES TO DIE

"The enemy's fire in the next room stopped momentarily now that we were behind cover, and I couldn't hear any movement," Kasal says. "It was just the dead insurgent, badly wounded Nicoll, and me in the room with an undetermined number and location of enemy right next to us."

Both Marines were bleeding profusely from multiple wounds, but each man carried only one pressure dressing. "I knew a tourniquet was needed on the legs of both of us in addition to the upper body wounds," Kasal says. "So this is where I made my first decision to die that day.

"I decided to use all our dressings on Nicoll so that at least one of us could live. I knew I was tough and what I was physically capable of, so I decided to try to gut it out while I stopped his bleeding. I also thought of the enemy next door and kept listening for sounds of movement.

"I realized that when friendly forces reached us they might not know who was inside the room. I was concerned that hearing our movements they might think we were the enemy. So I decided to use my M16 to mark the doorway. I knew any Marine seeing it would at least pause before spraying the room. I then pulled out my 9mm pistol and laid it on my stomach to use for defense."

Satisfied that he had accomplished all there was to do to protect them, Kasal turned his attention to saving Nicoll. As he did so his own blood was steadily seeping onto the sand-covered floor. Kasal struggled to put a tourniquet on Nicoll's leg to stop the bleeding. "Being in the position I was in I couldn't do a very good job but did manage to get a half-assed tourniquet in place," he says. Although he could barely move Kasal wrestled with Nicoll's gear, fighting to get a dressing on his upper body wounds.

"I was talking to him to try to help him remain conscious. It was then that I became aware of the enemy presence again—kind of like a sixth sense—and I heard a noise to my right. I rolled half over to get ready for whatever was next. When I looked down I saw a pineapple grenade lying about three feet away from me on the floor."

With nowhere to go and feeling too wounded to try, Kasal says he made his second decision to die that day.

"In all honesty I thought I was going to bleed to death from severe wounds and lack of medical treatment anyway," he says. "So out of instinct—and love for the Marine next to me—I did the only thing any Marine would do if faced with the same situation: I protected my brother. I rolled over, pushed Nicoll down, and lay on top of him, using my body to shield him from the grenade blast.

"The grenade went off, sending sharp pain from shrapnel into my legs, buttocks, and lower back and causing my head to spin and my ears to feel like they had just burst. But my gear absorbed some of the blast, and the closeness of the grenade caused much of the blast to go above me. Those two things probably saved me."

MITCHELL MAKES HIS MOVE

Mitchell knew Kasal and Nicoll were trapped in the small room on the other side of the house and he intended to get to them. As he started to cross the main room of the house the insurgent at the top of the stairs sprayed the open space with his AK. The 7.62mm slugs whacked into walls and scampered about the floor, each impact a sharp crackling explosion. Movies that have filmed such attacks simply can't capture the sound of a high-power automatic weapon on full-auto in an enclosed space. It is literally numbing. Yet Mitchell scarcely noticed.

"I had to cross that danger area—4 or 5 feet—in that middle room," he says. "An insurgent on the roof had it covered through the skylight. When I came running in he started shooting. Bullets were hitting all around me. I just remember small-arms explosions until I got into the room with Nicoll and First Sergeant."

Mitchell found Kasal facing the doorway with his pistol at the ready. "It was spooky," he says. "I ran into that room. If I remember right I had to pull Nicoll—one of them—out of the doorway a little bit. I don't think Nicoll was conscious. He slipped in and out. I could see he was hurt real bad."

Kasal was still trying to shake off the concussive effects of a grenade exploding 3 feet from his prone body. "I tried to shrug it off and get back in the fight," he says. "I was thinking that the enemy would follow it up with more or even come in after us. Then out of nowhere Mitchell came bursting into the room. He stopped in the doorway and immediately enemy fire began impacting all around him. He was immediately hit with some of the shrapnel from the exploding rounds as they hit the wall. He managed to get out of the way and joined us in the room.

"In my opinion—and I'll say this to my grave—Mitchell was the true hero that day. I did what I had to do because it's called survival and the right thing to do. I had no choice. But Mitchell voluntarily ran through enemy fire and joined us in a room that was sealed off from rescue and covered by enemy fire to try and help us. He is the true hero."

CLASSIC KASAL

Mitchell has another point of view: "Kasal was being First Sergeant Kasal. He told me, 'We need help.' He didn't sound excited or out of control; he was strictly business. He gave me a strict assessment of the situation. To me it was like getting an order from the First Sergeant when I came into the room. He told me I needed to concentrate on saving the lives of as many Marines as I could, save Nicoll, and then get the fuck out. He had control of the doorway and I knew that he was going to be fine."

So Mitchell turned his attention to Nicoll and tried to get a pressure bandage on him. "I had a hard time getting off his vest," he says. "I was having trouble using my arms.

"Then Kasal started talking to us just to keep us from blacking out while I was attending him and Nicoll. They took the brunt of that grenade. Kasal was bleeding out from his back and Nicoll was bleeding out from his leg and his stomach. I tried to help them. I thought Nicoll was going to die."

Mitchell says he has no memory of the grenade blast that sent seven pieces of shrapnel into his left leg. "I guess it happened when I was running across the main room. It was only five or six steps. Kasal asked me if I was hurt and then I saw the blood on my leg. It really didn't hurt that bad. I looked down and saw blood. I saw I was peppered with some pretty good-size pieces. My adrenaline was going strong so I didn't feel too much. Every wound I got was like that. It never hurt me until later."

All in a day's work: CAAT Platoon Marines regroup in the shade of a building that shows the scars of their onslaught.

Through backyards and blind alleys, amid rubble and ruins, Marines take the fight into the city's insurgent strongholds, rooting out the enemy.

Sgt R. J. Mitchell reacts to a sudden commotion behind him while studying a map with Lt. Jesse Grapes.

LCpl Alex Nicoll gets a moment's rest behind the shelter of a war-torn wall as the din of battle surges through the city.

Kneeling in the foreground with bayonets ready for close-quarters fighting, Nicoll (left) and Mitchell react to gunfire.

Inside the notorious "House of Hell," Marines fire through a doorway, fighting toward where Kasal and others are trapped.

Deeper into the building, one of the wounded is pulled back to safety as fellow Marines prepare to move forward.

The body of one insurgent bears silent witness to the gunfight.

Lt Jesse Grapes drops to the blood-covered floor, firing toward enemy fighters stationed overhead.

With handgun at the ready, Kasal emeges grim faced and horribly wounded. Assisting him are Christopher Marquez and Dan Schaeffer.

Marines prepare to move Nicoll from the room where he and Kasal were trapped.

After the house had been reduced to rubble, someone inside still managed to lob a grenade out at Marines, who responded with necessary final force.

Stalwart Marines prepare to press on, taking the fight to another sector, another day.

Treated at the field hospital, Kasal awaits transport to facilities where he will undergo the first of many surgeries. His leg wound reveals the devastating damage to tissue and bone.

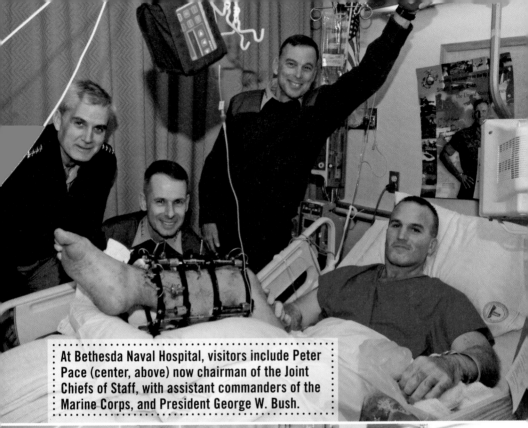

At Bethesda Naval Hospital, visitors include Peter Pace (center, above) now chairman of the Joint Chiefs of Staff, with assistant commanders of the Marine Corps, and President George W. Bush.

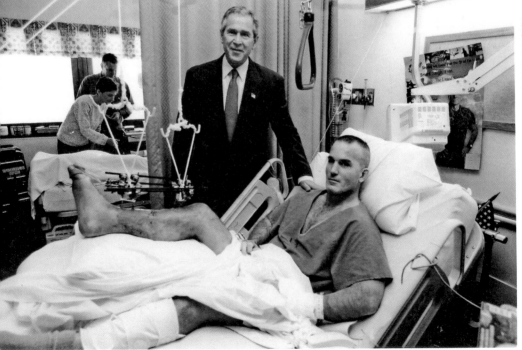

To Brad Kasal
With respect and appreciation,

Back in California at last, Kasal joins in the joyful homecoming of his Marines in January 2005.

Brothers in arms, in calmer times: GySgt Chad Wade, left; 1st Sgt Tim Ruff and 1st Sgt Wayne Hertz, below, with Hertz's young son, Mathew.

Kasal's parents, in foreground above, were present with other family to see him honored by the Iowa legislature. Kasal speaks with legislators, below.

Byron Norwood, killed on the day Kasal was injured, is never far from his thoughts.

Kasal receives the Navy Cross in formal ceremonies at Camp Pendleton, California.

Kasal's parents stand behind him as he is introduced in the Iowa State Senate, which responded with a thunderous ovation.

On the mend: Kasal enjoys time at home in Iowa with visiting relatives on his deck and with friends Linda and Jim Arslanian.

"I WASN'T GOING TO FAIL"

Even at that point Kasal was more worried about Nicoll and Mitchell than he was about himself. He was afraid they were going to bleed out and he wasn't going to be able to help them. He figured the only thing he could do was maintain his composure.

"I wasn't scared and I was never unconscious or losing consciousness," he says. He never yelled out in pain or panic, which some might credit to that classic Kasal toughness. But Kasal offers a second reason for his steely calm. "That is what leadership is," he explains simply. "If I had been screaming or hopeless, how reassuring would that have been to Nicoll?"

Besides, he adds, "I never felt hopeless as long as I had a weapon, as long as I had a bullet left, as long as I had some fight in me. Sometimes, for a second or two I thought I might not make it out because of blood loss, but I wasn't going to let that thought seep in. Nicoll's life depended on me and I wasn't going to fail."

Once Mitchell arrived Kasal was encouraged. "Mitchell, in my eyes, is not an ordinary Marine. He was an above-and-beyond NCO, so having him there gave me more reassurance because of the brotherhood of Marines, that camaraderie of Marines.

"Mitchell's first reaction upon arriving was to ask us about our wounds while ignoring his own," Kasal continues. "I told him bluntly, 'Don't worry about mine; just treat Nicoll'—as I couldn't do a very good job—'and I'll watch the door to keep the little bastards back.' Mitchell then put his full efforts into treating Nicoll as I faced the doorway.

"I knew how much punishment I could take. That is why I refused medical attention. I was determined to fight until I was dead or until all three of us were medevac'd."

Mitchell was equally unaffected by their predicament. He was more worried about a satchel charge or fragmentation grenade arriving airmail from somewhere outside the door than of dying from his shrapnel wounds. He figured that Kasal had the door, and as long as Kasal could hold a weapon nobody was going to get past him. The only way Mitchell figured anyone was going to get them while they were in the room was to either throw in a frag or rush the room and shoot them. All he could do in the meantime was sit tight and try to help.

"YOUR RIFLE AIN'T WORTH A SHIT"

Random gunfire continued even though the insurgents couldn't see the wounded Marines. But in the midst of their predicament, wounded and trapped, Mitchell actually laughed when he found out his rifle had been wrecked by an enemy bullet.

"Even though it worried me I had to laugh because the way I found out was pure Alex Nicoll," Mitchell says. "He was always making fun of a bad situation. I had been there with Kasal and Nicoll for a half hour or 45 minutes when he looks at me. He was lying on his back up against the wall. He had been floating in and out, kind of lying there with his eyes opening and then closing again. Every once in a while he would moan or sigh, something like that. He never screamed.

"Out of the blue he says, 'You know, Mitchell, your rifle ain't worth a shit.' I looked at it and there was a hole in the bolt! It was shot to shit, useless. I had to laugh. It wasn't what he said; it was the way he said it."

Finally Mitchell remembered he had a radio, a small civilian-style Motorola unit that all the squad leaders were issued to stay in communication with the platoon sergeants and platoon leaders. Up until then he had forgotten about it.

"I got on my radio, a PRC-148 about the size of a cell phone. I was on the same freq as Grapes. I let Grapes know that Kasal, Nicoll, and me were wounded and pinned down in the little room off to the left of the main entrance. I told him Nicoll was really serious and so was Kasal. I think I told Grapes there were other wounded Marines in the house but that I was unaware of their situation. Since I got in the room with Kasal and Nicoll there had been constant shooting inside the house."

ATTEMPTING A RESCUE

Mitchell's call for help galvanized Grapes and Lopez into renewed action. Along with Navy Corpsman Douglas "Doc" Williams they tried to reach the trapped men.

Lopez was ready to try anything. He says: "Me and Doc Williams dismounted. Grapes was already standing there. Doc Williams went over to treat Pruitt, who was wounded in the arm and leg. I went with Grapes to the gate outside the building and looked up on the roof and through the door. We knew there was an insurgent up there from Pruitt, but we couldn't see him because there was a foot-high wall around the edge of the roof. He could move around on the roof and we couldn't see him."

Grapes told them to get on top of a little one-story shack across the street. "We ran out in plain sight to get to the building," Lopez says. "Our adrenaline was pumping. There was shooting going on all over the place. We jumped up on the shack to see if we could get a shot at the guy on the roof. The shack had a slanted roof that didn't offer much protection and wasn't high enough for us to see anything."

The insurgents' building was taller and had a catwalk inside. "They used that catwalk to go outside and peek out around the roof," Lopez says. "We could see the roof but it was not good enough for a shot."

The rescuers knew that time was running out for the pinned-down men inside. "I wanted to find out about my missing Marines," Lopez says. "I didn't know what had happened to First Sergeant Kasal except that he was hit. He was one of the best Marines I had. He had a lot of heart and always tried harder than anybody in my section.

"About that time the QRF [quick reaction force] from 2d Platoon showed up [commanded by Lieutenant John Jacobs]. Then I heard we had a KIA [killed in action]. That is when I found out that there were also more injured inside. We knew we had to get into the building to get them out.

"Lieutenant Grapes told us to go around to the side of the building. First we went to the main entrance but we couldn't go in that way. We already knew it was covered by fire from Mitchell telling us on the radio. We went around the side of the building. Grapes tried to knock a hole in the building with a sledgehammer."

Kasal heard Grapes pounding on the wall with the sledge. Pretty soon pieces of concrete started busting loose from the inside wall and pummeling the three men trapped in the room.

"I told Lieutenant Grapes to stop," Kasal says. "Mitchell had a radio and he had a direct line with Grapes. I was relaying stuff to Mitchell who would then relay it to Grapes. At first we said, 'Yeah, try and bust a hole through the wall.' But that didn't work because debris was hitting us, so we told him to stop and try something else."

Grapes had another idea. He sent Lopez and another Marine with bolt cutters to a nearby window to cut through the bars that covered it.

"It took a little effort," Lopez says, "but we got them cut. While I was doing that Grapes and some other guys were shooting up toward the insurgents while the rest of the Marines moved up to get the casualties."

Some of the Marines were trying to force a passage through the front door. Among them was Sergeant Byron Norwood, one of the missing Marines Lopez was concerned about. Norwood had entered the foyer of the house to help out.

Before the Fallujah fight Norwood had commanded a CAAT vehicle with a .50 cal on it that Colonel Toolan used for transport.

After Toolan went home Norwood was assigned to Iscol's CAP (Combined Action Platoon), so he didn't even have to be there. He could have stayed with Iscol advising the ING, but that didn't offer enough action for the 25-year-old former trumpet player and amateur actor from Pflugerville, Texas. He kept hounding Iscol and Buhl to let him go back into combat until they relented.

Norwood had only been in the house a few moments when he poked his head around the foyer door to see what was happening. In that instant an insurgent shot him in the forehead. Norwood died instantly. The same burst that struck him also hit Wolf in the chest, knocking him out of the doorway but not hurting him badly.

At the back of the house Chandler and Severtsgard decided they had to get out of the kitchen. Chandler was bleeding and in terrible pain from his wounded leg. It was twisted around from his hip to his ankle in a spiral fracture. Despite their injuries the two Marines pried open a door panel just enough to squeeze through the opening. The effort caused Chandler to scream in agony but at last they were outside. Within seconds they got assistance from Lance Corporal Steven Tatum. For them the fight was over.

STILL TRAPPED

That still left Marines—including Kasal, Mitchell, and Nicoll—trapped in the house. Grapes and Jacobs held a powwow to come up with a plan. Grapes' first idea was to use flashbang grenades to confuse the insurgents while they crept inside to rescue the trapped Marines. That didn't work. They threw the flashbangs but the insurgents were not confused and let loose with a tremendous volley of fire.

Their next plan involved squeezing through the window Lopez had cut open. Grapes and Private Justin Boswood stripped off their gear and squeezed through. Lopez and another Marine handed them their weapons. Grapes and Boswood knew approximately where the three wounded Marines were holed up, but until they got inside the house they couldn't be sure exactly where everything was. Kasal couldn't see them either, but he knew something was going on.

"He [Grapes] wasn't able to see me because my back was to the wall. I was turned toward the door with my pistol so if anybody came through the door, I could shoot them. I heard him and Boswood right outside my door," Kasal recalls.

What Kasal heard was Boswood dragging a dead insurgent out of the doorway. When the opening was clear Grapes slid on his back into the main room with his weapon pointed up at the stairwell. Boswood knelt over him with his weapon pointed skyward. In the back bedroom window Lopez and Jacobs covered the area where the insurgents were hiding. At the same time Lance Corporal Christopher Marquez and Lance Corporal Dan Schaeffer got ready to run through the kill zone and extract the three wounded Marines. Inside the room Kasal was wondering if he was going to remain conscious. He knew he was bleeding at a prodigious rate.

"Mitchell kept up his efforts in relaying to his platoon commander our situation and giving him intel as I guarded the doorway," Kasal says. "As tough as I knew I was and as determined as I can be, thoughts would slowly creep into my head that I would not make it out due to loss of blood—or to a still-unknown enemy force next to us.

"I remember also looking down at my wounds and especially at my shattered right leg. I thought for sure I would lose it even if I made it home; my foot was pointing a different direction than my leg. But I'm a Kasal and I'm from Iowa, so I never give up.

"And then out of nowhere, again I heard Marines who I later learned to be Grapes and Boswood. They had made it to an adjacent room near our doorway and were laying down suppressive fire trying to shoot up into what I now realize was the second floor where the enemy was located."

FIRE AND RESCUE

When everybody was in position Grapes gave the order to fire. Simultaneously all the shooters opened up on the stairwell, forcing the insurgents back while Marquez and Schaeffer sprinted across the kill zone. In seconds they appeared in front of Kasal.

"As they suppressed the enemy two young Marines came storming into the room," Kasal says. "They came to pull us out and I remember the first thing I noticed about them was they weren't carrying any weapons. I also knew the only way out of there was right back through the kill zone that the enemy had covered by fire.

"As they grabbed me I kept hold of my 9mm pistol, thinking if the enemy started shooting then at least I could fire back and, hopefully, get them first. I was now worried about the two young Marines who were helping me. Still under the suppressive fire laid down by Grapes and Boswood, the two young Marines and I started across the room and toward the outside door. Due to the enemy being pinned down we were able to make it without incident."

When they came out the door Lucian Read snapped his now famous picture.

After recovering Kasal the two young Marines made two more trips to bring out Mitchell and Nicoll. That left Sanchez, Rodriguez, and Carlisle still in the back room. Corporal Jensen, having completed bandaging Weemer, came up with a plan to get them out. He attached a long chain to a Humvee and pulled the bars off the back bedroom window to give them an escape route. As soon as the window was clear Sanchez and Rodriguez passed Carlisle's unconscious form through the window, then bailed out through it themselves. Once they were clear Boswood and Grapes made a firing retreat out of the main room. For the moment the insurgents had the house to themselves.

MEDEVAC

The two young Marines cleared the door and set Kasal down on the outside steps where Doc Williams, a Navy corpsman, and Lopez from Weapons Co., along with other Marines grabbed him and laid him in the back of a Humvee to be evacuated. He was placed into the Humvee next to Chandler, who also was wounded, and they were rushed to the Battalion Aid Station outside the city.

Lopez ran around to the front of the house after Kasal and the others were rescued. There he saw his friend Byron Norwood being carried out on a poncho.

"I didn't recognize him when they pulled him outside the courtyard. I knelt right down beside him and looked at him," Lopez says. "I am never going to forget him."

Weemer was also evacuated but not until later. "I tried four or five times to get back in the fight," he says. "I knew I wasn't going to die. Doc Edora, who had also treated Eldridge, came by to check me out. Later he would work on Nicoll and Carlisle. After that he just sat around watching the war swirl around him until the fight was over. Then he helped with the casualties.

"Once we finally got Carlisle and Nicoll, they pulled Norwood out. I helped put him in the back of the Humvee. Then I got in the back with Norwood. There were three or four vehicles full of casualties. When we got everybody loaded we took off."

Mitchell was in on exploding the house. "I didn't go back to the BAS until two hours later," he says. "One of the docs gave me a Percocet and I went back to the firm base. It was still in the mansion. We all went back there after everybody else was medevac'd and we blew up the house. We had so many casualties. We had 11 people from Kilo hit, and Norwood was killed. I had stuff to do—accountability for weapons, personnel equipment, gear that was lost.

"I told Grapes I had work to do. He said I didn't and that I had done enough and needed to go to the BAS. When I got there I got a shot of morphine. They sent me to Bravo Surgical Team and then I went home. I had been wounded four times.

"I always thought three Purple Hearts was an automatic ticket home. That ain't true. I got to go home but not because I had the Hearts but because I was hurt bad enough."

Grapes was appalled by the casualties. He said the confrontation at the House of Hell changed the way Kilo, 3/1 cleared houses in Fallujah for the rest of the battle.

"As it turned out my platoon had suffered the most casualties of any platoon in my company," Grapes says. "Our platoon lost its combat effectiveness due to casualties. After that we never entered a house until we threw something in it that exploded."

"SIR, I FOUND SOME TROUBLE"

Even as he was being transported, Kasal was still testy and full of fight. He was worried more about his men. He still didn't know how many casualties there were, but he knew it was a substantial number. He already knew about Norwood and he could see many of the men from Kilo being medevac'd out to the BAS at the same time he was transported.

"There I was given my first shot of morphine and medical treatment," Kasal says. "Throughout the entire process from beginning to end, I never lost consciousness despite the wounds and severe blood loss. I forced myself to stay awake as I knew a Marine's survival and my own depended on it.

"My adrenaline was still flowing when I got to the BAS. Until I knew that all the other Marines were safe and made it I didn't let my guard down. Once I found out that everybody else was out and everybody else was safe, and medevac'd, and going to be okay, then I finally let my guard down. Then I finally let them take my weapons off me, take my gear, and put morphine in me. Even back in the BAS I didn't part with my 9mm until all that happened.

"Two days before I was wounded I ran into Lieutenant Colonel Buhl in the center of Fallujah, and he asked me if I was 'staying out of trouble.' I told him 'of course.' The next time I talked to Lieutenant Colonel Buhl I was lying bloody on the stretcher, and he asked me what happened. 'Sir,' I replied, 'I found some trouble.'"

CHAPTER 16
★ ★ ★

RECOVERY AND RECOGNITION

Kasal reportedly lost more than half of his blood before he arrived at the Battalion Aid Station in the Fallujah train depot. He and Chandler made the trip to the BAS in the back of a Humvee on a mad, 20-minute dash through the still-dangerous city streets.

Nicoll, near death and floating in and out of consciousness, was in another Humvee in the same convoy. He couldn't have known at the time that one Marine was dead and 10 more were wounded in the 90-minute clash.

Doctors assessing his wounds were afraid Nicoll might end up the second KIA of the fight. He was gut shot, had fractured ribs, and shrapnel had cracked his spine and punctured a lung. At the very least he was going to lose his lower left leg.

The rest of Kilo continued fighting for another week with a dangerous glint in their eyes. It was an unfortunate insurgent that encountered Kilo's Marines after the House of Hell, Grapes says. Before they were finished with their fight a week later, more than 1,000 Iraqis in 3/1's area of operations would die.

Weapons Co. continued operating effectively without Kasal's personal stamp, probably the highest compliment a leader can be paid. Even so, the men missed their First Sergeant. He had been the Weapons Co.'s center of balance. Wade was made temporary First Sergeant and did a fine job. 3/1's battle continued unabated until the mission at Fallujah was accomplished. No one in the Marine Corps is indispensable. Not even Kasal.

AT THE BAS

While the remainder of 3/1's Grunts were taking Fallujah, other Marines had transformed the hulking train station into the nerve center of the Thundering Third. It had its own air force of miniature spy planes, an intelligence headquarters, a logistics base, a control tower that talked to dozens of airplanes and helicopters moving through its air space, an aerial medical evacuation facility, and a variety of weapons experts, artillerymen, and engineering specialists advancing the war in a dozen deadly ways.

Most important the complex was home to a mini hospital called the 3/1 Battalion Aid Station, overseen by two very young doctors grandly called battalion surgeons. They were aided by a score of Navy corpsmen under a grizzled chief hospital corpsman named Pete Dominquez and collectively had more practical experience in emergency medicine than a division of civilian technicians working in Level One trauma centers in the United States. If someone had to be shot or blown up, BAS was the place to be.

Kasal arrived still wearing his gear and still armed with his 9mm pistol. The people who saw him first remember he was a bit pugnacious, not ready to give up his gear before he knew his Marines were safe. Kasal hadn't accepted any pain medication yet; he wanted to remain alert. He remembers the pain in his leg as manageable, although the lower limb was nearly severed.

Kasal was still up on his elbows looking around, gruffly refusing entreaties to lie back and take it easy when they put him on an examining table.

Twenty-nine-year-old Lieutenant Commander Robert Sobehart was the battalion surgeon who initially treated Kasal. Six months before, he had been an intern in Pittsburgh, Pennsylvania. As a football player and medical student at the University of Dayton, Sobehart had wanted more out of medicine than a standard progression. Through the recruiting program, he'd heard about Marine Corps medicine from the other battalion surgeon—another 29-year-old, Lieutenant Commander Matthew Shepherd, the senior doctor in 3/1. Shepherd had been practicing medicine an entire year. It was more than a coincidence that Shepherd and Sobehart found themselves together on the outskirts of Fallujah treating grievously wounded Marines.

Both doctors relished serving in the military. Shepherd's dad was a retired Marine Corps staff sergeant and Vietnam veteran who passed on his reverence for the Corps to his son. Sobehart wanted to enter Navy medicine so he could be a flight surgeon, the glamorous arm of naval medicine, or a general medical officer. Either avenue would allow him to practice the kind of medicine he was looking for. But first he had to pay his dues.

Before taking on their new responsibilities the two doctors received a few weeks of orientation into Marine Corps medicine followed by a week of orientation in Iraq. Then they were elevated to the final authority on medicine within the 3/1. Shepherd had more field training than Sobehart because he had deployed with 3/1 stateside so he could see how Marines worked during training exercises.

In the course of the Fallujah fight the two men treated dozens of casualties a day. According to Sobehart, nothing in civilian medicine is comparable to what doctors in Iraq routinely experience. At the civilian hospital where Sobehart is now training, for example, the busiest day ever has been 17 admissions. In Iraq, he says, "by the end of the first week, we had seen over 250 cases.

"By the end of our first four days in Iraq it was as bloody as bloody can get. You get a little used to that. Chief Dominquez told me Kasal was one of the casualties," Sobehart says. The doctors knew all the first sergeants from battalion meetings, and among them, Kasal stood out. "Kasal was not as intrusive as some of the other first sergeants. He was the quintessential Marine.

"I knew it had been more than an hour before they made it to the BAS. That made him unusual because most of the time the casualties were pulled out of the cities immediately. He came in with about eight or 10 other Marines.

"His only concern was how the rest of his men were doing. He insisted we care for the other men before we treated him. That wasn't possible. We needed to get a tourniquet on him. After we did that most of the arterial bleeding stopped. He lost about 4 inches of bone in the tibia." He also had severe blood loss and many other wounds.

It was obvious to the doctors that amputation was a distinct possibility. "He had a gaping hole in his leg," Sobehart says. "We had another officer with a similar injury who didn't want to go through the years of surgery and recovery; he allowed his leg to be amputated."

Kasal was at the BAS just long enough for the medics to get him stabilized, relieve some pain, and put dressings on his many wounds to protect them from infection. That is what Battalion Aid Stations do, and they do it well. Almost all the Marines who made it to the BAS survived. Without it many more would have died.

PUC Gallogly, wearing pants this time, arranged Kasal's evacuation from the BAS. "When Kasal was evacuated, it was an urgent," PUC says. "We had quite a few casualties at once—eight or 10 urgents if I remember correctly—and we had just started coordinating it. Urgents are Marines who will die within 20 minutes. The pilots did a great job. I would have the helo inbound while the corpsmen were stabilizing the wounded Marines."

Dominquez was in charge of stabilizing the urgents after the Humvees and armored ambulances skidded to a halt. "That man saved dozens and dozens of lives," PUC says. "He had been in the Corps as long as Kasal had. He was phenomenal. I would tell him urgents are coming—head wounds, IED injuries, whatever it was—and Dominquez would be ready for them."

CAMP TQ

Within two hours of being wounded Kasal was in a helicopter headed for "Camp TQ"—Al Taqaddum Air Base—about 74 kilometers west of Baghdad. At the field Naval hospital he had the first of more than 20 surgeries and dozens of painful procedures he would endure over the next year.

Lieutenant Commander (LCDR) Paul J. Girard, the orthopedic surgeon who later treated Kasal at Balboa Naval Hospital in San Diego, says the doctors at Camp TQ focused on saving the leg. "There was no concern over the blood supply, no blood pressure issues, no absolute reason to take his leg off," Girard says. "He was stable. They were able get a temporary fixator on his leg— something very simple intended to stabilize his wounds."

Kasal was relieved to learn he still had a chance to stay intact. "Up to that point I thought I was going to lose my leg for sure," he says. "The doctor who looked at it said he thought I was going to get to keep my leg because I was still getting blood flow to my foot even though it was just hanging there by flesh." On the evening of the 13th he was flown from Camp TQ to Balad Air Force Base north of Baghdad where he spent the night in a field hospital before being flown to Germany.

On the 14th, Kasal was put on an Air Force C-17 evacuation flight bound for Germany. The plane was filled with Marines and soldiers too severely wounded to recover inside Iraq.

Kasal certainly qualified. His right leg was nearly severed from his body by gunshot wounds. His buttocks were perforated by both shrapnel and bullet holes, including three lacerations approximately ½ inch wide, 3 to 4 inches long, and 2 inches deep. The back of his legs, buttocks, lower back, groin, and arms were also filled with shrapnel holes. Doctors eventually determined that Kasal had seven gunshot wounds and 44 shrapnel wounds.

BACK IN THE USA

On November 18 Kasal arrived at Bethesda Naval Hospital in Maryland, where he would spend the next two months as a patient in Ward 5C. From his admittance until just before Christmas, Kasal says he was pretty much "out of it" from pain medications. He was enduring surgery every other day to clean out his wounds. There were a few days, however, that he does remember—such as the time his family came to see him for the first time since he had been wounded.

On November 23, Kasal's family—Mom, Dad, and brothers Randy, Kelly, and Kevin—came to visit. "They stayed until Thanksgiving Day before they had to return home. It was good to see family and it gave me a respite from the hospital life.

"My little brother, Kevin, I remember, was heavily focused on a piece of shrapnel in my right foot that was working its way back to the surface. It was just under the skin so I let him dig it out, much as you would a splinter. He kept it as a souvenir and I looked at it as one less piece of shrapnel in my body."

His father, Gerald Kasal, remembered the visit just as vividly. He had been terribly worried about Brad since the Marines notified him of Brad's injuries. He notified the local papers that Brad was wounded and received many concerned telephone calls from his relatives and Brad's childhood friends. When Lucian Read's famous picture showed up on the front page of the *Omaha-World Herald* and the *Des Moines Register*, the Kasal home was flooded with more calls. When Gerald actually got to see Brad for the first time, he was relieved to see that his son did not look as bad as he had imagined.

"He was a little pale and looked thinner, but he didn't look too bad except for his leg," Gerald recalled. "He was very quiet. He was pretty drugged up from the pain medications they had given him, but he wasn't completely out of it. He just seemed very tired. He even joked around some, especially when Kevin was fooling with his foot."

Gerald added a father's emphasis to a sentiment shared by many back home: "I am very proud of him."

After his family left Thanksgiving Day, Kasal didn't do any feasting. He was in the operating room before dinner was served. When he came to the ward dinner was over and he was receiving a celebrity visitor.

FAMOUS GUESTS

"That afternoon, Arnold Schwarzenegger and his family came to the hospital to visit all the wounded Marines and sailors," Kasal recalls. "I remember thinking very highly of Mr. Schwarzenegger, that he spent his Thanksgiving at the hospital with us."

During the holidays a number of famous people came to visit America's wounded warriors at Bethesda. It was a thrill for Kasal and all the patients they visited. Despite their fame and status Kasal found these people to be warm, friendly visitors who genuinely cared for the wounded veterans.

"From the time I arrived to the hospital on November 18th and through New Year's 2005, we were flooded with support," Kasal says. "I want to thank all the people who spent their free time and even their holidays to come and visit the other wounded Marines and me. We had celebrities from Arnold Schwarzenegger to Cher, Hilary Duff, Donald Rumsfeld, Brian Dennehy, ZZ Top, the cast from *The Sopranos*, and many, many more. But it was the everyday, average people who really were the best. People just came to show their support and I will always remember them."

Still the most memorable visitor to Kasal's bedside was President George W. Bush. He came to visit quietly and without fanfare during December when the patients at Bethesda were feeling their bluest. Many of their families were far away and even Kasal had to resist the urge to feel down about his situation. The president's visit went a long way to lift his waning spirits.

"There was a certain aura about him," Kasal says. "And the first thing he did was show leadership right off the bat. I had a roommate at that time who was a junior-ranking Marine. He was also severely wounded but my bed was closest to the door. Yet President Bush did what any good leader would do and walked past me stating, 'I'll get to you next, First Sergeant,' and he went first to the junior Marine.

"He spent about five minutes with the young Marine and then came to me. He also spent five minutes with me, making a joke, asking me how I was doing, and wishing me well. Two things I will always remember about his visit are his deep sincerity and the fact he did not come into the room with an entourage.

"I was expecting reporters and people in suits and a big crowd with him. I'm sure they were around. But President Bush came into the room with just himself and his photographer to take a picture with each Marine to send to the families and one close personal friend. I've been a leader at various levels for over half my life, and I sensed nothing but leadership and sincerity from the president that day."

All that time Kasal really missed the men in his battalion and felt as if he should be with them. The feeling was mutual: Lopez and the other staff NCOs from Weapons Co. still in Iraq were just as anxious to talk to Kasal. Things just weren't the same without him, Lopez says.

"I remember when we evacuated him, he talked to Major Rob Belknap on the telephone. Belknap assured him that everything was going to be good and that we would stay in touch. After he went back to the States, to Bethesda, all the staff NCOs got on the satellite phone, and we all called him. He wasn't feeling sorry for himself; he wanted to know about his Marines. We got a new first sergeant eventually, but it wasn't First Sergeant Kasal."

TREATMENT OR TORTURE?

December was memorable for another reason as well. That's when Kasal was fitted with a diabolical-looking contraption called an Ilizarov frame. Dr. Girard says the Ilizarov frame, named after the Russian orthopedic surgeon who invented it, has helped mend millions of broken and deformed legs. The device is also horribly painful and ungainly, especially when the patient has a hole in his leg big enough to put both hands in.

That's a memory Kasal can't shake: "The orthopedic surgeon came into the room and started taking these big metal rings and holding them up against my leg. I asked him, 'What the hell is that?' He said, 'This is what's going to go on your leg.'" Kasal's leg still had the fixator that had been installed in Iraq. He couldn't imagine this new device taking its place.

On about December 7 doctors used a skin graft from Kasal's hip to mend some of the gaping wound on his leg. "It closed up some of the hole; then they were able to sew the rest of the wound together," he says. "A couple of days after that they took my metal fixator off and put the Ilizarov frame on."

A 4-inch piece of donor bone was used to replace the bone in his lower leg that had been shattered beyond repair. The eight metal rings of the Ilizarov frame attached to the bone sections by rods, wires, and screws to hold the pieces together. Steel rods similar to bicycle spokes were drilled into both ends of his tibia and into a bone graft the surgeons hoped would grow between them. The screws were adjusted one turn every day while the bone was healing to obtain the required length and shape.

"The fact that he had a large soft-tissue wound made the procedure more complicated," Girard says. "It speaks a lot to his strength of character. Most people would not be able to endure this treatment. Kasal was able to see far enough down the street to see it ultimately helping him."

Not that Kasal actually embraced the device. After the surgeons finished the installation he had plenty of questions about the bizarre contraption.

"My first question was 'How am I going to drive?' Kasal says. "He replied, 'You don't!' 'How am I going to go to the gym?' 'You don't!' 'How am I going to do this?' 'You don't!' Everything I came up with that was normal to me, he said, 'You don't!'"

In addition most of the doctors Kasal spoke with told him he would probably be wearing the contraption for 12 to 18 months. It was very disheartening news, Kasal recalls.

"During my recovery phase I had a second opinion from a civilian doctor. She didn't recommend that procedure. She told me to amputate but that I would never run again." In true Kasal fashion, he says, "I didn't want to accept that. I had to try."

Kasal continues: "I said there was no driving, no this, no that. How was I going to survive? I live alone; I am single, blah, blah, blah. My main orthopedic surgeon was more optimistic; he said he thought it would be off by April. At the time that sounded good to me, but it wasn't going to come true."

As difficult and painful as the wounds and surgeries were, Kasal says they were nothing compared to the long road of recovery. "I'm a warrior and a very independent person," he says, "but just like that, in the blink of an eye, my whole world changed forever.

One minute I was as strong and hardy as they get, and in a split second I was a bloody, broken mess."

FIERCELY INDEPENDENT

His fierce independence and pride would sometimes jeopardize his recovery. But ultimately he credits those traits for helping him fight back—against indignities as well as against the effects of his wounds.

"Many times before I was wounded I used to joke that if I ever became injured or sick I'd try to maintain as much of my dignity as I could," he says. "And one thing I swore I'd never do was to use a bedpan or have someone else helping me with the bathroom. But suddenly there I was, lying in a field hospital—a bloody and broken person with one leg hanging by flesh and gaping wounds in my backside. I still got up on crutches and used the bathroom on my own. And I kept doing that even throughout my long hospitalization at Bethesda Naval Medical Center."

Even right after a surgery, Kasal would hobble into the bathroom on his own, leaving the lights out so the nurses wouldn't know. "They had given me direct orders to never get out of bed on my own," he says. Of course whenever the nurse came in and saw his empty bed, it was obvious there was only one place he could be. "So I'd hear this knock on the door followed by stern warnings to never do it again," he says. "As painful as this was, my own sense of dignity and pride were more important to me. You can break a Marine's body but never his spirit."

The severity of his wounds forced Kasal to accept treatments that tore at his pride. The lacerations across his back and buttocks were too deep to simply stitch shut at the surface. So each day Kasal had to roll over as a nurse came and packed his wounds with gauze. He had to endure this treatment daily or every other day for about five months before the wounds finally healed enough to need no further dressings.

"There's not much dignity in this procedure," he says.

But Kasal insisted on doing as much for himself as was possible, often to the chagrin of the nurses whom he appreciated and respected. "I felt the only way I was going to get better was to keep my spirit and be as strong as I could," he explains. "I figured I had two choices: be stubborn and do everything I could to get back to health or give up and let the grim outlook come true. I chose to fight."

His motivation was as direct as an order: "I wanted my life back," he says simply. "I wanted my Marines back. And no matter what it took I was going to win.

"I'd take the pain of the wounds and the many surgeries any day over the emotional pain I was feeling about being away from my Marines and from doing what I loved most, which was leading Marines. My body may have been broken, but it was nothing compared to the pain I felt in my heart from not being with my Marines. I actually felt guilty lying there in the hospital."

A WHEELCHAIR FOR CHRISTMAS

Kasal spent the holidays laid up in his room at Bethesda. But after a month of every-other-day surgeries, just days before Christmas, he was finally able to get out of bed and use a wheelchair for an hour or two at a time.

"That brought my spirits up tremendously," he says. He used his new mobility to visit with young Marines recuperating in rooms nearby. "Seeing and talking with them made me feel like a leader again," Kasal says. "That was a great help.

"I would even go get them food if they were unable to get out of bed. Every day for the next month I went from room to room to reassure them, talk to them, and just ask how they were. This was my best time."

Christmas was still a rough ordeal emotionally. By then he had been hospitalized for 42 days and was still mostly bedridden. An hour or two of mobility each day couldn't get Brad Kasal where he needed to be.

"I only wanted to be one place that Christmas," he says, "and that was back in Iraq with my Marines. They were still over there spending their Christmas engaged with the enemy and away from their families. That was the only place I wanted to be, and it was tearing me up that I couldn't be with them."

But there was no escaping Christmas. Holiday decorations were everywhere and Christmas scenes were on every television set. And the images only reminded Kasal of his far-off Marines.

"There was no place to forget," he says, "only to think. And it was the worst place to be."

In early January Kasal got word that his unit was going to be coming home at the end of the month. "All I wanted was to be there to see them home," he says. "I kept telling my doctor, Commander McGuigan, that he had to get me out of there and back home to Camp Pendleton by the end of January or I would push my bed out of the hospital myself and find a way home!"

The medical team responded to Kasal's determination. On January 22, he was cleared to go home. Follow-up hospitalizations and surgeries would be at Balboa Naval Hospital in San Diego. "As anxious as I was to leave," Kasal says, "I also felt a tinge of sadness as I had grown very close to the nurses and staff at Bethesda and realized how much I would miss them. They were truly committed to their jobs and cared greatly for each patient. I will forever be grateful for their care."

On at least one occasion, however, he had been able to take care of them as well. "I became very loyal to my nurses and corpsmen," he says. "I remember one instance in particular where I had an older roommate who was having a kidney stone removed. Being right next to him for two days, I heard every piece of advice the nurses gave him. It was all right on. And I saw the patient ignore them and not follow their advice. On the third night of his stay he started complaining very loudly to the nurse on deck about pain and the inability to go to the bathroom. His complaining started about 11 and continued until around 2:30 in the morning.

"Each time he got worse and louder, and each time the nurse tried to remain polite and professional with him, giving him instructions that he had to drink water and other things he failed to do, which were causing all his symptoms. I saw how rude and mean he was being to the nurse each time and how professional yet frustrated and rattled the nurse was becoming. Plus the rude patient was keeping me awake with his consistent whining. So I politely asked the nurse to leave and close the door behind her. She did, and once the door was closed, I grabbed my crutches, painfully got out of bed, and walked over to my roommate's bed.

"I pointed my crutch at him and said, 'Listen to the nurse. She's right. And if I hear one more peep out of you the rest of this night, I'm going to shove this crutch up your ass and give you some real pain to complain about.'

"With that said, I got back into bed and fell asleep. I never heard one more word from him the rest of the night, and he quietly got up the next morning and left to go home without a word." Kasal pauses. "Those were my nurses, and nobody gives them a hard time."

FRIENDS AND COMRADES

After more than three months in Maryland the day finally arrived for Kasal to return to his home in California. On January 22, 2005, he began a two-day journey aboard an Air Force medevac flight. The first night he landed at Travis Air Force Base and spent the night there. Early the next morning he left Travis for Marine Corps Air Station North Island, followed by a short ambulance ride to Naval Hospital Camp Pendleton (NHCP).

"When I arrived at NHCP the first thing I saw when I pulled up and they opened the doors was a welcoming party," Kasal says. "There were a whole bunch of my former Marines who had been wounded and were sent home early waiting for me. They found out I was being flown in and they all showed up at the hospital.

"That was pretty emotional and touching. It was kind of overwhelming because that was the first time I had seen any of them since I got wounded."

After getting a quick physical and a careful examination of his leg, Kasal was discharged to go home. As eager as he had been to return home, he realized that his physical needs and his pride were going to make for a difficult transition to recovery in California, where he would have to rely on the help of friends.

"Again, being as independent as I am, it was very hard for me to ask for or accept help," he says.

Since his high school days, Kasal had always seen himself as the helper or the protector. "I'd help any way any time but never asked for help. And now I realized I'd have to become almost reliant on others. It would be a long time before I could drive, run errands, cook, or even clean my own house. That was the hardest part, having everything you know stripped away from you.

"Fortunately I was blessed with so many friends, fellow Marines, and volunteers who for the next 14 months did everything I was unable to do. Of course, I'd still try to do anything I could possibly do on my own. And sometimes friends would give me an ear full, telling me I was risking my health and to just let them do it. What they didn't understand was how my health actually depended on my taking these risks. Anything I could do for myself, even if small, helped me feel like I was getting back to normal."

Dr. Girard was assigned to treat Kasal after he settled into his new life as an outpatient at the Balboa Naval Hospital. Navy doctors like Girard specialize in making wounded service members whole again, but it is a tough environment for both the patients and the doctors. For Girard it is never an easy task to treat otherwise healthy young men who have gone from being perfectly normal to permanently injured in the blink of an eye. "Unfortunately," he says, "it is getting a little easier now. The only way that you see these injuries are in wartime. They are only associated with military rifles and blast injuries. At the beginning of the war it was a little more startling. My colleagues and I—and Navy medicine as a whole—are on the forefront of treating these kinds of injuries."

Before Dr. Girard could move forward with his plan for treatment, he had to make sure Kasal understood the tremendous hurdles he would have to climb over just to keep his leg, much less stay in the Marine Corps.

"From the beginning he understood that pain was going to be a big part of his life," Girard says. "He had been on pain medication until he got out of Bethesda. After that he was trying to step that down so he could be more and more lucid. It is unusual for people to do this if you look at the population as a whole. But for the part of the population Brad is in, it is less unusual than it is in the civilian sector. Trying to get off medication is a common thread to folks like him."

A MODEL FOR OTHERS

Girard sees Kasal as a model for other severely injured patients. "How he has dealt with this shows his tremendous strength of character," the doctor says. "I use his story a lot when I meet these guys. I use him and some other Marines of equal caliber as examples that people can get better."

Kasal's public strength of character was sometimes clouded by his secret reservations about what lay ahead for him and many other Marines who had suffered similar fates.

"I didn't know if I was fighting a battle to lose," he concedes. "The doctors talked to me about amputation. They told me, 'If you amputate we can have you back running in six weeks.' I would always second-guess and wonder if I should just do that. My whole life consisted of fear of the unknown and second-guessing. Should I get it over with and just amputate?"

Girard said the ghosts that secretly haunted Kasal and other wounded warriors during their odyssey of pain are not unusual among men struck down by debilitating injuries in their prime.

"These young men—strong, healthy go-getters—are injured in an instant and their life is changed," he says. "They don't have any time to accommodate or get used to what is going on. Their expectations are naturally very, very high. They want to get back to right where they were a split second before they were shot. Generally it is not realistic."

Realistic or not, Kasal was determined to regain his independence, his strength, and his career. But for the next 14 months he would have to rely on friends and volunteers for almost everything he needed. They shopped for him, drove him to appointments, cleaned his house, helped with his laundry, and did myriad other tasks he simply could not do himself. It was both a gratifying and humbling experience for a proud, self-reliant Marine.

Some of his helpful friends were his comrades-at-arms from Iraq. Wade helped a lot, as did Mortimer and his wife, Chris; Fox and his wife, Sarah; Lopez; and a large group of civilians who volunteered to help Kasal and other wounded Marines who were flooding into Southern California from the combat zones and needing special personal care the Marine Corps could not provide.

Among these volunteers was Lou Palermo, a former airline flight attendant and museum worker who just wanted to meet a real Marine; Ed Sparks, a retired Navy chief; Geoff and Clyrinda Milke; and Jim Arslanian, a retired Massachusetts cop and one-time sailor, and his wife, Linda. They all remain close friends and often visit each other. Linda still likes to cook for Kasal. He and Jim share sea stories, conversation about books, and all the other things that make Kasal such an interesting man.

BATTLING DOUBTS

Recovery brought a series of new challenges into the life of Brad Kasal, including doubt and depression. "A lot of the depression was caused because I had always been independent and now all of a sudden I could hardly do anything for myself," he says. "I was used to being active—skiing, mountain climbing, running, camping, scuba diving, just always on the go. Now all of a sudden my life consists of watching TV, playing video games, and watching movies. I was in constant pain and everything else, so depression was a big factor that would kick in sometimes."

A lot of that depression was caused by fear of the unknown, Kasal says: "For most common injuries, the doctors can tell you what to expect. If you tear your ACL, for example, doctors can predict what you'll experience and how you'll recover. But my injuries were so severe and uncommon that it was mostly guess work. And none of the guessing was promising.

"Throughout my long and painful recovery, every doctor said that I'd never run again, that I would walk but with a cane, and I'd never be normal again. And that was their good news! I got numerous recommendations to amputate my leg and get on with my life. But I chose to gut it out. I chose to fight and prove everyone wrong.

"But sometimes doubt and fear would set in, followed by depression. And sometimes I wished I would have died back in that house on November 13th. At least then I would have gone with dignity and honor rather than wasting away in a bed and relying on others for even the simplest of tasks.

"And I'd wonder: What if the doctors are right? What if I will never be normal again? What if I'm enduring this long, painful process just to fail in the end and have them be right? I wondered if maybe I should just amputate and get it over with.

"Then as quickly as the doubt crept in, I'd dismiss it, bite down, and just get more determined. And I'd do something, anything, to try to make myself better. Even if all I could do was grab the phone book and curl it in bed to get stronger in some way."

Doubt and fear of the unknown are powerful enemies, Kasal says, but in the end the heart is an even more powerful force. "I became determined to get my life back and get back into uniform, no matter what it took. I had never failed anything before and I wasn't going to fail now with so much at stake. "

Still, progress came slowly, one goal at a time. Kasal was in a hospital bed for 14 months unable to lie flat on his back or on his side. He had to lie with his head and legs constantly elevated. "When I was finally able to lay in a normal bed for the first time, it was like heaven," he says. "At 15 months I drove for the first time and after 17 months I finally walked without a crutch or cane."

And after 18 months of misery and indignity, Kasal dared to challenge himself and challenge what every doctor had said he could never do: run. "I wanted to try to run just 50 feet to see if I could do it," he says. "But I wanted to do it in privacy, because I was embarrassed about my condition."

He sought out an empty parking lot behind a Kmart store. With a bad foot and grim determination, Kasal charged forward. "I made it for five minutes of a kind of shuffling run," he says. "It was such an awesome feeling. It was just 50 feet, but I had come so far! Being able to shuffle for five minutes after what I went through felt like completing a marathon."

Since then Kasal has kept pushing. And on November 9, 2006—almost two years to the day from when he was wounded— he ran a Marine Corps physical fitness test consisting of a 3-mile run, pull-ups, and crunches! Kasal not only passed but earned a first-class score.

His doctor urged him not to run, warning that he would risk further setbacks and long-term degeneration of his damaged leg. Kasal feels he had no choice: "To me it's about having that sense of normalcy back. And now that I'm back in uniform and once again leading Marines, it's also about setting an example."

Impressions can be misleading, however. Most people who see him get the impression that he's almost back to 100 percent. "In reality I'm about 40 percent of what I used to be," he confides. His pride and legendary toughness help him hide most of the difficulties, and he refuses to show pain or even discomfort.

"Some may call that macho or stubborn," he admits, "but it's just a way of accepting and dealing with my injuries and moving on—and trying to be as normal as I can.

"The truth is, I will always have pain, limited use of my right leg, and a limp. My ankle doesn't move and I can't lift my right foot. The circulation is bad in my lower leg due to the trauma and loss of veins, which causes swelling and discomfort. I get frequent migraines from the concussion and effects of the blast, and my hearing is shot."

Kasal is quick to add, however: "As bad as things may seem, they could always be worse; for more than a year the outlook was that I would never recover to the level I have."

Beyond that, Kasal has adopted a wait-and-see attitude for the time being. "I have to wait for the next couple of years to pass so I can find out if I will be able to deploy again," he says hopefully. "I want to be able to return to the operating forces."

That goal requires a return to full mobility if not full strength. Yet Kasal is determined to get back to combat duty with his beloved Corps. "I won't stay in unless I am capable of being deployed like any other Marine," he insists. "I've got two years to find out." At the time of this writing, he is overseeing Marine Corps recruiting efforts in the upper midwest, based in his home state of Iowa.

Dr. Girard thinks that Kasal may be an exception to the unkind fate that befalls many such men and women who have been injured so severely. Even so, Girard worries that Kasal will never reach the pinnacle of fitness he occupied before he was shot down at Fallujah. The human body simply doesn't make exceptions for people no matter how hard they try. If Kasal succeeds he will have beaten all the odds.

"He has done extremely well," Girard says. "But for him to be able to return to what he was doing before he was injured—as far as the running and wearing packs and leading people and doing what he was doing—is probably unrealistic. It is hard to imagine that on that leg, that ankle, and that foot he is going to be able to do what he did before."

Kasal isn't so sure. It is against his nature to give up and he doesn't intend to start now.

"I am not yet back to what I used to be, but it is better now. I am going for 100 percent. That is my goal. Will I get there? Who knows? Nobody thought I would get this far, so who is to say I won't get to 100 percent eventually? What I tell young Marines or soldiers or anyone else in this situation is this:

• "One, do not be afraid to ask for help because there are a lot of people out there who want to help.

• "Two, don't be afraid to talk about what you are thinking and doing because depression is going to set in no matter how strong you are. It happens to everyone at some point. It may be for 10 minutes or it may be for 10 days, or it may be the whole process. But everybody is going to get depressed sometime. Don't think you are abnormal for that; talk to somebody.

• "Three, listen to what the doctors tell you, but know that it is all on you also. You are going to succeed or fail based on your own willpower. How bad you want it is going to dictate how much you get back. Whether you will ever be back to 100 percent, who knows? But how good you want to get depends on you."

RECOGNITION

On May 1, 2006, in a ceremony at Camp Pendleton, Brad Kasal stood at rigid attention in front of his beloved 3/1 Marines while Major General Michael R. Lehnert, Commanding General of Marine Corps Installations West, awarded him the Navy Cross. It is the nation's second-highest decoration, behind only the Medal of Honor, and as of this writing, only 14 Navy Crosses have been awarded for heroism since the end of the Vietnam War.

Attending the ceremony were the 1st Marine Division's past and present commanding generals, Lieutenant General James N. Mattis and Major General Richard F. Natonski, the architects of the campaign leading to Fallujah. Their presence alone was high praise indeed.

Kasal's citation is brief and to the point—the way he likes things, he says. It reads:

The President of the United States takes pleasure in presenting the Navy Cross to First Sergeant Bradley A. Kasal, United States Marine Corps, for service as set forth in the following citation:

For extraordinary heroism while serving as First Sergeant, Weapons Company, 3d Battalion, 1st Marine Regiment, Regimental Combat Team 1, 1st Marine Division, I Marine Expeditionary Force, U.S. Marine Corps Forces Central Command in support of Operation IRAQI FREEDOM on 13 November 2004.

First Sergeant Kasal was assisting 1st Section, Combined Anti-Armor Platoon as they provided a traveling overwatch for 3d Platoon when he heard a large volume of fire erupt to his immediate front, shortly followed by Marines rapidly exiting a structure. When First Sergeant Kasal learned that Marines were pinned down inside the house by an unknown number of enemy personnel, he joined a squad making entry to clear the structure and rescue the Marines inside.

He made entry into the first room, immediately encountering and eliminating an enemy insurgent, as he spotted a wounded Marine in the next room. While moving towards the wounded Marine Sergeant Kasal and another Marine came under heavy rifle fire from an elevated enemy firing position and were both severely wounded in the legs, immobilizing them. When insurgents threw grenades in an attempt to eliminate the wounded Marines, he rolled on top of his fellow Marine and absorbed the shrapnel with his own body.

When First Sergeant Kasal was offered medical attention and extraction, he refused until the other Marines were given medical attention. Although severely wounded himself, he shouted encouragement to his fellow Marines as they continued to clear the structure.

By his bold leadership, wise judgment, and complete dedication to duty, First Sergeant Kasal reflected great credit upon himself and upheld the highest traditions of the Marine Corps and the United States Naval Service.

After pinning on the medal, shaking Kasal's hand, and offering a few brief remarks, Lehnert concluded the ceremony.

"Some may call a basketball player a hero for scoring the winning goal or a celebrity for donating a small portion of their earnings to a good cause," Lehnert said, "but Kasal is a true American hero."

PERSONAL REFLECTIONS

FROM SERGEANT MAJOR BRAD KASAL, USMC

I would like to thank the countless friends, fellow Marines, people, and organizations who have helped me during my long and difficult recovery from the wounds I received on November 13, 2004. I want to thank our nation's leaders for allowing us to take the fight to the enemy versus on our own soil; my fellow Marines and our Navy corpsman brothers I've served with over the past many years; and the Navy nurses who worked round the clock to provide care while I was hospitalized. Most of all I thank the members of the 3d Battalion, 1st Marines, and all service members worldwide who are serving overseas locating, closing with, and destroying the enemy while keeping the wolf away from the door and maintaining our freedom.

After serving 19 of my last 21 years of service in an infantry unit, I've served beside some of the finest men I've ever known. Their heroism, courage, and selfless sacrifices truly make them the next greatest generation. While serving this last time in Iraq I witnessed young Marines who would one day watch their buddy become a serious casualty and the next day go right back out on patrol without any hesitation. And to watch young 20-something NCOs step up and serve in billets usually reserved for a rank of one and sometimes two higher in a stressful combat situation was phenomenal. Marines by the names of Sergeant Comeau, Sergeant Carter, Sergeant Monohan, Sergeant Martinez, Sergeant Hankins, and many others achieved tasks of great stress and responsibility time and again over a very tense and dangerous combat tour. I remember many times going out with them on different missions and wondering "Where do we get these fine men?"

I'd watch these young Marines perform and my chest would swell with pride as a father's would for his sons. The Marines I had the pleasure to serve beside—in CAAT Platoon and 81s Platoon, Weapons Co., 3/1—were the best, and I cherish the time I had with them. I miss them dearly and these men are the reason I love the Corps so much. I truly had the best job in the world.

Even more amazing were the young PFCs and lance corporals who threw themselves into harm's way only for the love of their fellow Marines and who assumed greater responsibilities when the situation dictated. My company had our 81mm mortar platoon split up to provide approximately 18 to 20 Marines at two different Iraqi National Guard compounds. The Marines' responsibility was to train more than 200 fresh Iraqi troops in infantry tactics, MOUT (Military Operations on Urban Terrain), and marksmanship skills so they could take over security of their own country. I would make constant trips out to each ING (Iraqi National Guard) compound in order to check on my Marines and go along with them on whatever missions they were assigned to conduct with the Iraqi National Guard troops.

The responsibility fell upon a handful of NCOs and mostly junior Marines to train these Iraqi soldiers. It is a testament to the caliber of these young PFCs and lance corporals who were 0341 mortarmen and fresh out of their own infantry training as they taught 0311 basic rifleman skills to the Iraqi soldiers as if they were seasoned and veteran NCOs. These were young men with names such as Gomez, Perez, Lu, Jensen, Roiger, and many more. Across the entire battalion, wherever I went as I traveled throughout our area of operations, I saw Marines and our Navy corpsmen performing meritorious and heroic acts of courage and selfless sacrifice. I also saw daily examples of how leadership in combat was vital to the success of the mission.

As combat is inherently dangerous to everyone involved, I believe in leading from the front and placing myself in the same danger and hardship as even the most junior troops when the situation allows. This enables me to keep things in perspective and never forget what they're experiencing and to learn more about my Marines and provide them with reassurance. Having your Marines see you endure the same conditions as they are will lift their spirits in even the hardest of times. I enjoyed time with any Marines, and I figured I could lead by a radio farther back or I could lead by a radio with my Marines.

As a senior Marine leader I was also cautious not to get too involved. I wasn't there to run the squad, platoon, or section. I was there to be with my Marines. So I would become just another rifleman and let the team leader do his job. Afterward when we returned from a mission, I would then pull the young leader aside—separate from his Marines—and give him any input I had. It was also important to be consistent in going out even during the late night or on seemingly boring missions, not just the high-profile ones. In doing so the Marines welcomed my presence and the subordinate leaders never felt threatened or as if they were being overly supervised. Although I was involved in countless large-scale combat operations at the company and battalion level, it was the opportunity to go out on these smaller missions, led by a young staff sergeant or other NCO, that I enjoyed the most. I will never forget the young Marines I served with in Weapons Co. I was blessed with SNCOs such as Staff Sergeants Mortimer, Fox, Lopez, and Viklund and Gunnery Sergeants Wade and Christiansen who made my job as a first sergeant easy.

Leading from the front does have its risks, however. The day I was wounded I certainly didn't start out thinking I should kick in a door and engage practically hand-to-hand with the enemy. However as I was with my Marines going street by street and house by house, upon learning that wounded Marines were trapped inside a building with terrorists, I knew every second counted. So several other Marines and I charged forward rather than waiting for someone else. To this day many consider it a miracle that I lived after the severe blood loss and trauma caused by seven gunshot wounds and several dozen shrapnel wounds. I simply see it as just the love for a fellow Marine and a little bit of toughness and stubbornness

Throughout this entire ordeal from the time of being wounded until I was medically evacuated close to an hour later, and despite the multiple wounds and loss of blood, I never lost consciousness or quit my post while guarding that doorway. While some may call this heroic, I just call it loyalty. It was because I loved the Marine next to me that I was determined to do anything it took to keep him alive, even at my own risk. He would have done the same for me. It's called being a Marine—we're all brothers and a family.

Many times since my injuries occurred people have labeled me a hero. I beg to differ—I believe the true heroes that day were Sergeant Robert Mitchell, Corporal Schaeffer and Corporal Marquez, Private Justin Boswood, and the men of Kilo 3/1 and Weapons Co., 1st CAAT section, who fought to get us all out of the building now called the "House of Hell." I will be forever indebted to these fine professionals.

The word "valor" is often used to describe the actions of many of these Marines. And it is commonly understood to mean "extreme courage." But valor is more than the extreme courage of a single individual. It does take courage to do a valorous act, but that courage is made possible by camaraderie and esprit de corps—of not wanting to leave their fellow man behind. I watched young men do amazing things in order to protect the man next to them. For example, Sergeant Mitchell voluntarily trapped himself inside the same room as myself and Lance Corporal Nicoll. Lance Corporal Marquez and Lance Corporal Schaeffer, the two young Marines who carried me out of the house, ran into the room without their weapons, leaving themselves defenseless so they could have their hands free to carry me out. That showed how much trust they had in the Marines who were covering them.

After seeing many news reports on what is currently happening overseas, I decided to have this book written and tell this story. I remember once while out on patrol we had an embedded reporter from the *New York Times* along with us. I asked the reporter why his newspaper didn't report the complete story and all the positive things going on over there. And he replied, "I see it, but my editor only wants to hear about deaths and disasters. Helping the Iraqi people doesn't sell papers."

The biased media have made an impression on the American citizens and the terrorists themselves. Every time the media give airtime to a protestor, it gives another victory to the terrorists rather than to the protestors. And people believe what they read in the paper because it is all the information they have to go on. One time while I was at dinner with a few friends a lady approached me and asked what happened to my leg. At that point I looked like something out of a horror movie and was in a wheelchair. At first she was very concerned. But as soon as I told her I was in the military and injured overseas, she began to go into a long antimilitary tirade about how we don't need a military, and how there's never a reason for a war, and all the service members are dying unnecessarily. Biting back my anger for all the fine men who gave the ultimate sacrifice that she just dishonored, I simply replied with "Ma'am, you're very welcome; I'm sure what you meant to say was 'thank you' to myself and all the other service members who have made sacrifices to give you the freedom to openly make whatever statement you desire."

I'll be the first to say, as I've seen it numerous times firsthand, that war is an ugly thing. But sometimes you have to fight for what you believe in. We are facing a worldwide enemy who has only one agenda: the complete annihilation of the American way of life. And that enemy will stop at nothing short of that goal.

Freedom has never come free. Whatever your beliefs or political stance, our young service members of all branches are performing remarkably and making a difference. In Iraq combat was only a small part of our overall role. Military service members performed countless humanitarian projects ranging from large-scale items—such as building new schools, hospitals, and community services—to everyday things as small as handing out candy and pencils to children or helping a farmer with a flat tire.

These valiant young men are helping to bring freedom to a country that was previously without it. They are constantly facing the dangers of IEDs, suicide bombers, and ambushes while they capture or kill terrorists who have no regard for human life.

Many people are amazed that I wish to return overseas as soon as I'm healthy again. But serving my country is where my heart is. It is my wish that the American media would show the true and complete story of what is really going on overseas and tell the story of how our service members are performing selfless acts of heroism and helping to bring freedom and a better way of life to a country.

During OIF 1 General Mattis wrote, "A U.S. Marine—no better friend, no worse enemy." I strongly believe in those words and would tell my young Marines to be the most fearsome warriors the enemy has ever faced, but when given the chance and without compromising security, to show compassion for the Iraqi people and their children. The future of Iraq was in those children. I would tell my Marines to kill an enemy and make a friend every day.

So as this book is written, I pray the words can be found to do proper honor to describe the many men with whom I've served. I think we all can learn from these young men who wear the uniform of a Marine. We label a basketball player who sinks a last-second shot or a football player who scores the game-winning touchdown a hero. But the true heroes are serving overseas. We watch politicians argue for political gain and our streets escalate in violence. Meanwhile service members have learned to put aside differences such as race, religion, ethnic backgrounds, and social status to serve together in defense of this great country.

To all Marines and sailors, past and present, and especially to the men of the Thundering Third, continue to kick ass, and you will forever be a part of this old warrior's spirit and heart.

Brad Kasal

GLOSSARY
★ ★ ★

AAV—Amphibious assault vehicle

ACR—Armored Cavalry Regiment (U.S.A.)

AC-130H—U.S. Air Force "Spectre" gunship used at night over Iraq to interdict insurgent forces

AEV—Armored engineer vehicle

AFV—Armored fighting vehicle

AH—Attack helicopter

AH-1J "Cobra" Attack Helicopter —The initial Marine AH-1s were Army G models modified only with Navy-compatible radios, Marine green paint, and a rotor brake for shipboard operations. Later Marine models such as the twin-engined AH-1J were specifically designed for Marine aviation requirements.

AK-47—7.62mm Russian-designed assault rifle used by insurgents

Amph—Amphibious

ANGLICO—Air and Naval Gunfire Liaison Company

AO—Area of operations

Armorer— Someone who works on weapons and in the armory

Arty—Artillery

ARV—Armored reconnaissance vehicle

ASAP—As soon as possible

"Aye, aye"—Acknowledgment of an order

....

Barracks—Building where single Marines live or a duty station where they serve

BAS—Battalion Aid Station

BDA—Bomb damage assessment; given to fixed-wing pilot by airborne AO at end of air-to ground-support mission

BDE—Abbreviation for a U.S. Army brigade

BLT—Battalion Landing Team; main body of infantrymen that make up an MEU

Blues—Dress blue formal uniform

BN—Battalion

Booby trap—Military slang for any of a huge variety of explosive devices, often homemade, hidden and designed to kill or wound unsuspecting Marine upon hitting a tripwire or other triggering device

Boondocks—Swamps, small towns, middle of nowhere; also called boonies

Boot—A brand-new Marine

Boot camp—Marine Corps basic training

Boot mistake—Rookie mistake

Brass—Senior officers

Butterbar—A second lieutenant; refers to the gold rank insignia

....

CAAT—Combined Anti-Armor Team Platoon

CASEVACs—Casualty evacuations via helicopter

for Marines in need of urgent medical care

Casualty—Any person who is lost to the organization by reasons of having been declared dead, missing, captured, interned, wounded, injured, or seriously ill

CG—Commanding General

CH-46 "Sea Knight"—A twin gas turbine-powered medium helicopter that replaced the CH-53A

CH-53D "Sea Stallion"—A twin gas turbine-powered heavy helicopter for the retrieval of downed aircraft, as well as the movement of heavy and large equipment such as trucks and artillery. The CH-53D was the improved version with more powerful engines.

Civilian—Anyone not in the military

CMC—Commandant of the Marine Corps

CO—Commanding Officer

COC—Command Operations Center

Colors—American flag; also the ceremonies of raising and lowering the flag

Combat stack—A closed-up formation used by assaulting infantrymen to enter buildings and other dangerous areas

Comm(s)—Communications

Corpsman—Navy medic who serves with Marines; also called "doc"

CP—Command Post in the field

CPO—Chief Petty Officer in U.S. Navy

CWO—Chief Warrant Officer; also called Warrant Officers in all branches of service

---

Deck—Floor

Dependent—Legal term used for a person receiving all or a portion of necessary financial support from a service member; alternative term is family member

Deployment—Date/time when a Marine's unit departs home base for an extended period of time, which can be weeks or months depending on the mission

Detachment—Group of Marines from one unit assigned to another unit

DI—Drill instructor

DIV—Division

DOD—Department of Defense

Doggie—Slang for U.S. Army soldier

Dragon Eye—A $10,000 unmanned aerial vehicle (UAV) flying camera that feeds live pictures back to the COC in real time

---

FAC—Forward air controller

FAST—Fleet Anti-Terrorism Security Team

First Sergeant—Term used for the senior enlisted member of some units; also a rank (see Officer Ranks chart)

Float—Deployment at sea (as in "a six-month float") usually on an MEU

FMF—Fleet Marine Force

FMFPAC—Fleet Marine Force Pacific

FOB—Forward Operating Base

FOC—Forward Operations Center

FTX—Field Training Exercise that provides an opportunity for a unit to practice away from the home station

....

GBU-43/B—Massive ordnance air blast bomb (MOAB); a 21,000-pound GPS-guided bomb nicknamed the "Mother of All Bombs"

GPS—Global positioning satellite

Gung ho—Ready, fired up, enthusiastic

....

Hatch—Door

Head—Bathroom

HESCO—Name of the manufacturer that was adopted as the generic name for a prefabricated, multicellular defense system made of galvanized steel mesh and lined with nonwoven polypropylene bags filled with sand

HML—Marine Light Helicopter Squadron; the H means helicopter, the M means Marine, the L means light

HMM—Marine Medium Helicopter Squadron; the first H means helicopter, the first M means Marine, the second M means medium. Three numbers following these letters usually identify the original parent Marine Aircraft Group and the sequence in which the squadron was first commissioned

HMMWV—High mobility multipurpose wheeled vehicle that replaced the Jeep; pronounced and often spelled "Humvee"

Hump—Field march

....

IED—Improvised explosive device

Ilazarov frame—An external medical stabilizing device made from eight series of circular rings and pins that go around and into the leg

ITBn—Infantry Training Battalion

....

Javelin—A man-portable, fire-and-forget antitank missile employed by dismounted Marine infantry to defeat current- and future-threat armored combat vehicles

....

KIA—Killed in action

....

Ladder well—Stairway

LAV—Light armored vehicle

Leave—Vacation time

LPD—Landing platform dock; a Navy amphibious ship capable of supporting and operating a small number of helicopters for an extended period of time

LPH—Landing platform helicopter; a Navy amphibious ship capable of supporting and operating a squadron of helicopters for an extended period of time, as well as transporting and off-loading a battalion of Marines

LST—Landing ship, tank

LZ—Landing zone; an unimproved site where helicopters land in the performance of their assigned missions

....

M1A1 Abrams—60-ton U.S. main battle tank

M2A1 and M3A1—Bradley fighting vehicle systems (BFVS); tracked armored personnel carriers that replaced the M-113

M2—Browning .50 caliber belt-fed heavy machine gun

M9—Beretta 9mm pistol; designated sidearm of U.S. military that replaced the M1911 .45 caliber semiautomatic pistol

M16A2—5.56mm basic Marine weapon

M40A1—7.62mm Remington sniper rifle used by USMC snipers in Iraq

M60—Belt-fed automatic weapon

M-113—Vietnam-era tracked armored personnel carrier

M203—40mm grenade launcher that mounts on an M-16 assault rifle

M240G—Medium machine gun; a belt-fed automatic weapon that replaced the M60

MAG—Marine Air Group

MARDIV—Marine Division

Mark-19—U.S.-made 40mm automatic grenade launcher

MAW—Marine Air Wing

MCRD—Marine Corps Recruit Depot

MEB—Marine Expeditionary Brigade

MEF—Marine Expeditionary Force

MEU—Marine Expeditionary Unit; group of Marines organized for a float that is designated a Special Operations Capable Marine Expeditionary Unit

MIA—Missing in action

MOPP—Mission-oriented protective posture suits designed to protect against gas, biological, and chemical agents

MOS—Military Occupational Specialty; a combination of numbers and letters that identifies a Marine Corps member's specific military skill. Infantry MOS designators include:

0311 Rifleman

0331 Machinegunner

0341 Mortarman

0351 Assaultman

0352 Antitank Guided Missileman

MOUT—Military Operations on Urban Terrain warfare training

MP—Military Police

NCO—Noncommissioned Officer

NCOIC—Noncommissioned Officer in Charge

NH—Naval Hospital

NHCP—Naval Hospital Camp Pendleton

NRMC—Naval Regional Medical Center

....

OEF—Operation Enduring Freedom combat operation in Afghanistan

OIC—Officer in Charge

OIF—Operation Iraqi Freedom combat operations in Iraq

OJT—On-the-job training

OOD—Officer of the day

Op Tempo—Operational Tempo; how frequently a unit deploys or goes to the field

Ops—Short for operations

....

PCS—Permanent change of station; moving to another base

PFT—Physical fitness test

PKC—7.62mm belt-fed, Russian-designed light machine gun favored by insurgents

PL—Phase Line; an imaginary line on a map used to designate a geographical place

Psyops—Psychological operations

PT—Physical training

PX—Post exchange (same as MCX)

QRF—Quick Reaction Force

....

Rack—Bed

Rappel—To descend by rope

RCT—Regimental Combat Team

Recon—Reconnaissance

Recruit—An individual attending boot camp

ROE—Rules of Engagement

Round—Bullet or shell

RPG—Rocket-propelled grenade

....

S-1—Administrative Section of a unit

S-2—Intelligence Section of a unit

S-3—Operations and Training Section of a unit

S-4—Logistics and Supply Section of a unit

SAW—Squad automatic weapon; a 5.56mm light automatic weapon that is both belt- and magazine-fed capable

Scuttlebutt—Rumor, gossip

Secure—Lock up, close, take care of, or finish for the day

Semper Fi—Short for "Semper Fidelis," which is Latin for "Always Faithful"

Sick bay—Hospital, clinic, or office of medical personnel

Sick call—Assigned time for ill Marines to go to sick bay, usually first thing in the morning

Skivvies—Underwear

SMAW—Shoulder-launched multipurpose assault weapon

SMAWNE—Shoulder-saunched multipurpose assault weapon—novel explosive

SNCO—Staff Noncommissioned Officer

SOC—Special-operations-capable group of Marines assigned to a Marine Expeditionary Unit

SOI—School of Infantry

SOP—Standard operating procedure

Sound off—Shout very loudly

Squad bay—Large room where many Marines live

Squared away—Prepared, taken care of, or sharp looking

Squid—Navy person; also called a "swabbie"

SRB—Service Record Book

SSN—Social Security number

SVBIED—Suicide vehicle-borne improvised explosive device

....

The word—Confirmed information

TOW—M-220 tube-launched, optically tracked, wire-guided missile

....

UA—Unauthorized absence

UAV—Unmanned aerial vehicle

UH-1E/N—The "Huey"; the standard Marine helicopter able to operate from shipboard

Unsat—Unsatisfactory

UXO—Unexploded ordnance

....

VA—Slang for Department of Veterans Affairs, formerly Veterans Administration

VBIED—Vehicle-borne improvised explosive Devise

VMA—Marine Corps designation for aviation attack squadron

VMF—Marine Corps designation for aviation fighter squadron

....

Warrant Officer—A person who holds a warrant in a warrant officer grade

WESTPAC—Western Pacific tour, such as Okinawa

WIA—Wounded in action

WM—Woman Marine

WO—Warrant Officer

....

XO -- Executive Officer; 2d in command of a unit

OFFICER RANKS

Credit: United States Marine Corps

RANK	USMC	USA	USAF	USN/ USCG	USN/USCG RANK
General	Gen	GEN	Gen	ADM	**Admiral**
Lieutenant General	LtGen	LTG	Lt Gen	VADM	**Vice Admiral**
Major General	MajGen	MG	Maj Gen	RADM	**Rear Admiral (Upper)**
Brigadier General	BGen	BG	Brig Gen	RDML	**Rear Admiral (Lower)**
Colonel	Col	COL	Col	CAPT	**Captain**
Lieutenant Colonel	LtCol	LTC	Lt Col	CDR	**Commander**
Major	Maj	Maj (MAJ)	Maj	LCDR	**Lieutenant Commander**
Captain	Capt	Capt (CPT)	Capt	LT	**Lieutenant**
1st Lieutenant	1stLt	1LT	1st Lt	LTJG	**Lieutenant Junior Grade**
2nd Lieutenant	2dLt	2LT	2nd Lt	ENS	**Ensign**
Chief Warrant Officer 2-5	CWO2-5	CW2-5	N/A	CWO2-5	**Chief Warrant Officer**
Warrant Officer	WO	WO1	N/A	N/A	**N/A**

ENLISTED RANKS USMC

PAY GRADE	RANK/TITLE	ABBREVIATION
E-9	Sergeant Major of the Marine Corps Sergeant Major Master Gunnery Sergeant	SgtMajMC (SMMC) SgtMaj MGySgt
E-8	First Sergeant Master Sergeant	1stSgt MSgt
E-7	Gunnery Sergeant	GySgt
E-6	Staff Sergeant	SSgt
E-5	Sergeant	Sgt
E-4	Corporal	Cpl
E-3	Lance Corporal	LCpl
E-2	Private First Class	PFC
E-1	Private	Pvt